D0425464

13 BY SHANLEY

APPLAUSE

APPLAUSE AMERICAN MASTERS SERIES

13 BY SHANLEY

COLLECTED PLAYS • VOLUME I

JOHN PATRICK SHANLEY

APPLAUSE
❧ B O O K S ❧

All inquiries concerning stock and amateur stage performing rights should be directed to the DRAMATISTS PLAY SERVICE, Inc., 440 Park Avenue South, New York, NY 10016.

All inquiries concerning publication rights should be addressed to Rights Department, Applause/Hal Leonard, 7777 West Bluemond Rd., Milwaukee, WI 53213.

Library of Congress Cataloging-in-Publication Data

Shanley, John Patrick
13 by Shanley : thirteen plays / by John Patrick Shanley.
    p.   cm. — (Collected plays; v. 1) (Applause contemporary masters series)
    ISBN 1-55783-129-7 : $27.95. — ISBN 1-55783-099-1 (pbk.) : $12.95
    I. Title. II.Title: Thirteen by Shanley. III. Series. IV. Series: Shanley, John Patrick. Plays ; v. 1
PS3569.H3337A19 1992
812' .54—dc20

92-4492
CIP

Applause Theatre & Cinema Books
19 West 21st Street, Suite 201
New York, NY 10010
Phone: (212) 575-9265
Fax: (212) 575-9270
Email: info@applausepub.com
Internet: www.applausepub.com

Applause books are available through your local bookstore, or you may order at www.applausepub.com or call Music Dispatch at 800-637-2852

Sales & Distribution:

North America:
Hal Leonard Corp.
7777 West Bluemound Road
P.O. Box 13819
Milwaukee, WI 53213
Phone: (414) 774-3630
Fax: (414) 774-3259
Email: halinfo@halleonard.com
Internet: www.halleonard.com

Europe:
Roundhouse Publishing Ltd.
Millstone, Limers Lane
Northam, North Devon
EX 39 2RG
Phone: 01237-474474
Fax: 01237-474774
Email: roundhouse.group@ukgateway.net

CONTENTS

In the third scene of "the dreamer examines his pillow", Dad says, "The individual life is a dream." For me personally, this is a most moving idea. It frees me from my fear of death. It puts my ego where it belongs, in a place of secondary importance. It binds me to the human race, and binds the race itself to the atoms in the stars.

Who am I? This is a courageous question. As a writer and as a man I am involved in one central struggle — to discover and accept who I am. I believe all fear has its roots in denial. I have, at one time or another, denied everything. Every fact of my specific self. My parents, my Bronx origin, my Americanness, my Irishness, my appetites, my mortality, my need for love and acceptance, my jealousy, my violence, my anger.

I am not a courageous person by nature. I have simply discovered that, at certain key moments in this life, you must find courage in yourself, in order to move forward and live. It is like a muscle and it must be exercised, first a little, and then more and more. All the really exciting things possible during the course of a lifetime require a little more courage than we currently have. A deep breath and a leap.

Writing is acting is directing is living your life. I have told you the things I have just told you so that you would know something of my approach to playwriting. I see no difference between writing a play and living my life. The same things that make a moment in my life succeed, combust, move, these same things make a moment in my playwriting have life. And when I move in my writing, I have moved in my life. There is no illusion. It is all the same thing.

Acting is the same as playwriting.

— John Patrick Shanley

Danny and the Deep Blue Sea

An Apache Dance

"DANNY AND THE DEEP BLUE SEA" was presented at the Circle in the Square Theatre, in New York City, June 6, 1984. It was directed by Barnet Kellman; the scenery was designed by David Gropman; the lighting was designed by Richard Nelson; and the costumes were designed by Marcia Dixey.

The cast was as follows:

Roberta .... June Stein
Danny .... John Turturro

"DANNY AND THE DEEP BLUE SEA" received its professional premiere at Actors Theatre of Louisville in February, 1984.

"DANNY AND THE DEEP BLUE SEA" was originally presented as a staged reading at the 1983 National Playwrights Conference at the Eugene O'Neill Memorial Theatre Center.

This play is dedicated to everyone in the Bronx
who punched me or kissed me,
and to everyone whom I punched or kissed

CHARACTERS

Roberta: 31 years old. Blue jeans, a cheap dress-up blouse that's gotten ratty. She's physically depleted, with nervous bright eyes.

Danny: 29 years old. Chinos and pullover shirt. He's dark and powerful. He finds it difficult to meet Roberta's gaze.

About both characters: They are violent and battered, inarticulate and yearning to speak, dangerous and vulnerable.

A DEFINITION
An Apache Dance is a violent dance for two people, originated by the Parisian apaches. Parisian apaches are gangsters or ruffians.

STYLE
This play is emotionally real, but does not take place in a realistic world. Only those scenic elements necessary to the action should be on stage. Only those areas that are played in should be lit.

11

SCENE I

Two tables, each illuminated by its own shaded light. Roberta sits at one in a vacant sulk, nursing a beer and picking at a bowl of pretzels. Enter Danny, with a pitcher of beer and a glass. He sits at the other. His hands are badly bruised, and one of his cheeks is cut. He pours himself a beer. A moment passes.

Danny: How 'bout a pretzel?

Roberta: No. They're mine.

Danny: You ain't gonna eat all of 'em. Lemme have one.

Roberta: Fuck off.

Danny: All right.

Roberta: You wanna pretzel?

Danny: Yeah.

Roberta picks up the bowl, takes it to Danny's table, and goes straight back to her seat.

Roberta: You can have 'em. I'm finished with 'em.

Danny: Thanks.

Roberta: You're welcome.

Danny: You want some of my beer?

Roberta: No.

Danny: Some fuckin bar. Nobody here.

Roberta: That's why I like it.

Danny: What's the matter? You don't like people?

Roberta: No. Not really.

Danny: Me neither.

Roberta: What happened to your hands?

Danny: Fight.

Roberta: Who'd you fight?

Danny: I don't know. Some guys last night. Tonight too.

Roberta: Two fights?

Danny Yeah.

Roberta: How come?

Danny: I don't know. Guys bother me, I start swinging.

Roberta: I don't get it. Did they say something to you?

Danny: (*Exploding.*) Who the fuck asked you to get it! Ain't none a your fuckin business I lock horns with anybody! Nobody crosses my fuckin line, man! They can do what they want out there, but nobody crosses my fuckin line!

Roberta: All right.

Danny: They asked me where I was going.

Roberta: Who?

Danny: The guys I was fighting tonight.

Roberta: They asked where you were going.

Danny: That's right. So I decked the first guy. Hit him in the nose. You hit 'em in the nose, they can't see.

Roberta: Why not?

Danny: I don't know. But it's true.

Roberta: All right.

Danny: But while I was hittin on him, the other guy got me with his belt.

Roberta: That musta hurt.

Danny: Yeah. I made him eat that fuckin belt!

Roberta: Where you from?

Danny: Zerega.

Roberta: Yeah? I used to catch frogs from over at Zerega.

Danny: Ain't no frogs 'round Zerega.

Roberta: Not now. When I was a kid.

Danny: Ain't never been no frogs 'round Zerega.

Roberta: Yes, there was. There used to be a little like marsh over on Zerega, and it had frogs in it.

Danny: When?

Roberta: A long time ago.

Danny: How old's that make you?

Roberta: Thirty-one.

Danny: I'm twenty-nine. When I turn thirty I'm gonna put a gun in my mouth and blow my fuckin head off.

Roberta: Do it in the bathroom. It's easier to clean up.

Danny: I'm gonna do it!

Roberta: Why you say a thing like that?

Danny: I don't know.

Roberta: Ain't no different to be thirty.

Danny: It's gotta be different.

Roberta: I'm thirty-one.

Danny: I heard ya. That's you! Me, I'm twenty-nine and I can't stay the way I am for too fuckin long.

Roberta: Why not?

Danny: Cause I can't!

Roberta: You from Zerega whaddaya doing here?

Danny: There's nothing goin on over Zerega.

Roberta: Nothing going on here.

Danny: Yeah, well maybe I like that. Peaceful.

Roberta: You don't look peaceful to me.

Danny: I'm peaceful. But people fuck with me.

Roberta: Why don't you come over, sit with me.

Danny: I don't wanna. This is good where I am.

Roberta: All right.

Danny: I'm sorry.

Roberta: That's all right.

Danny: Is that guy looking at me?

Roberta: Who? Fred? No, he's sleeping. He's drunk. Can't you see, his mouth's open.

Danny: Oh, yeah. There's light on his glasses. I couldn't see his eyes. I thought he was looking at me.

Roberta: What if he was?

Danny: I'd beat his fuckin face in.

They both laugh.

Danny: You from here?

Roberta: Yeah.

Danny: Where?

Roberta: Right up the block.

Danny: What, you married?

Roberta: Divorced.

Danny: Gotta kid?

Roberta: Yeah.

Danny: Who's takin care of the kid?

Roberta: My mother. My mother always takes care of the kid.

Danny: That's a good deal.

Roberta: Yeah. You gotta friend, you know, a girlfriend?

Danny: No.

Roberta: No?

Danny: We broke up.

Roberta: What was her name?

Danny: Cecilia.

Roberta: Italian?

Danny: Yeah.

Roberta: I'm Italian.

Danny: She gave me a pain in my ass! She was very fine, but she'd make me go to her house. Sit around with her fuckin parents. And she'd talk in this totally fuckin phoney-ass way when her parents were around. Would you like a glass of soda, Danny? Oh, please be careful with your cigarette, Danny. Like she wasn't the same one I humped inna pay toilet! I'm sorry. I gotta bad mouth.

Roberta: Maybe she had to play phoney cause her parents were drivin her crazy?

Danny: I don't think so.

Roberta: I hate my father. If I thought I wouldn't get in bad trouble I'd take a big knife and stab him in the face about fifty times.

Danny: I hate my father, too.

Roberta: Yeah?

Danny: He's dead, but I hate him anyway. He was a meatpacker. He used to get real mad all the time. One time he got so mad cause somebody did something, that he just fuckin died.

Roberta: I wish my father would die. He was the one who made me get married. This guy I knew got me pregnant. I was like eighteen. And my father made me get married to him. He wasn't a bad guy. We moved into this apartment. I was scared. But it was nice, too. I started, you know, to decorate. And then my parents started comin over all the time. This is how you put up curtains. This is how you wash the floor. My fuckin mother started cookin the fuckin meals! And this guy, my husband, he was like, What the fuck is goin on? His parents were cool. Just like called once in a while on the phone. I felt so bad. Sick in the morning. Mother knockin on the door by twelve o'clock. My father comin in after work. And the guy, my husband, when he got there. It was like, Who the fuck are you?

Danny: What's your name?

Roberta: Roberta.

Danny: Mine's Danny.

Roberta: Sometimes I just start screaming, you know? For no reason at all. My mother thinks I'm crazy. Maybe you're right. Maybe I shoulda shot myself in the head when I turned thirty.

Danny: You want some beer?

Roberta: Sure.

Danny brings over pitcher, pours some beer, and then goes back to his table.

Roberta: You waitin for somebody?

Danny: No.

Roberta: Me neither.

16

Danny: I don't know anybody anymore.

Roberta: I got a girlfriend. Shirley. She lives next door to me. Always has. Never got married. We used to have good times when we were kids. We both had long hair and we'd go bicycle riding. I have a picture home. We looked great. She's a pig now. She goes to these bars up in the two hundreds. They got live bands. Guys pick her up. She goes in cars with 'em. She'll get in any guy's car. We used to sniff glue in my bedroom and get fucked up. She uses a lotta dope now. I use some, but she uses a lot.

Danny: I think I killed a guy last night.

Roberta: How?

Danny: I beat him up.

Roberta: Well, that's not killing a guy.

Danny: I don't know.

Roberta: What happened?

Danny: I was at this party. A guy named Skull. Everybody was getting fucked up. Somebody said there was some guys outside. I went out. There were these two guys from another neighborhood out there. I asked 'em what they were doing there. They knew somebody. One of 'em was a big guy. Real drunk. He said they wanted to go, but something about twenty dollars. I told him to give me the twenty dollars, but he didn't have it. I started hitting him. But when I hit him, it never seemed to be hard, you know? I hit him a lot in the chest and face but it didn't seem to do nothing. I had him over a car hood. His friend wanted to take him away. I said okay. They started to go down the block. And they started to fight. So I ran after them. I hit on the little guy a minute, and then I started working on the big guy again. Everybody just watched. I hit him as hard as I could for about ten minutes. It never seemed like enough. Then I looked at his face … His teeth were all broken. He fell down. I stomped on his fuckin chest and I heard something break. I grabbed him under the arms and pushed him over a little fence. Into somebody's driveway. Somebody pointed to some guy and said he had the twenty dollars. I kicked him in the nuts. He went right off the ground. Then I left.

Roberta: You probably didn't kill him.

Danny: I don't know.

Roberta: I seen a lotta people get beat up. They looked real bad, but they were all right.

Danny: It don't matter.

Roberta: You ever been in jail?

Danny: No.

Roberta: I wonder what it's like. Maybe it's crazy, but sometimes I think I'd like it.

Danny: Why?

Roberta: I don't know. Just a change of scenery to keep me from going off my nut.

Danny: I don't get it.

Roberta: What?

Danny: You don't make me mad.

Roberta: So?

Danny: Everybody makes me mad. That's why I don't ever talk to nobody. That's why I'm sittin in this fuckin bar. I don't feel like walkin home. I feel like I'm gonna have to fight everybody in the whole fuckin Bronx to get home. And I'm too tired to fight everybody.

Roberta: You live with your mother?

Danny: Yeah.

Roberta: Think she's worried?

Danny: My mother's a fuckin dishrag. Dishrags don't worry.

Roberta: Is she stupid?

Danny: I don't know.

Roberta: Well, what's she like?

Danny: She works in a bakery. She gotta get up real early. When she comes home, she throws up.

Roberta: Why?

Danny: From the sweetness. The smell of the sweetness is too much, and it makes her puke.

Roberta: My mother's nervous. There's something wrong with her thyroid.

Danny: Why don't you rip her fuckin thyroid out?

Roberta: I don't know.

Roberta comes over and joins Danny at his table.

Danny: What are you doin?

Roberta: I'm lonely.

Danny: I think you're makin me mad.

Roberta: Cause I'm sittin here?

Danny: Cause you want something, and I am definitely not up to fuckin nothin! You don't understand! I'm jumpin out of my fuckin skin! Everything hurts! I could bite your fuckin head! Leave me alone! Everything hurts!

She grabs him by the shirt.

Roberta: You're crazy, you know that?

Danny: Yeah, I know.

Roberta: You're lucky you don't stutter. You're lucky you don't bite your fuckin tongue! You're a lucky guy!

Danny: What the fuck you sayin?

Roberta: Nothing you could understand, alright?

Danny: You calling me stupid?

Roberta: I'm calling you crazy, Crazy! But what you don't know is I'm crazy, too! Yeah. You don't know me! I could do anything. I did something so awful. I ain't even gonna tell you what. If I told you, you wouldn't even look at me.

She lets go of his shirt.

Danny: There ain't nothing you coulda done would seem like anything to me. What'd you do?

Roberta: I'm not gonna tell you.

Danny: Look, I think I killed a guy. What could be worse than that?

Roberta: Suckin off your father.

Danny: What?

Roberta: A daughter suckin off her father. That'd be worse than killin somebody, wouldn't it?

Danny: Did you do that?

Roberta: Answer me!

Danny: I don't know. No. Did you do that?

Roberta: Yeah.

Danny: I thought you hated the guy?

Roberta: Yeah, I always did. I always hated him and wanted to run away. But then, after, I hated him different. So I wanted to stick a butcher knife in his nose. Ja! Right in the middle of his nose. And then pull down slow till I got to his mouth.

Danny: That wouldn't kill him. I don't think it would.

Roberta: It'd be good. People'd ask him why I did it, and he'd say, I don't know. But he'd know.

Danny: I'm havin trouble breathin.

Roberta: Why? What's wrong?

Danny: I start thinkin about it. Whenever I start thinkin about breathin, I can't breathe right.

Roberta: So forget it.

Danny: A guy told me, if you think you're gonna have a heart attack, if you keep thinkin about it, even if your heart was alright to begin with, in the end, you'll have one. You can make your heart go bad.

Roberta: That's bullshit.

Danny: It's true!

Roberta: How do you know?

Danny: I can feel it happening! I don't wanna die like that. I don't wanna die from my own mind. I gotta think about something else. Davy Crockett. (*Sings.*) Davy! Davy Crockett ... !

Roberta: He came into my room. He was drunk. It was real real dark. He was mad cause I'd gone out partyin and my mother was away and nobody'd been watching the kid. He was yellin at me and I was thinkin, He yells and I do nothin. So I started cryin and sayin I was sorry. He put his hand on my face. I put my hand out

20

and I touched him. There. He got quiet. That's what did it. I made him get quiet. I could never make him do anything. That's why I did it. So I could make him do things. That was the only time. There was one other time after that when he wanted me to, but I wouldn't. And that was good, too. Right then.

Danny: I was supposed to marry this girl Cecilia. I called her Sissy. She liked that, but she wouldn't let me call her that in front of her parents. I don't know what was with her and her parents.

Roberta: Did you hear what I told you about me and my father?

Danny: Yeah, I heard.

Roberta: Would you be able to kiss a girl who'd done that?

Danny: It don't mean nothin to me.

Roberta: Really?

Danny: Sure really.

Roberta: Would you kiss me?

Danny: What, you don't get kissed?

Roberta: Nobody knows but you.

Danny: What'd you tell me for?

Roberta: I don't know.

Danny: Well, I won't tell nobody.

Roberta: That don't help.

Danny: What d'you want?

Roberta: How am I gonna get rid of this!

Danny: What?

Roberta: What I done!

Danny: I don't know.

Roberta: I can't stay like I am! I can't stay in this fuckin head anymore! If I don't get outta this fuckin head I'm gonna go crazy! I could eat glass! I could put my hand inna fire an watch the fuckin thing burn and I still wouldn't be outta this fuckin head! What am I gonna do? What? I can't close my eyes, man. I can't close my eyes and see the things I see. I'm still in that house! I wouldn't a believed it but I'm still in that house. He's there and I'm there. And my kid. Who's nuts already. It's like, what could happen now? You know? What else could happen? But somethin's gotta. I feel like the day's gonna come when I could just put out my arm and fire and lightning will come outta my hand and burn up everything for a thousand miles! It ain't right to feel as much as I feel.

Danny: What you tellin me for?

Roberta: No reason, all right?

Danny: You want something.

Roberta: So what. Don't you?

Danny: No.

Roberta: Liar.

Danny: Hey, you wanna smack? I don't lie!

Roberta: So what if you did, it ain't so terrible.

Danny: I don't lie!

Roberta: All right.

Danny: I'm tellin you the truth. I don't want nothin from you.

Roberta: I got a good deal in my house. I got somethin it's almost like my own apartment. When you get to the top of the stairs, there's a separate door to the room I sleep in. Don't have to deal with my parents at all if I go right in that room. I'd never deal with 'em if it weren't for the kid.

Danny: I'm not goin anywhere with you.

Roberta: Who asked you to? So what are you goin to do?

Danny: Stay here, drink my beer.

Roberta: All night?

Danny: That's right.

Roberta: The place closes.

Danny: So when it closes, I'll go someplace else!

Roberta: All the places close.

Danny: I'll go someplace else!

Roberta: And get in a fight, right?

Danny: Maybe. If people fuck with me!

Roberta: Ain't no maybe. You're gonna haveta fight. Because you were right. You're gonna haveta fight every motherfuckin body in the Bronx. And even it probably won't get you home.

Danny: You don't know.

Roberta: I know.

Danny: Get off my case, bitch!

Roberta: Come home with me.

Danny: What for?

Roberta: Cause you're the one I told.

Danny: That ain't no reason.

Roberta: Oh, yes it is! It is to me.

Danny: No.

Roberta: Let me ask you something.

Danny: I ain't tellin you shit.

Roberta: Tell me why your hands are all ripped up.

Danny: I got in a fight!

Roberta: And that mark on your face.

Danny: I got in a fight, I told ya!

Roberta: Yeah, you told me.

Danny: That's right.

Roberta: And you think you killed somebody.

Danny: That's right, too.

Roberta: Why?

Danny: Shut up!

Roberta: I wanna know.

Danny: What are you, a fuckin social worker! Shut up I said!

Roberta: Why don't you tell me before somethin happens and you can't tell me no more?

Danny: You're tryin ta cross my fuckin line, man!

Roberta: That's right! I am. I've been sittin here starin at a spot on the wall for about a thousand years, and if I don't talk to somebody about somethin, somethin that means somethin, I'm gonna snap out! You understand? I'm gonna snap the fuck out!

Danny: Don't you work no shit on my head or I'll kill ya, understand?

Roberta: I understand, okay? I just don't give a flyin fuck.

Danny: You can do what you want out there, but don't you cross my line or you'll be dead!

Roberta: Then I'll be dead. That scares me about as much as Halloween.

Danny: Don't push me.

Roberta: Why not? What else I got to do to pass the fuckin time!

Danny: Don't, I'm tellin ya!

Roberta: I know, I know. You're a cold killer with a hair trigger and I better tiptoe outta your way before I get wasted. Pardon me if I don't faint.

Danny: Please!

Roberta: You don't scare me, asshole. I see worse than you crawlin around in my sink. You're about as bad as a faggot in his Sunday dress! Your mama probably still gives you her tit when you get shook up! (*She starts slapping him.*) What's the matter, badass? Somebody get your matches wet? This your time of the month? Huh? Huh? You don't remember how to pop your fuckin cork? Huh? Or do you get off on pigs rubbin their shoes on your ugly dick-lick face, you lowlife beefcake faggot!

Snapping out, he roars and chokes her. She doesn't struggle.

Danny: I told you! I told you!

Roberta: I ... got ...

Danny: You can't push me!

Roberta: Harder.

Danny: (*Lets her go in horror.*) Jesus!

Roberta: Why'd you stop?

Danny: Don't talk to me.

Roberta: Who am I gonna talk to if I don't talk to you?

Danny: (*Starts to cry.*) Leave me alone.

Roberta: No.

Danny: Everybody leave me alone.

Roberta: Why you so quick with your hands?

Danny: I don't know.

Roberta: You know.

Danny: I'm too full.

Roberta: What?

Danny: I'm too full ... for anything ... to move right. I can't ... Watch out.

Roberta: Talk.

Danny: Watch out. Listen. I can't stop myself if I hit you.

Roberta: That's all right. I don't care and I'm not scared.

Danny: People can't talk to me anymore.

Roberta: I hear you.

Danny: I can't work anymore. They don't want me on the truck.

Roberta: I hear you.

Danny: It's like they don't listen to what they say to each other. If they was listenin, they'd have to start swingin. They'd have to.

Roberta: But you listen.

Danny: I don't want to.

Roberta: But it ain't a question a want.

Danny: No.

Roberta: It's how you are.

Danny: They talk to each other. Nobody talks to me. I'm alone wherever I am.

Roberta: Me too.

Danny: I start to think, I'm breathin, I'm breathin, and then that gets hard to do cause I'm thinkin about it, and I start to think about gettin a heart attack, and I feel pain, O NO, everything hurts! Everything hurts! Why does it keep on when I can't do anything. Somebody help me!

Roberta: I'll help you.

Danny: Somebody help me.

Roberta: I'll help you, baby.

Danny: Everything hurts all the time.

Roberta: I know, I know.

Danny: The only thing that stops it is when I hit on somebody. Then I'm nobody and it's just the other guy I see. I can just jump on him and outta me. Make it go out, out!

Roberta: I'm gonna take you home, baby.

Danny: I don't wanna.

Roberta: Yes, you do.

Danny: What for?

Roberta: For love.

Danny: Love?

Roberta: We're gonna love each other.

Danny: I can't do that.

Roberta: We're gonna love each other. I hear the birds in the morning at my window. It always hurts me. We'll hear the birds in the morning.

Danny: I gotta go home.

Roberta: You got no home.

Danny: Yes, I do.

Roberta: You got no home. Just like me.

Danny: I gotta go home.

Roberta: My poor sweetheart. He's gotta go home but he's got no home.

Danny: No. You're right. I don't.

Roberta: Me neither. I got no home neither. But I'm gonna take you home, baby, and it's gonna be there.

Danny: The guys I work with. The guys on the truck. They call me the Beast.

Roberta: No.

Danny: They call me the Beast.

Roberta: Come on. Let's get outta here. Let's go home.

They exit, slowly and quietly. The lights go down.

SCENE 2

Roberta and Danny on a mattress on the floor of a little room with no right angles. Somewhere above them is a small, crooked window. The colors of the room are slate blues and dove grays. A little lamp sits d.r., on a little stool; it's lit. There's some shelving, left. A doll, dressed as a bride, stands on one of the shelves. They've just finished.

Roberta: So what's your name?

Danny: Danny. What, you forget already?

Roberta: No, I remember now.

Danny: Yours is Roberta.

Roberta: You got a good memory.

Danny: No big deal.

Roberta: You didn't mind?

Danny: What?

Roberta: Doin it with me?

Danny: No.

Roberta: After what I told you? About my father?

Danny: No. Why would I care?

Roberta: Don't be stupid. You want somethin to drink?

Danny: Whaddaya got?

Roberta: I got some red wine.

Danny: Okay.

She gets up, goes to a little shelf, pulls out a bottle of wine and a metal cup.

Roberta: I only got the one cup.

Danny: That's okay. I'll drink outta the bottle.

Roberta: No. Would you mind? We could both drink from the

27

one cup.

Danny: No, I don't mind.

She pours, sips, and passes the cup to him. She watches him a moment, till he drinks.

Danny: It tastes like piss.

Roberta: I'll light a candle.

Danny: All right.

Roberta: You like my room?

Danny: Yeah. It's good.

Roberta: It used to be a closet. I painted it myself.

Danny: Uh-huh.

Roberta: I light this candle and I close this door … You see that round light up on that roof?

Danny: Yeah, I see it.

Roberta: The guy who lives over there put that light up because he's got a pigeon coop, and people were stealin his pigeons. Don't you think it looks like the moon?

Danny: No.

Roberta: Come on, look at it!

Danny: All right. Yeah, it does a little.

Roberta: Like a full moon every night.

Danny howls.

Roberta: Shut up! What are you doin?

Danny: Howlin at the moon.

Roberta: Oh. Well, you ain't no wolf out in the woods, so keep it down. My father will hear you.

Danny: Fuck 'em.

Roberta: You got the most beautiful eyes.

Danny: Shut up.

Roberta: I mean it.

Danny: Shut up.

Roberta: Are you blushin?

Danny: Fuck no. What the fuck you think I am?

Roberta: You are!

Danny: I wanna ask you somethin.

Roberta: What?

Danny: Who ... I mean, how old are you?

Roberta: I already told ya! And you have a good memory!

Danny: Right, right. So how old's your kid?

Roberta: You're just tryin to change the subject.

Danny: So what if I am? No, really. I wanna know How old is he?

Roberta: He's gonna be thirteen.

Danny: Old.

Roberta: Yeah. He's got big hands and feet. He's gonna be a big guy. Now he's gonna be in high school ...

Danny: Wow, you're gonna have a kid in high school.

Roberta: Yeah, ain't that a laugh? I hope he does better than I did. But he won't.

Danny: Why not?

Roberta: He's all fucked up.

Danny: What's wrong with him?

Roberta: He's a jerk. He's got me for a mother.

Danny: It ain't his fault.

She slaps him, suddenly furious.

Roberta: You're gonna be a wiseass why don't you just get the fuck outta here! I don't need that! I don't need anything like that!

Danny: What's the fuck's with you?

Roberta: Sayin shit about the way I raise my kid!

Danny: I didn't say nothin! You said it. And keep your hands to yourself or you could lose 'em!

Roberta: That kid was just born crazy, that's all. My mother don't understand that. Anyway, if anybody got him nuts it was her. All the time with the eyes. All the time not lookin at anybody ...

Danny: HEY! I never said nothin about your motherhood.

You're probably good.

Roberta: No, I'm not.

Danny: You probably are though.

Roberta: You think so?

Danny: Sure.

Roberta: Thanks.

Danny: You got some smack.

Roberta: You all right?

Danny: No big deal. It almost felt … I feel good.

Roberta: So do I.

Danny: It does look like the moon.

Roberta: You think so?

Danny: Yeah. I was out in the country once. At night you never seen so many stars. It gave me a fuckin headache. Really. But then I saw there was this one bunch that looked like a big fish. A tuna or some shit. A big fish jumpin around in the stars. And cause I could see something in there, you know, somethin that added up, the whole thing didn't gimme a headache no more. That sound stupid?

Roberta: You must like the country.

Danny: I hate the fuckin country.

Roberta: Why?

Danny: All those fuckin trees. They smell bad.

Roberta: No!

Danny: Yeah. They stink up everything out there like aftershave. And bugs all over the place. Mud. Rocks in your shoes. You can keep it.

Roberta: You're funny.

Danny: Who's laughin?

Roberta: Not me.

Danny: I had this teacher. He said I was stupid. Right in front of everybody. So I punched him in his fuckin eye. It swelled up real good. So they sent me to this camp in the woods to straighten my young ass out. I don't know what they was thinkin about. Gettin bit by a buncha bugs and sloppin through the fuckin mud whadn't about to change my mind about some asshole teacher in James Monroe High School.

Roberta: I went to the deli this mornin to get a roll. Chinese guy put it in the bag. I looked at his face. And he was happy, I could tell. Bad things happen, I guess, to him sometimes, but you could see things whadn't bad for him.

Danny: Let's go throw a rock through his window.

Roberta: No. I got another idea. Let's be like him, Danny. For tonight anyway. Let's be happy.

Danny: Whaddaya talkin about?

Roberta: Let's be romantic.

Danny: What?

Roberta: Let's be romantic with each other! Say things to each other!

Danny: No. Like what?

Roberta: I don't know. Like ... If you love me, I'll love you, too.

Danny: I can't say shit like that.

Roberta: Sure you can! Oh, I don't know. Sure I do! Let's be romantic to each other, Danny! We've got a bed and we've ... done love, and there's a candle and some kinda moon ... What do we got? What do we got? Touch me. Put your hand on me nice and talk to me.

   Danny, with difficulty, touches her.

Danny: You're a nut, huh?

Roberta: Nice?

Danny: You're a ... You ... You're ... good-lookin.

Roberta: No I'm not.

Danny: Don't contradict me when I'm tellin you somethin!

Roberta: I'm sorry.

Danny: You're good-lookin.

Roberta: Okay.

Danny: (*Pause. He's working hard.*) You got a nice nose.

Roberta: A nice nose?

Danny: Yeah. It's like … It looks at ya. That's right! It looks right at ya, your nose, and it says Hello! That's right! And you got a nice chin, too. When you, when you smile, it goes up. Yeah. Like a balloon. No. Better. Like a bird. Like some kinda bird.

Roberta: Thank you.

Danny: Shut up! I ain't finished yet!

Roberta: You're not?

Danny: No. What are you kiddin? I gotta tell you about your mouth. It's … It's … beautiful. Like a flower. That's right! A bird flyin and a flower, right there on your face. And all the time your nose sayin Hello.

Roberta: Stop!

Danny: You know what?

Roberta: What?

Danny: Say your name!

Roberta: Why?

Danny: Just say it!

Roberta: Stop. Roberta.

Danny: Say it again!

Roberta: Stop. Why?

Danny: I wanna watch your mouth say your name. Say it again!

Roberta: Roberta.

Danny: Again.

Roberta: Roberta. What are you doin?

Danny: Watchin your beautiful mouth say your beautiful name.

Roberta: That's nice! You're bein so nice to me!

Danny: Roberta.

Roberta: Stop!

Danny: Why?

Roberta: It's like ... tickling me.

Danny: All right.

Roberta: Now I'll be nice to you!

Danny: Nah.

Roberta: Yes, I will.

Danny: You don't have to.

Roberta: Yes, I do too. I'll save your eyes for last. You did so good, I don't know what to say.

Danny: Don't do nothin.

Roberta: Your hair! Your hair is very sexy.

Danny: Shut up.

Roberta: Very sexy. Cause it's like strong and soft at the same time, and it feels good when you touch it.

Danny: Comon, comon, let's talk about somethin else.

Roberta: All right. You got friendly ears.

Danny: I ain't got friendly anything.

Roberta: You got friendly ears. They make me feel friendly. They make me feel like, I wanna shake hands.

Danny: This is so fuckin silly.

Roberta: Don't ... curse.

Danny: Okay.

Roberta: I was savin your eyes. Cause your eyes are very dark and beautiful. And I don't think I know how to say things about 'em. Your heart. I can see your heart.

She leans forward to kiss him, very slowly. As their lips are about to meet, in a panic, he slaps her.

Danny: No!

Roberta: (*Unshaken.*) Don't be scared, baby.

This time she succeeds in kissing him, first on his lips, then on each of his bruises.

Danny: (*Weakly.*) No, no. Don't touch me. It burns.

Roberta: Somebody hurt my baby. Somebody hurt him. Somebody hurt his hands. Somebody hurt his face. I love you, Danny. I love you. I know you hurt, baby. I love you.

Danny: What you doin to me?

Roberta: (*Kissing him.*) I'm lovin you.

Danny: Stop.

Roberta: No.

Danny: It's too much.

Roberta: Come on.

Danny: I'm breathin.

Roberta: No you're not.

Danny: I'm breathin too much.

Roberta: Don't worry about it.

Danny: I'm gonna die from this.

Roberta: It's just an idea in your mind. Look at me. Look at me.

He looks at her.

Danny: I ... I ... You're good ... to be with.

Roberta: Oh, thank you, baby! Thank you!

He slaps her.

Danny: No! I can't ...

She goes right on kissing him.

Roberta: You don't have to be scared. You don't have to be. I'm not gonna hurt you. I'm never gonna hurt you.

He chokes back a sob.

Danny: I'm the Beast!

Roberta: No you're not. No you're not.

Danny: Why you doin this for?

Roberta: I'm not doin nothin you ain't doin, too.

Danny: Yeah?

Roberta: That's right. Do you really think you killed that guy?

Danny: I don't know.

Roberta: I hope not.

Danny: He was a real mess.

Roberta: But it takes a lot to kill somebody, right? I mean lots of people've been hurt worse than you hurt that guy, I bet, and they didn't die. Sure! That's right. Babies fall outta windows five stories high and go right on cryin. Old ladies get run over by buses and pop right back up. You hear about it all the time.

Danny: I don't know. He wasn't … He wasn't dead when I left.

Roberta: Then you probably didn't kill nobody at all.

Danny: I coulda killed him. Even if I didn't. Ain't that the same?

Roberta: Between you and me, yeah. It's the same. One way or the other. (*A distant boat horn sounds.*) Listen! (*It sounds again, and then once more.*) There. You hear it?

Danny: What is it?

Roberta: Big boats.

Danny: Ain't no boats around here. There's no water.

Roberta: Yeah, there is. It's not a block over or like that, but the ocean's right out there. (*The horn sounds again.*) See? That's a big boat goin down some like river to the ocean.

Danny: Whatever you say.

Roberta: That's what it is. There's boats right up by Westchester Square. What's that, twenty blocks? Look sometime, you'll see 'em. Not the real big ones, but big. Sea boats. I met a sailor in the bar one time. In the outfit, you know? I was all over him. But he turned out to be nothin—a pothead. He giggled a lot. It was too bad because … Well, it was too bad. When we got married, me and Billy, that was my husband, we smoked a ball of opium one night. It really knocked me out. I fell asleep like immediately. And I dreamed about the ocean. It was real blue. And there was the sun, and it was real yellow. And I was out there, right in the middle of the ocean, and I heard this noise. I turned around, and whaddaya think I saw? Just about right next to me. A whale! A whale came shootin straight outta the water! A whale! Yeah! And he opened up his mouth and closed it while he was up there in the air. And people on the boat said, Look! The whales are jumpin! And no shit, these whales start jumpin outta the water all over the place. And I can see them! Through one a those round windows. Or right out in the open. Whales! Gushin outta the water, and the water gushin outta their heads, you know, spoutin! And then, after a while, they all stopped jumpin. It got quiet. Everybody went away. The water smoothed out. But I kept lookin at the ocean. So deep and blue. And different. It was different then. 'Cause I knew it had all them whales in it.

Danny: What if you ... Nah, I ain't gonna say that.

Roberta: What were ya gonna say?

Danny: Somethin I'm not gonna say. (*Referring to the doll.*) Is that you?

Roberta: That? It's just a doll.

Danny: Yeah, I know that. But is it supposed to be you?

Roberta: Yeah, I guess so. Shirley gave it to me. My friend. When I was gonna get married.

Danny: It don't look like you.

Roberta: No kiddin.

Danny: It don't have your nose.

Roberta: No?

Danny: No. Did you get in the whole white outfit, you know, when you got married?

Roberta: Not really. We got married at City Hall. My mother was pissed. She's religious. But we wanted to get that part over with. I was showin. It woulda been stupid in white. It's an ugly room, though, when they marry you at City Hall. It's like school.

Danny: Why you keep the doll?

Roberta: It ain't much to keep.

Danny: It's pretty.

Roberta: You think so?

Danny: Bein a bride. All in white and everything. Flowers. I was at a weddin once. They left through this garden. All these roses all around. I never seen so many roses. Bees buzzin. Lotsa other flowers, too. They came out. Everybody was throwin rice.

Why do they do that?

Roberta: I don't know.

Danny: And then the bride came out. The groom was nothin. He looked good. (*Picks up the doll gently.*) But it was the bride. Here comes the bride, here comes the bride. I was sittin on this stone bench, waitin for 'em to come out. When I saw the bride, I stood up. She was so ... I stood up. This big white dress. A veil. Flowers in her hand with ribbons blowin around. Little ribbons. And all around her. All these roses. And the bees buzzin. And nice girls. And everybody dressed in good clothes. Then everybody started throwin rice. Not hard. Nice and easy. Friendly. I forgot to throw mine. You wanna hear somethin really crazy? I mean, nuts?

Roberta: What?

Danny: I'm not gonna tell ya.

Roberta: Comon, what?

Danny: All right. I wanted to be the bride.

Roberta: That is nuts.

Danny: I wanted to be the bride. Walkin out the big doors. All dressed in white. Music. Flowers all around. Everybody bein nice. Special, you know? Special. Yeah, I wanted to be the bride.

Kisses the doll and places it gently back on the little shelf.

Roberta: Me too.

Danny: You wanna marry me?

Roberta: Don't kid around.

Danny: I'm serious.

Roberta: Stop it.

Danny: Square business. You wanna marry me?

Roberta: No. Now let's talk about somethin else.

Danny: Inna church? I wanna get married in that church with the garden. The one I was at.

Roberta: I told ya, don't kid around! Please!

Danny: I ain't kiddin! I want you ... to be a bride ... with me.

Roberta: I got a kid.

Danny: Let your parents take care of the kid.

Roberta: My parents.

Danny: That's right! They fucked up your last marriage and they owe you somethin! Well comon, collect!

Roberta: I can't.

Danny: Roberta. You got the right to somethin. Hey. Say your name for me.

Roberta: Roberta.

Danny: Yeah. Roberta. That's you. And who am I?

Roberta: Danny.

Danny: That's right. That's me. Will you marry me?

Roberta: All right. I mean, yes.

Danny: You will?

Roberta: Yeah. I mean, yes.

Danny: No! Yeah?

Roberta: Yeah!

Danny: All right! Good! That's good! I feel like I won a prize or somethin.

Roberta: And will I wear a white dress?

Danny: Yeah! Sure you will!

Roberta: And you'll wear the bow tie and everything?

Danny: Yeah, yeah. The whole outfit.

Roberta: You think we could?

Danny: Why not? People get married like that left and right!

Roberta: And we can go through the garden with all the flowers.

Danny: That's right. I wanna go through the garden.

Roberta: And people will be throwin rice.

Danny: Yeah, nice an easy. Underhand.

Roberta: And music. No guitars or anythin like that. An organ. A church organ.

Danny: Okay.

Roberta: And we won't invite my father. We won't invite anybody we know. Maybe Shirley. No, not even Shirley. Just people we don't know. Nice people who go to weddings and throw rice.

Danny: I gotta invite my mother.

Roberta: That's okay. I don't know her.

Danny: And she could probably get us the cake. You know, cause she works in a bakery.

Roberta: A weddin cake. With the little you an the little me standin on top. An that thing around us.

Danny: That's right.

Roberta: Where will we live?

Danny: We'll get a place. Maybe out by Zerega. There's some nice places out by Zerega.

Roberta: Can I decorate it?

Danny: Sure! Who else?

Roberta: I don't want anything Mediterranean. My mother's got all Mediterranean stuff.

Danny: Okay. No Mediterranean.

Roberta: I like American furniture, you know? Maple. Shirley's got a maple chest a drawers. It's real nice. And solid! You could kick it and you'd just break your foot.

Danny: I've been havin a lotta trouble on my job, you know? Cause I ... Not a lotta trouble, you know, just some. Cause I fight a lot. The other guys play rugby, an they think I don't know nothin cause I don't know nothin about it. But I wouldn't have anymore trouble, you know, if I was married, you know? Settled down. And I pull down pretty good money, too. I ain't got nothin in the bank cause I never had no reason to save anything, you know? No reason to put nothin by. But we could save some money. It wouldn't take long. Buy some stuff. Lamps.

Roberta: And no kids!

Danny: No?

Roberta: No.

Danny: I thought I might like a kid.

Roberta: I don't want any.

Danny: All right.

Roberta: Kids take all the money and you can't go nowhere. And if they get crazy or they're born crazy, everybody blames you, and they're around your neck like a rock on a chain. Just you and me, okay? Is that good with you?

Danny: You got it. Gimme your hand. You're with me now. Everything I make, you get half. Everything I feel, I'm gonna tell you. When I walk down the street, you'll be walkin with me.

Roberta: All right.

Danny: Maybe, like on Sunday, we can go to Hampton House. Have breakfast. They gotta special breakfast. People go there.

Roberta: We're gonna haveta announce the weddin.

Danny: Yeah?

Roberta: Yeah. You gotta have an announcement for a church weddin. Banns.

Danny: Oh yeah, right. So we'll do that.

Roberta: Ah no, we can't get married inna church, though.

Danny: Why not?

Roberta: I'm divorced.

Danny: So?

Roberta: They won't let ya.

Danny: We won't tell 'em.

Roberta: They'll find out.

Danny: No, they won't.

Roberta: There's papers you gotta do an stuff. They'd know.

Danny: Hey, my mother's Protestant. We'll get married Protestant.

Roberta: They don't care?

Danny: No. You can be divorced.

Roberta: Really? I guess that's right.

Danny: It don't make no difference to Protestants.

Roberta: And are their churches like, real?

Danny: Yeah. They're great!

Roberta: And I can still wear the white an everything?

Danny: Yeah, sure.

Roberta: My parents'd go through the roof if I got married Protestant. I bet my mother'd go off her nut.

Danny: They're not invited, remember?

Roberta: That's right.

Danny: Fuck 'em.

Roberta: Yeah.

Danny: You're with me now.

Roberta: Okay.

Danny: The moon just went out.

Roberta: He's got it on a timer.

Danny: It's almost the mornin.

Roberta: Seems like it couldn't be.

Danny: Why not?

Roberta: Too quick.

Danny: Yeah.

Roberta: I'm glad. I'm glad.

Danny: You tired?

Roberta: Yeah. I'm gonna sleep. You sleep, too.

Danny: Yeah.

> *She turns out the little lamp. Just the candle burns. Only Danny is visible.*

Roberta: Kiss me. (*He does.*) Thank you.

Danny: You're welcome.

Roberta: You talked to me nice, Danny. Romantic. I can never get to sleep good. Couldn't close my eyes, you know? Cause if I closed my eyes, I was just in my head. And I couldn't hack it. In my head. Buildin's burnin and people fallin in cracks in the ground. My father. My kid. My mother prayin. Rainin floods. You never know whether it's a puddle or you step in the wrong spot and you drown. But this is real good. My head's shuttin down. All I can see in here's the moon, floatin over everything quiet. Like a bride. All dressed in white. I can smell the roses. Can you?

Danny: Yeah.

Roberta: An the bees are hummin.

She hums "Here Comes the Bride" softly and falls asleep.

Danny: It's good. It's good. Hey, I didn't know that about what you told me, the ocean bein right here. Think a that. Maybe that's what we oughta do. Build a boat and sail the fuck away. Get married on some island where everybody speaks Booga Booga. Are you asleep? I love you.

Danny blows out the candle. The first hint of dawn is in the window. A bird gently sings the first notes of a morning song. The lights go down.

SCENE 3

Lights up. The bedroom. It's late morning. Roberta and Danny are asleep. Danny is snoring. Roberta wakes up. She touches Danny's face tenderly, then hits him with a pillow.

Roberta: Tag!

Danny: *(Snapping into a violent stance.)* What?!

Roberta: You're it. Good mornin!

Danny: Oh yeah. Good mornin.

Roberta: Keep it down a bit.

Danny: Why?

Roberta: My family.

Danny: Oh. Okay.

Roberta: They'll be gone inna minute. Then I'll cook you breakfast if you want.

Danny: Sure. Where they goin?

Roberta: The kid goes to school. At least he leaves here with books. My mother goes to work. My father goes to work.

Danny: What about you?

Roberta: I don't work. Not right now. I didn't like my last job so I quit.

Danny: What did you do?

Roberta: I was a secretary for a bunch a exterminators.

Danny: You're kiddin?

Roberta: Nope. They had this truck with a big dead roach on top, an they were real nasty to me, and at night, I used to dream the truck was chasin me an the roach was movin. So I quit. I gotta get somethin else, but I ain't started lookin yet. What about your job? When you gotta be there?

Danny: They don't need me till Wednesday this week. It's a slow time.

Roberta: So how do I look in the daylight?

Danny: Good.

Roberta: You still like my nose?

Danny: Oh yeah.

Roberta: You don't have to, you know.

Danny: Whaddaya mean?

Roberta: You know.

Danny: No, I don't.

Roberta: You don't haveta stick to nothin you said last night. It was nice that you said it at all. I slept good last night for about the first time inna fuckin century.

Danny: Whaddaya think I am?

Roberta: I think you're real nice. An I like ya. That's why I'm sayin what I'm sayin. So you won't haveta. You like eggs for breakfast? I think there'll be some.

Danny: I meant last night. What I said.

Roberta: You don't haveta say that.

Danny: I did!

Roberta: Aw comon, Danny.

Danny: I asked ya ta marry me last night square business an you said yes an I meant it!

Roberta: All right then, I didn't!

Danny: What?

Roberta: You heard me!

Danny: What?

Roberta: I was lyin cause I wanted a nice thing. Get serious. No way are you an me gettin married. That was strictly make-believe.

Danny: Don't do this to me!

Roberta: I gotta kid, a fucked up kid, no job, crazy parents. I'm crazy myself. I told you. Last night. Wake up. Open your fuckin eyes. I ain't got no serious way possible I could get married to anybody. Not anybody. No less a guy like you.

Danny: Whaddaya mean, a guy like me?

Roberta: Nothin, all right?

Danny: Tell me what you mean!

Roberta: You know.

Danny: I don't know nothin!

Roberta: Look at your hands, Danny, Why do you wanna make me say it? You're all fucked up. If ya didn't kill somebody the other night, ya will sometime. If I married ya, it could be me. Yud haveta be retarded not to see it! You're a fuckin caveman! Yud be bouncin me off the walls …

Danny: NO!

Roberta: You grabbed me last night. See the mark?

Danny: I'm sorry I hurt your throat.

Roberta: I'll make you breakfast. Then you'll go back to Zerega.

Danny: No.

Roberta: Then you'll go wherever, but you'll go.

Danny: I don't buy this line a shit, Roberta. Not just cause it makes me feel bad. It don't sound true to me.

Roberta: It don't matter how it sounds.

Danny: Yeah, it matters! I heard the way you really are last night. It whadn't this. Ya wanted to show somebody how ya really was last night. Ya showed me.

Roberta: This is how I really am! Last night was just time out.

Danny: You're lyin!

Roberta: And you're still dreamin!

Danny: No I'm not.

Roberta: I don't wanna talk. I don't care.

Danny: I care. I gotta care.

Roberta: Well don't bother me with it.

Danny: You gotta be straight with me at least.

Roberta: I don't gotta do nothin.

Danny: You do too! You were gonna marry me last night.

Roberta: I can't marry ya!

Danny: Tell me why!

Roberta: I told ya!

Danny: I know I'm fucked up! But I got control! Don't do this to me, Roberta! Ya kissed my hands. Ya kissed my hands. It ain't right ta do this to me. I got a heart in my body and it's gonna break and it's gonna be you that did it. What can I tell you? What can I tell you that'll make you like you were to me?

Roberta: Danny.

Danny: Anything. Don't just … just don't say no.

Roberta: I can't, baby. I can't.

Danny: Why not?

Roberta: Just leave it.

Danny: I can't go back.

Roberta: I heard the bird sing that sings outside my window. This mornin. When I was just gone asleep. I heard ya talkin an the bird singin. An it was the first time I could sleep right … since I was a young girl. But I'm sorry I told ya yes, cause I can't marry ya, baby. Just take it outta ya mind. It wouldn't be right.

Danny: There's a way ta make it right, if ya know enough! Tell me what's the matter an we'll make it right! There's people we can go to if we don't know enough between us. There's people an a way if ya want it bad enough, but ya just don't know how. An I want it bad an I think you do too! Do ya wanna marry me, Roberta?

Roberta: Sure. I mean no. I mean I can't.

Danny: What's the thing?

Roberta: Nothin.

Danny: What's the thing?

Roberta: I told ya.

Danny: Told me what?

Roberta: About my father.

Danny: So ya told me.

Roberta: Ya can't do a horrible thing like that, Danny, an not be punished. It was me that did it.

Danny: Whaddaya talkin about?

Roberta: I did a bad thing.

Danny: All right! So ya did a bad thing. Ya told me.

Roberta: An … An … nobody punished me.

Danny: Good.

Roberta: No! No, it ain't good! I did a bad thing an nobody punished me, and so … it stayed with me.

Danny: I don't get you.

Roberta: I made my father inta garbage. I made myself that way, too. It's all wrong. My mother don't know what happened, but she knows. Cause it stinks so bad. I can hear her prayin all the time. Crazy whinin prayin like needles. An when she's not prayin, she's lookin around like she lost somethin but she ain't lookin for anythin an SHE WON'T LOOK AT ME! At the floor the wall anythin but not me! An my kid. I did that an I got a kid. I had no right to do what I did! It was too bad a thing to do. There's no happy thing possible becausa me. It's my house. It's my garbage. I can't leave this house cause it's my crime.

Danny: That's crazy.

Roberta: So what? Just cause it's crazy don't mean it ain't true.

Danny: You can do whatever you want.

Roberta: I did whatever I wanted, an it killed my whole fuckin family! I don't mean ta spill my poison any further than I already have! Ya hear me? It's over. I'm through screwin everythin up. I went out last night cause I couldn't stand it in this room anymore. I couldn't stand bein by myself anymore, with myself anymore. I talked ta you cause I hadda talk to somebody, somebody, an there you were, so fucked up ya might listen.

Danny: Roberta ...

Roberta: No. An ya did listen. An I thank ya for it. An I slept last night so sweet, for the first time inna hundred years. Cause you were good ta me an talked nice. But that's it, man. That is strictly fuckin it. Cause this is my house. My house. And I gotta live in it.

Danny: I'm takin you outta here.

Roberta: Forget it. It ain't gonna happen.

Danny: I have to!

Roberta: You can't!

Danny: I love you.

Roberta: You just need ta say that for your own private fuckin reasons! You don't know me. It ain't possible ta know somebody that fuckin quick. I told ya last night, an I'm telling you now. I'm nuts! An I'll tell you what I didn't tell you then. I'm bad.

Danny: Oh comon, gimme a break.

Roberta: I gotta badness in me. I did what I did ta my father an my family cause there's a big mean bad feelin in me that like ta break an hurt, and I'd break and hurt you just the same. Just the same as I did them.

Danny: Get serious. You would not.

Roberta: You ain't nothin ta me! You ain't dog shit on my shoes! Get outta here, freak! With yar crazy fights. Go back to the cave ya crawled out of! Go beat up a wall! Go watch yar dishrag mother puke her dishrag guts! Ya fuckin Beast! Ya fuckin Beast! Ya got to screw the pig, and if ya'd played yar cards right, ya mighta got a free breakfast! But ya blew it, so get the fuck out! Get out! Get out! Get out, ya moron clown! Get the fuck outta here an leave me, leave me alone!

She collapses, sobbing. Quiets.

Danny: I ain't too good at people. But I gotta say somethin. A crazy thing. To you. An you gotta let me say it. (*Embarrassed.*) I … forgive you.

Roberta: What?

Danny: I forgive you. Everythin you done.

Roberta: You can't do that.

Danny: I gotta be able. You gotta let me be.

Roberta: I can't.

Danny: You gotta let go. Let go of it.

Roberta: You don't know what you're sayin.

Danny: I know. You told me … what you done. An I don't care. There ain't nobody else. An it's gotta happen. So I do it. I forgive you. You're forgiven.

Roberta: Whaddaya think you are, a priest?

Danny: I am whatever I gotta be. It's over now. You've felt bad long enough. You did a bad thing. An it's been bitin you in the head for a long time. It's a long enough time. You paid for what you done. That's why you got me last night. That's why you brought me here. You knew … you'd paid up. That's why you told me your bad thing.

Roberta: You can't forgive me.

Danny: Yes, I can.

Roberta: No!

He pulls her to him, and over his knee. He spanks her.

Danny: That's for doin what you did. All right? That's the punishment.

Roberta: I'm sorry. I didn't mean it. It just happened. It was ... I'm sorry, I'm sorry, I'm sorry. Please ...

Danny: (*Putting a hand on her.*) I forgive you. It's done. I've done it. It's done.

Roberta: Yeah?

Danny: Yeah.

Roberta: Thank you.

Danny: You're welcome.

Roberta: Thank you.

Danny: We were bullshit last night. It was bullshit. I'm not too good. At tellin the difference. I ain't been too good at people. Ever. But what we were makin believe, other people got.

Roberta: That's other people.

Danny: But if we want, why can't we?

Roberta: I don't know.

Danny: It ain't a lot, what I want. I don't see why I can't get it. I know there ain't no way my whole life's gonna turn a corner an be the perfect thing. Yours neither. But I can get a day, can't I? To start with? That seems like somethin I could get.

Roberta: What day?

Danny: Weddin day.

Roberta: No ...

Danny: Listen. We could have a weddin day. You be dressed in white. The flowers. Everythin we said. Pretty much. I gotta job. I'll get the money. If you get a job, that's good, too. We'll plan it out. There don't haveta be no hurry with it. It'd be somethin ta make happen.

Roberta: It don't make no sense ta do it.

Danny: Just cause it don't make no sense don't mean it ain't true. It could be true. If you want it. I ain't never planned no single fuckin thing in my life. I ain't never done nothin. Things happen to me. Me, you, what you did. We didn't do that stuff. It happened ta us. That's why you're sayin no, Roberta. It's cause ya think we can't do nothin. Like it's always been, right? But we can. We can plan a weddin, an the weddin'ill happen the way we plan. The only surprise will be that we knew.

Roberta: Yeah? You think so?

Danny: Yeah. I do. I definitely definitely think I do.

The lights fade.

THE END

Welcome
to the
Moon

And Other Plays

These little plays are dedicated to James Ryan,
for his friendship.

"WELCOME TO THE MOON and Other Plays" was first presented by The Ensemble Studio Theatre, in New York City, in the fall of 1982. it was directed by Douglas Aibel; scenic design was by Evelyn Sakash; costume design was by Michele Reisch; lighting design was by Mal Sturchio; sound design was by Bruce Ellman; the music director was Barry Koron; and the production stage manager was Teresa Elwert.

The company was as follows:

      Robert Joy
      Anne O'Sullivan
      John Henry Kurtz
      James Ryan
      Michael Albert Mantel
      June Stein

THE RED COAT

Night time on a side street. A street light shines down on some steps through a green tree. Moonlight mixes in the shadows. A seventeen year-old boy sits on the steps in a white shirt with a loosened skinny tie, black dress pants, and black shoes. He is staring off. His eyes are shining. A sixteen year-old girl enters, in neighborhood party clothes: short skirt, blouse, penny loafers.

John: Hi, Mary.

Mary: Oh! I didn't see you there. You're hiding.

John: Not from you, Mary.

Mary: Who from?

John: Oh, nobody. I was up at Susan's party.

Mary: That's where I'm going.

John: Oh.

Mary: Why did you leave?

John: No reason.

Mary: You just gonna sit here?

John: For awhile.

Mary: Well, I'm going in.

John: Oh. Okay … Oh! I'm not going in … I mean came out because … Oh, go in!

Mary: What's wrong with you, John?

John: I left the party because you weren't there. That's why I left the party.

Mary: Why'd ya leave the party 'cause I wasn't there?

John: I dunno.

Mary: I'm going in.

John: I left the party 'cause I felt like everything I wanted was outside the party … out here. There's a breeze out here, and the moon … look at the way the moon is … and I knew you were outside somewhere, too! So I came out and sat on the steps here and I thought that maybe you'd come and I would be here … outside the party, on the steps, in the moonlight … and those other people … the ones at the party … wouldn't be here … but the night would be here … and you and me would be talking on the steps in the night in the moonlight and I could tell you . . .

Mary: Tell me what?

John: How I feel!

Mary: How you feel about what?

John: I don't know. I was looking out the window at the party . . . and I drank some wine . . . and I was looking out the window at the moon and I thought of you . . . and I could feel my heart . . . breaking.

Mary: Joh . . .

John: I felt that wine and the moon and your face all pushing in my heart and I left the party and I came out here.

Mary: Your eyes are all shiny.

John: I know. And I came out here looking for the moon and I saw that street light shining down through the leaves of that tree.

Mary: Hey yeah! It does look pretty.

John: It's beautiful. I didn't know a street light could be beautiful. I've always thought of them as being cold and blue, you know? But this one's yellow . . . and it comes down through the leaves and the leaves are so green! Mary, I love you!

Mary: Oh!

John: I shouldn't 've said it. I shouldn't 've said it.

Mary: No, no. That's all right.

John: My heart's breaking. You must think I'm so stupid . . . but I can feel it breaking. I wish I could stop talking. I can't. I can't.

Mary: I never heard you talking like this before.

John: That's 'cause this is outside the party and it's night and there's a moon up there . . . and a street light that's more beautiful than the sun! My God, the sidewalk's beautiful. Those bits of shiny stuff in the concrete . . . look how they're sparkling up the light!

Mary: You're crying! You're crying over the sidewalk!

John: I love you, Mary!

Mary: That's all right. But don't cry over the sidewalk. You're usually so quiet.

John: Okay. Okay.

A pause. Then John grabs Mary and kisses her.

Mary: Oh . . . you used your tongue. (*He kisses her again.*) You . . . should we go into the party?

John: No.

Mary: I got all dressed … I tasted the wine on your … mouth. You were waiting for me out here? I wasn't even going to come. I don't like Susan so much. I was going to stay home and watch a movie. What would you have done?

John: I don't know.

Kisses her again. She kisses him back.

Mary: You go to St. Nicholas of Tolentine, don't you?

John: Yeah.

Mary: I see you on the platform on a hundred and forty-ninth street sometimes.

John: I see you, too! Sometimes I just let the trains go by until the last minute, hoping to see you.

Mary: Really?

John: Yeah.

Mary: I take a look around for you but I always get on my train. What would you have done if I hadn't come?

John: I don't know. Walked around. I walk around a lot.

Mary: Walk around where?

John: I walk around your block a lot. Sometimes I run into you.

Mary: You mean that was *planned*? Wow! I always thought you were coming from somewhere.

John: I love you, Mary. I can't believe I'm saying it … to you … out loud. I love you.

Mary: Kiss me again.

They kiss.

John: I've loved you for a long time.

Mary: How long?

John: Months. Remember that big snowball fight?

Mary: In the park?

John: Yeah. That's when it was. That's when I fell in love with you. You were wearing a red coat.

Mary: Oh, that coat! I've had that for ages and ages. I've had it since the sixth grade.

John: Really?

Mary: I have really special feelings for that coat. I feel like it's part of me … like it stands for something … my childhood … something like that.

John: You look nice in that coat. I think I sensed something about it ... the coat ... it's special to me, too. It's so good to be able to talk to you like this.

Mary: Yeah, this is nice. That's funny how you felt that about my coat. The red one. No one knows how I feel about that coat.

John: I think I do, Mary.

Mary: Do you? If you understood about my red coat ... that red coat is like all the good things about when I was a kid ... it's like I still have all the good kid things when I'm in that red coat ... it's like being grown up and having your childhood, too. You know what it's like? It's like being in one of those movies where you're safe, even when you're in an adventure. Do you know what I mean? Sometimes, in a movie the hero's doin' all this stuff that's dangerous, but you know, becausa the kind of movie it is, that he's not gonna get hurt. Bein' in that red coat is like that ... like bein' safe in an adventure.

John: And that's the way you were in that snowball fight! It was like you knew that nothing could go wrong!

Mary: That's right! That's right! That's the way it feels! Oh, you do understand! It seems silly but I've always wanted someone to understand some things and that was one of them ... the red coat.

John: I do understand! I do!

Mary: I don't know. I don't know. I don't know about tomorrow, but ... right this minute I ... love you!

John: Oh, Mary!

Mary: Oh, kiss me, John. Please!

John: You're crying!

Mary: I didn't know. I didn't know two people could understand some things ... share some things.

They kiss.

John: It must be terrible not to.

Mary: What?

John: Be able to share things.

Mary: It is! It is! But don't you remember? Only a few minutes ago we were alone. I feel like I could tell you anything. Isn't that crazy?

John: Do you want to go for a walk?

Mary: No, no. Let's stay right here. Between the streetlight and the moon. Under the tree. Tell me that you love me.

John: I love you.

Mary: I love you, too. You're good-looking, did you know that? Does your mother tell you that?

John: Yeah, she does.

Mary: Your eyes are shining.

John: I know. I can feel them shining.

The Lights Go Down Slowly.

DOWN AND OUT

Love, a woman in a shawl full of holes, stands at a table. On the table is a large candle burning brightly, and a red box. A distant storm rages without. Love is setting the table. There are two spoons and one paper napkin. Carefully, with trembling hands, she tears the napkin in half, and puts one half at each place. A knock at the door.

Love: Is that you, Poet?

Enter the Poet, in wet yellow rain gear.

Poet: It is I, my Love.

Love: How did you fare?

Poet: Not well.

He coughs.

Love: Still sick?

Poet: Worse. Though still, it is nothing.

Love: You must rest.

Poet: Yes. And yet, there is no possibility of rest.

Love: The book then, that you wanted, you could not get it?

Poet: The library was closed. The library used to be open at all times, but then less and less. Now it is open one half hour a week.

Love: What has happened to the world?

Poet: Cutbacks.

Love: Cutbacks.

Poet: The painters in the parks are bags of bones, the clowns are tired, the tragedians have succumbed to pettiness, and the poets ... What's for dinner?

Love: Water and beans.

Poet: Again?

Love: Yes.

Poet: Six days now we have eaten water and beans.

Love: Yes.

Poet: And yet, still the water is sweet.

Love: It is.

Poet: And still the beans are the true fruit of the earth.

Love: I love you.

Poet: And you are my love. Is it safe in the box?

Love: It is safe.

> *Violent knocking at the door. The door swings open. A shrouded Figure stands on the threshold.*

Figure: *(In a ghastly whisper.)* Are you the Poet?

Poet: I am.

Figure: Give here your library card.

Love: No! You can't take his library card! He's sick! He has no money! He eats nothing but beans! The library card is all he has!

Figure: Give here your library card.

> *The Poet gives the Figure his card and stands away. The door shuts. The Figure laughs madly from off. The laughter trails away.*

Poet: They have silenced the song of Shakespeare. They forbid me the comfort of Keats.

Love: Don't despond, my Poet. Though they have taken everything from you, and you are not well, don't despond.

Poet: It is not for these things I despond, my Love. As you well know. But because I cannot write.

Love: But you can!

Poet: No.

Love: But I know you can! There are a hundred songs I see in you.

Poet: Yes. That is true. But I cannot write them. Because I have no pencil.

Love: It will come!

Poet: I wait. Every day. I have put my soul away against the time. But the postman comes, and then he goes again. And no pencil.

Love: It will come!

Poet: Let's eat.

Love: All right.

> *Violent knocking at the door. It opens. A shrouded Figure holding a huge amount of money.*

Figure: *(In a ghastly whisper.)* Money! Money! Money!

Love: Look at all the money!

Poet: How wonderful!

Love: Look at how green it is! How green!

Poet: It's beautiful! Can I have it?

Figure: Give me your soul. Give me your soul.

Poet: *(Picks up the red box.)* My soul?

Love: NEVER! GET OUT GET OUT GET OUT!

The door slams. Mad laughter trailing away.

Poet: My soul? Why would they want my soul?

Love: You are a child. I forget sometimes. These days you are a child.

Poet: I remember when the wolf was at the door, and I was not afraid.

Love: Eat your beans.

Poet: Yes, I must eat my beans. I feel weak.

Love: Tomorrow I must sell this table. We must learn to eat without a table.

Poet: Whatever is necessary. I'm sorry. I'm sorry I ever wrote a poem.

Love: Don't say that.

Poet: But I am. I am silly and I have failed. No one wants my poetry. The man in the newspaper said I am an untalented fool. The man in the newspaper was right. We are alone. Unknown. We live on beans. They have taken my library card. And I have no pencil.

A civilized knock on the door. The door opens. It's the Postman. He has a small package.

Postman: Package for the Poet.

Love: *(Taking it.)* Thank you. *(Postman exits.)* It's your pencil. It's come.

He takes it from her, trembling. He unwraps it gently. It's broken.

Poet: It's broken.

Love: Oh. *(He breaks down and weeps.)* So, it has come. I have kept this key around my neck against this day, my Poet. For you are my love and I am your Love. The darkest thing has come, and led to a moment of despair. But look! See here! I am your Love who has never left you! I can turn a tiny lock and open up your soul again!

She opens the box, which is his soul. It plays music. The Poet is bathed in a powerful light. He rises up.

Poet: I will sharpen this broken pencil and I will write a line of poetry! And I will learn to eat without a table!

Love: Yes! Yes! *(A wolf howls without.)* Poet! Poet! The Wolf! The Wolf is at the door!

Poet: I am not afraid.

The lights depart.

LET US GO OUT INTO THE STARRY NIGHT

A cafe. Two tables. At the table left, sits a tormented young man surrounded by ghosts and monsters. They chew on his head, claw his stomach, whisper in his ear. He stares off, sipping a glass of wine. At the table right, sits a skinny earnest woman, and her girlfriend, who is a dummy.

Woman: Don't envy me because I'm skinny. I know you don't really, but you do say you do, which bothers me. If you knew why I was skinny ... I'm going to tell you why I'm skinny. I can't find nourishment. I'm not talking about food now, which I think you guessed. I'm talking about the world. The world does not nourish me. At least at the moment. Do you know what I'm talking about? You don't know. You don't have any idea. And the reason you're ignorant—because that's what you are, really—is that you don't care. If you cared, you would know what I'm talking about. Or, at least, I would find your stupidity more endearing. Because it would be stupidity of the head, which can be easily forgiven. But what you have - and it's very common and unforgivable - what you have is stupidity of the heart. *(All goes dark but for a spot on the woman.)* Why am I sitting here with this woman who does not love me? I am squandering something on this woman. An important energy of which I only have a certain amount, maybe. When I should be talking to that young man, at that table yonder. He looks like Dostoevsky. I'm not speaking cosmetically now. I mean he really looks like Dostoevsky. Time for resolve. For courage. I'm going to approach him. Make up an excuse to get away from the table. *(Lights up again. She picks up a glass of water from the table and pours it over her head.)* Oh, excuse me. I seem to have spilled some water on my head. I'll be right back. *(She goes to the young man's table.)* Hello, you don't know me, but could I borrow a cigarette never mind I don't smoke. I must look terrible. My hair's wet and you don't care, do you? I can tell. You're not concerned with outward appearance. What are these things that are bothering you? I can see them, even if no one else can.
Man: Ghosts and monsters.

Woman: You have a lot of them.

Man: Yes.

Woman: Are you lonely?

Man: I'm terribly lonely.

Woman: So am I.

Man: It's hopeless.

Woman: Why?

Man: Too many problems.

Woman: I have problems, too.

Man: I know. I can see that.

Woman: But you know why we're suffering? We're suffering because we are in direct contact with our lives. I can't believe that that's a bad thing. I'm skinny because my body honestly reflects my soul, which is famished. Listen, I must talk to you.

Man: Do you want to talk to me seriously?

Woman: Yes. Exactly. I want to have a serious conversation with you.

The ghosts and monsters stop working on the young man.

Man: That makes them quiet. They respect serious conversation. In fact, they contribute to a serious conversation.

Woman: Give me one minute to deal with matters mundane. I've got to get rid of my friend. No. I only want to do meaningful, truthful things now. I won't lie to her. I will make this a great act. An important moment in my life. *(Addresses the dummy.)* This supposed friendship between us has been an unconscionable lie. It symbolizes for me a lot of friendships I have had with soulless people who sneer at sincerity and honest intellectual pursuit. I hereby end all such friendships. Service! *(A box flies on from offstage. She grabs the dummy, chucks it in the box, nails the lid with great efficiency, slaps a sticker on the side that reads 'Irrelevant,' and boots the box offstage. She returns to the young man.)* Which one is that there? My God, she's ugly.

Man: That's the ghost of my mother.

Woman: Was she really that ugly?

Man: Oh no. She was just ordinary looking.

Woman: Then why does her ghost look so vicious?

Man: She doesn't look too bad today really. Some nights she visits me looking like a rotting side of beef and carrying a big knife in her hand. When the woman was alive, she bossed me around a lot, so now that she's dead, she's an ugly ghost. It's very neat, really. If you brood about these things enough, it all gets very neat. The ghost of my mother that I have made is ugly. Her revenge on me is to frighten me with her ugliness.

Woman: It's a relief to talk to a man like you.

Man: You're looking for romance?

Woman: Yes.

Man: It's hopeless.

Woman: But you are lonely?

Man: Terribly.

Woman: Then you should share with me what torments you, and I will help you find peace.

Man: What's in it for you?

Woman: Seriousness. I need to be serious. I'm tired of taking things lightly. Do you believe in God?

Man: No. But I do feel there is a spirituality in the world.

Woman: Yes, so do I! I think that everything in nature and in psychology is explainable, predictable, and that that's incredible! Where does all that logic come from? Imagine a mind big enough to contain all this logic around us. Maybe it's the mind of God, I don't know. What a relief to say these things even if they're sophomoric. I think there's a sophomore in a lot of people, just waiting to get out.

Man: I have tried to live with women. I have tried to have women for friends. It never works. It always ends up very painful.

Woman: Of course it was painful. To live, to honestly live, is very painful. My sister has never lived. She denies her ghosts and monsters, even though they're the most interesting thing about her. She distracts herself by cleaning things and having babies. The point I was about to make isn't true. I was about to say that my sister, because she doesn't confront life, isn't in pain. But she is. Of course she is. She's in agony. The difference between you and her is that she's in dumb agony. She doesn't admit to it, and her heart is stupid about it. So I guess the point is that everything is painful, so why not be honest about the pain?

Man: I feel better. When I first saw you, you looked like everyone else. But now I can see that you are beautiful.

Woman: There is a special light on you, I think.

Man: It's coming from your eyes.

Woman: We've reached it. Come with me. Let us go out into the starry night.

A drop of stars and planets unrolls with a thud.

Man: You're not as you were before.

Woman: Neither are you. Your ghosts and monsters are gone.

Man: Look at the sky. The stars and planets. It's beyond belief that such beauty could exist. And yet we go for years and never see it.

Woman: I wanted to travel through the universe and meet other beings.

Man: That was my dream!

Woman: Tonight I feel as if that dream has been fulfilled.

Man: How can we bring each other such joy? And it seems so easy. The stars and planets are always up there, aren't they?

Woman: Yes.

Man: And people are always lonely, aren't they?

Woman: Yes.

Man: And we have this potential, which I feel tonight, for the first time in so many years, this potential for joy.

Woman: Champagne. *(They make a popping sound, finger in mouth.)* It's delicious.

Man: It tastes like I'm drinking little sparks.

Woman: I'm alive. There are tears in my eyes. Kiss me.

They don't kiss, but it's as if they have.

Man: Why can't I stay here?

Woman: Don't think about it.

Man: How did we get here? Maybe if I knew how we got here, I could find my way back here again.

Woman: Stars and planets.

Man: How did we get here?

Woman: We got here by being serious.

They reach toward each other. The lights fade.

THE END

OUT WEST

The sound of wind blowing. The lights reveal a Cowboy.

Cowboy: O, I love the land when it's livin', the heart when it's young, the wind when it's blowin', the campfire, out on the prairie night, and the stars all bright, but small and many, like a busted-ta-bits-moon! I say that I am a free man, and the water in the lake, and the animals on the shore, and the mountain men who live in caves like holy saints or bears say back to me again that I am a free man. Hallelujah!

The lights reveal a Girl.

Girl: I am a girl. I live in a coffin called a room. I live in a tomb called a house. I live in a graveyard called a town, with fathers and cousins and mothers and uncles and brothers and aunts and sisters, like cold dead key-clutchin' jailers; but I have a window, and I have seen the stars, and far fires on prairie nights, and wild men singin' in the dark — Cowboys they call them — and I have pressed my soul to the glass so that it may have sight, and I have fixed my heart with a star like a pin to the bosom of the night, so that my heart is not in me, but out upon the Wild West! And that is why, even though I am a slave and I am dead, something of me is free, too. Something of me is altogether free!

Cowboy: Look upon me, young girl, prisoner of the town. Look upon me and know there is another way to be, another mind to think other thoughts, another heart to beat, another soul to fly out into the hub of the Wild West! Look upon me and know that I am a free man! I am a Cowboy!

Girl: Hallelujah!

Cowboy: And can you see me as I am?

Girl: I can see you, Mister.

Enter Betsy, a dance hall girl.

Betsy: I can see you, too, Mister.

Cowboy: Who are you?

Betsy: My name's Betsy. I'm a dance hall girl. Can I buy you a drink?

Cowboy: You sure can, honey.

Girl: No, no. Don't.

Cowboy: What's this?

Girl: You shouldn't drink, and you shouldn't talk to girls like her.

Cowboy: Well now, why shouldn't I?

Betsy: Because she has her own ideas 'bout what a Cowboy is.

Girl: You are special. You are pure. You are a dream. You have lived like a priest under the prairie moon. Don't let the town spoil you.

Cowboy: I reckon I'll have a drink.

The Girl runs out, crying. The wind stops blowing.

Betsy: Well, she's a tender thing, ain't she?

Cowboy: She could only see one part of me.

Betsy: Barkeep!

Enter the Barkeep. A saloon piano starts up.

Barkeep: Yes, Betsy?

Betsy: Whiskey for me and the Cowboy.

Barkeep: Sure thing, Betsy. You gonna get him drunk and promise him upstairs, then steal his money and leave him just a broken-hearted fool?

Betsy: Naw, Pete. I'll get him drunk and promise him upstairs, all right. But this is a real Cowboy, just in from the mystery of the Wild West. I'll promise him upstairs and I'll give him upstairs. And then he'll leave me, though I begged him to stay, and I gave him all my money, and I'll be the brokenhearted fool.

Barkeep: Here's your whiskey. Have you ever killed a man?

Cowboy: Yes, I have killed a man.

Betsy: Down the hatch, pardner.

Barkeep: Who was it?

Cowboy: Stagecoach Johnny.

Enter Stagecoach Johnny's brother, his gun drawn.

Brother: Did I hear you say you killed Stagecoach Johnny?

Cowboy: That's what I said. Who are you?

Brother: I'm his brother. Stand up.

Cowboy: I ain't got no quarrel with you, pardner.

Brother: You killed my brother didn't ya? Stand up.

Enter Girl, at a run.

Girl: No, no. You can't fight!

Brother: Get outta here, Sally!

Girl: I tell you ya can't draw on him, Billy! He hasn't gotta chance. You'll kill him!

Brother: You're talkin' like you're sweet on him.

Girl: Sweet on him? No, I don't care nothin' about him. He's just some saddle bum who drinks whiskeys in the saloon and fools with cheap women.

Betsy: Who you callin' cheap!

Cowboy: Hush, Betsy. Let's keep the women outta this.

Brother: That's all right by me. Sally, get outta here.

Barkeep: Yeah, come on missy. I'll walk ya to your carriage.

Girl: I'm not leavin'! O, dammit Cowboy, Billy was right. I am sweet on you.

Brother: First you killed my brother, and now y'ar stealin' my girl! Get outta the way, Sally!

Cowboy: He's right. You'd better move outta the way. This fella means ta draw on me.

Girl: I won't, I tell you! I won't!

Brother: Pete, get her outta the way.

Barkeep: Alright missy, why don't you jus' come on outside with me.

They move to door, but go no further. Piano stops.

Brother: Now its just you and me.

Betsy: Wait a minute!

Brother: What in thunder do you want?

Betsy: *(Kisses Cowboy.)* Now just wait a minute. *(Takes off garter.)*

Cowboy: What are you doin', Betsy?

Betsy: *(Giving him the garter.)* Keep this in your pocket for luck. I'll be upstairs ... waitin'. Come on up after the fight.

Brother: Hey Betsy, I'm the one who's gonna win this here shootin' match.

Betsy: *(To Cowboy.)* I'll be upstairs. First door on your right. Don't bother to knock.

Betsy exits.

Cowboy: Let's get this over with.

Brother: That suits me fine. Draw on the count a three. You count, Pete.

Barkeep: I don't wanna count.

Brother: Well, you jus' go ahead and count anyway.

Barkeep: Okay. One, two ...

The Brother begins to draw on the count of two. The Girl breaks away from the Barkeep.

Girl: No, no, don't kill him!

She throws herself in front of the Cowboy and is shot. The Cowboy shoots the Brother.

Cowboy: You shouldn't have done that.

Girl: I have been living in my room all my life waiting for the world ta notice me. I have been a slave to my parents. The only dreams I had were from lookin' out at the prairie. I never was alive until I saw you. At least now I'm dyin' after I was alive.

Cowboy: Poor little thing. She's dead.

Barkeep: *(Checking the Brother.)* So's this one. He started drawin' his gun when I was countin' two. She saved your life, Mister.

Cowboy: I know.

Barkeep: Well, I reckon you'll be goin'up ta see Betsy now. She's waitin' for ya.

Cowboy: Naw, I think I'd better be goin' along now.

Barkeep: What'll I tell Betsy?

Cowboy: I reckon you can tell her I'm joinin' up with the wagon train. I'm goin further West.

Barkeep: She ain't gonna like it none.

Cowboy: Well, I guess there ain't nothin' I can do about that. I'm a Cowboy.

The Cowboy, whistling one of the old Cowboy tunes, slowly exits.

A LONELY IMPULSE OF DELIGHT

Night time. Two guys, Jim and Walter, are crouched at the edge of a lake. Light from the water makes patterns on their faces.

Jim: What are we doing out here, Walter?

Walter: Shh.Just keep your eyes open, all right?

Jim: All right, Walter. But what are we doing out here?

Walter: Come on now, don't get boring, Jim. You came, and I thank you that you came. Now relax. And keep your eyes open.

Jim: But what am I looking for?

Walter: Never mind and just trust me and look!

Jim: I'm not into blind faith. It doesn't appeal to me.

Walter: You're my best friend in the world, Jim. If there's anybody who understands me it's you. If there's anybody I trust it's you. That's why you're here. Because you're my best friend in the world.

Jim: I'm sitting at a nice silly party. I'm about to get somewhere with a nice silly woman. And my friend Walter takes me by the arm, and leads me to Central Park Lake.

Walter: It's pretty. Enjoy it.

Jim: It's two o'clock in the morning.

Walter: Two-ten. Listen. How quiet. "And the spirit of God moved upon the face of the waters."

Jim: Look at that duck. It's asleep. It's mouth's hanging open.

Walter: Did you ever have a dream? Something in your head. A feeling. Something you wanted but you knew you could never have?

Jim: Probably. But nothing comes to mind.

Walter: Something's happened to me, Jim. Something that could never happen has happened to me. And it's the most wonderful thing. And the saddest. And nobody knows.

Jim: All right, I'll bite. What?

Walter: I'm in love.

Jim: Aw, give me a break!

Walter: I am!

Jim: I believe you. All right? But so what? Did you really have to ruin my shoes and break up my night to tell me that? So you're in love. I'm sure it seems very important to you, Walter, but really, get serious.

Walter: You don't understand.

Jim: No doubt I don't.

Walter: She's a mermaid.

Jim: What?

Walter: She's a mermaid. The woman I'm in love with. She's a mermaid. And she lives in Central Park Lake.

Jim: In the lake.

Walter: Yes.

Jim: Well, that makes sense. If she's a mermaid. That she would live in a lake. A fresh-water mermaid, huh?

Walter: Don't make fun.

Jim: But it's so easy. What are we doing here?

Walter: I want you to see her.

Jim: Why didn't you invite your parents so she could meet the family?

Walter: I've seen her twice now. Always between two and two-thirty.

Walter takes out a little plastic pumpkin.

Jim: What's that?

Walter: A small plastic pumpkin.

Jim: Ask a silly question. *(Walter turns it on. It lights up.)* Oh, and it lights up! Very nice.

Walter: It's our signal. I turn this on, and I call her name.

Jim: And how did you hit on this sophisticated system?

Walter: It came to me in a dream, Jim.

Jim: A dream.

Walter: Yeah. It's amazing how quickly you accept all these things once you've seen her.

Jim: I'll bet.

Walter: Sally. Sally.

Jim: What are you saying?

Walter: I'm calling her name.

Jim: Sally?

Walter: That's right.

Jim: Sally the mermaid?

Walter: That's right. Sally? Sally?

Jim: I'm leaving.

Walter: No. Don't go. She should show up any minute. I want you to see her. I'm desperate for you to see her really. You see, I've always had a terrible longing in me. A color. A feeling. And I didn't know what it was. Now I do. I'm a man who loves a mermaid. And she loves me. And it's wonderful. But it's sad, too. It's really sad for a man to love a mermaid. You can see that? And it's even worse if it's a dream. To love somebody you can't have is bad enough. But to love somebody you can't have, and she's a dream, too ... That's too sad. Do you know what I'm talking about, Jimmy? You're my best friend in the world. If you don't know what I'm talking about then there's nobody.

Jim: I don't know what the fuck you're talking about.

Walter: Just wait a minute. Just one more minute. Sally? Sally? Please?

Jim: There's no one out there, Walter.

Walter: She's out there. Sally?

Jim: No. There's nothing out there. Why don't you come with me? You should go home and get some sleep.

Walter: No. No.

Jim: All right.

Walter: 'Member back in the days when we saw everything the same way? And nothing was impossible? And we loved each other?

Jim: I'm worried about you, Walter.

Walter: I'm okay.

Jim: No, you're not. You're not.

Exit Jim.

Walter: Sally, why didn't you come? He was my best friend. He was my friend. Sally? O God. Lonely.

A ghostly woman's voice is heard. Light comes from the source of it, illuminating Walter's face.

Sally: Walter! Walter!

Walter: You've come!

Sally: I love you!

Walter: And I you. My solitary, unprovable, deepest only love.

FADEOUT

WELCOME TO THE MOON

A lowdown Bronx bar. Vinnie, an Italian guy in his early thirties, is sitting on a stool, nursing a beer. Artie, the bartender, a wasted old Irishman, sits in the corner, reading the paper. Enter Stephen, gaunt, dark-eyed.

Vinnie: Steve?

Stephen: Vinnie! How are you?

Vinnie: Good! Good! How you been, man?

Stephen: Alright.

Vinnie: You look like shit. It's been three years, man. I've been sitting here counting.

Stephen: Too long.

Vinnie: Damn right it's too long. Artie, give Steve a beer.

Artie silently does so.

Stephen: Thanks. So where is everybody? This used to be the big hangout.

Vinnie: Everybody split a long time since. The Bronx is dead.

Stephen: Where'd they all go?

Vinnie: Upstate.

Stephen: How come you didn't go?

Vinnie: Guess I'm lazy. Got the job at the Post Office. It's good. And I just don't like upstate. Fuckin' Poughkeepsie. Fuckin' Nanuet. Gimme a break.

Stephen: You like the Bronx.

Vinnie: That's right.

Stephen: I like the Bronx, too.

Vinnie: Now that does not compute.

Stephen: What d'you mean?

Vinnie: You were the first one to go.

Stephen: It just worked out that way. I went in the army, and by the time I got out . . .

Vinnie: Yeah, I know. By the time you got out, time and tide had you by the balls, and you were on your way to who knows where. Anyway, why would you come back to the Bronx? The Bronx is dead.

Stephen: There's still some neighborhoods that seem okay.

Vinnie: The Bronx is like one a those moon craters, man. Another couple of years, they're gonna be sendin astronauts up here. Guys from Houston 'ill be collecting rocks on Tremont Avenue. So how's Manhattan?

Stephen: Manhattan's all right. It's good. Exciting. Always a lot going on.

Vinnie: Uh-huh.

Stephen: Good museums.

Vinnie: Museums. Yeah, they're electrifying.

Stephen: I can walk to school.

Vinnie: Still in school! Ain't that some shit!

Stephen: Well, I wasn't in right along. There was the service. And then a lot of shitty jobs.

Vinnie: And then you got married.

Stephen: Yeah.

Vinnie: What is she again?

Stephen: A Speech Pathologist.

Vinnie: A Speech Pathologist. It sounds fuckin' hideous. I live with a Speech Pathologist.

Stephen: Very nice.

Vinnie: Sorry. I'm hungry. Artie, what do you got to eat?

Artie: Canadian bacon and cheese.

Vinnie: Gimme one. You want one?

Stephen: All right.

Vinnie: Two.

Artie: *(Puts sandwiches in a little oven.)* It'll take twelve minutes.

Vinnie: We're not going nowhere.

Stephen: Vinnie ...

Vinnie: Yeah?

Stephen: Vinnie ... It's good to see you, man.

    Starts to Cry.

Vinnie: It's good to see you, too, man. Time goes by, and everybody goes away, and you see what you had.

Stephen: It's true.

Vinnie: You went out and stood on the corner, and everybody you ever knew was hanging there with you.

Stephen: You know ...

Vinnie: It was your neighborhood. It was something to be inside of. You could do anything because you knew the fuckin' rules.

Stephen: You know, I think I left my wife.

Vinnie: What d'you mean, you think you left your wife?

Stephen: Things have been bad for a long time. I don't know why. School is driving me up the wall. I can't seem to ... I can't seem to find ... There's nothing left that I enjoy.

Vinnie: I'm sorry.

Stephen: Nothing happened. That's the really strange thing. I just told her I felt like going ... coming to the Bronx, you know, the old neighborhood, and she said okay. And I walked out.

Vinnie: Don't sound final to me. You can go back.

Stephen: I don't think I can. I don't want to.

Vinnie: It's your life.

Stephen: We were ... We're friends, Vinnie. I know I didn't call you for three years, and I know I didn't keep in touch much for years before that, but, we're friends.

Vinnie: Yeah.

Stephen: I don't really have any friends in Manhattan. I know people, but ...

Vinnie: Shut up.

Stephen: Yeah.

Vinnie: Look, Steve. How do you feel?

Stephen: I'm all right.

Vinnie: Yeah?

Stephen: Yeah.

Vinnie: Cause when I got your call, I thought you might like to see some of the old crowd. So I phoned around. A couple of the folks should be here in a minute. Is that gonna be okay?

Stephen: Who?

Vinnie: Ronny.

Stephen: Ronny. Yeah, I'd like to see Ronny. How's he doing?

Vinnie: Bad. Ronny's always doing bad. Tried to kill himself.

Stephen: No!

Vinnie: Three times.

Stephen: Really?

Vinnie: Yeah. I make him come around. He comes to my house sometimes. A few beers. Whatever. To keep him from thinking.

Ronny: Hi, Steve.

Stephen: Hi, Ronny.

Ronny: Long time, no see.

Stephen: Yeah. How you been?

Ronny: Bad. Real bad.

Stephen: Me too.

Ronny: Artie. Gimme whatever Steve's drinking.

Artie: He's drinking five shots of tequila.

Ronny: All right! Give us a round.

Artie: One. Two. Three. Four. Five. One ...

Vinnie: Hey, Artie, could you count to yourself!

Artie: Okay. *(Whispers.)* Two. Three. Four. Five.

Vinnie: Ronny, you shouldn't be drinking a drink like that. You know how you get.

Ronny: You're right, Vinnie. *(Drinks it down; then to Stephen.)* I'm an attempted suicide. I've tried to kill myself three times. First time, I tied my feet to this big rock, and jumped in the Bronx River. But the water was only two feet deep. I stood there all day. I thought maybe the pollution would kill me. Buncha Spanish kids came and made fun of me. I finally went home. Then last year, I cut my throat. Right there. But I had to stop because it hurt. The third time, I threw myself in front of the A train, but the fuckin' thing broke down before it got to me. Lately I've been eating in all the restaurants that have health violations. That might do it. Who knows? I've missed you, Steve. I wasn't much when you left, but I'm a total fuckin' disaster now.

Stephen: At least you've had the guts to ...

Starts to cry again.

Ronny: What's the matter with him?

Vinnie: He just left his wife.

Ronny: That's the mouth disease lady, right?

Stephen: Speech Pathologist!

Goes back to crying.

Ronny: Right.

Vinnie: You ain't gonna believe this, but he's still in love with Shirley Dunbar!

Ronny: Really?

Vinnie: He's been in love with her for fourteen years without seeing her.

Stephen: I can see her in my mind!

Goes back to crying.

Ronny: Sure you can, man! Sure you can! I know what's the matter with him, Vinnie, and it's real bad.

Vinnie: What?

Ronny: He's obsessed, man! He's got his fuckin' self an obsession.

Vinnie: How do you know?

Ronny: I know. I want you to do me a favor, Vin. I want you to give me five minutes with him. Take a walk around the block. I can help him. I know about this.

Vinnie: You do?

Ronny: Yeah.

Vinnie: But Shirley's coming. I invited her. She should be here any minute.

Ronny: All the more reason, man. Gimme five minutes right now, before she gets here, to straighten him out. I can do it, Vinnie. Gimme the chance!

Vinnie: Alright. *(To Steve.)* I'm going out for a few minutes, okay?

Steve nods through his tears. Exit Vinnie.

Ronny: Steve! Steve! You gotta listen to me, Steve. There isn't much time. I know how you feel. You love Shirley, right? Shirley don't love you, right? It's a tragedy, right? You don't have to tell me. I know it's a tragedy. I know … cause I got the same thing. I'm gonna tell you what I've never told anybody. And you gotta understand quick cause there's no time! I'm in love with Vinnie. That's right! And I always have been. But I know it can't work so I never told him. That's why I'm a suicide attempt. Because my life is ruined from loving someone who don't love me.

Stephen: Me too.

Ronny: I know! I know! And that's why I want you to commit suicide with me.

Stephen: You do?

Ronny: It's perfect! We both kill ourselves right now, and then they find us. The two idiots who are responsible! Will you do it?

Stephen: How?

Ronny: A really good way. Plastic bags. *(Pulls two plastic bags with drawstrings out of his jacket.)* We just put these over our heads and die.

Stephen: How long will it take?

Ronny: Not long! How much air could be in a little plastic bag?

Stephen: All right, I'll do it!

Ronny: *(Handing him a bag.)* We ain't got much time. We'll die quicker if we do exercise. That makes you breathe faster. *(Ronny and Stephen don their bags, and do jumping jacks. Then they run up and down the length of the bar. Ronny urges Stephen along, shouting 'Faster' and 'Run' and such. They both grow weak.)* This is it! This is it!

> *Ronny lays down on the bar, and Stephen lays down on the floor. Artie watches all this without concern. Enter Shirley, blond, a little plump, big round eyes. She takes it all in and screams.*

Shirley: They got bags on their heads! *(Enter Vinnie.)* Everybody's got bags on their heads!

Artie: I don't have a bag on my head.

> *Vinnie rips the bags off their heads. They are both a little dazed, but otherwise fine.*

Vinnie: That was very immature, Ronny.

Ronny: Four times.

Vinnie: And Steve, I'm surprised at you.

Ronny: Four times.

Stephen: It really seemed like the right thing to do.

Shirley: Is that you, Stephen?

Stephen: Shirley?

Shirley: Hi.

Stephen: Hi. My hair's all messed up.

Shirley: That's all right.

Vinnie: *(To Ronny.)* Are you okay?

Ronny: Yeah.

Vinnie: Why do you keep trying to kill yourself, Ronny?

Ronny: Do you really wanna know?

Stephen: You look great.

Shirley: You too. You got great color.

Stephen: That's cause I was suffocating.

WELCOME TO THE MOON & OTHER PLAYS

Shirley: Oh.
Ronny: I'm in love with you.
Vinnie: You're what?
Shirley: Did you hear what he said?
Ronny: I'm in love with you.
Shirley: He said it again.
Vinnie: That's impossible.
Shirley: Oh my God, he's a faggot!
Stephen: Shirley, I love you.
Shirley: I never woulda guessed it! I knew Ronny was crazy, but a crazy faggot?
Ronny: I loved you ever since we were little boys. On the see-saw. Playing curb ball. I never said nothing cause I knew it would hurt your feelings and you wouldn't like me anymore. I figured it was easier just to kill myself.
Vinnie: I don't know what to say.
Ronny: What could you say?
Vinnie: I love you … too?
Shirley: Oh my God, Vinnie's a faggot, too!
Ronny: You what?
Vinnie: I guess I love you, too.
Shirley: And they're brazen! They're brazen faggots!
Ronny: Why didn't you ever say anything?
Vinnie: Why didn't you?
Ronnie, Vinnie: I was afraid.
Stephen: Shirley.
Shirley: You are straight, right?
Stephen: Yeah, I'm straight.
Shirley: That's a relief.
Stephen: Shirley, I love you.
Shirley: You do?
Stephen: Yes.
Shirley: Still?
Stephen: Yes.
Shirley: Why?
Stephen: I don't know.
Shirley: It's been about a hundred years now you've been loving me.

Stephen: I know.

Shirley: And I've never loved you.

Stephen: I know.

Shirley: The old crowd's together again.

Stephen: Yes.

> *Artie sings 'When You Were Sweet Sixteen.' He has a lovely tenor. The two couples look into each other's eyes with sweet sadness.*

Artie: *(Singing.)* When first I saw the love light in your eyes
I dreamt the world held nought but joy for me
And even though we've drifted far apart
I never dream but that I dream of thee
I love you as I never loved before
When first I saw you on the village green
Come to me 'ere this dream of life is o'er
I love as I loved you when you were sweet
When you were sweet
Sixteen

> *The lights go down.*

THE END

Savage
in
Limbo

A Concert Play

"SAVAGE IN LIMBO" was originally presented as a staged reading at the 1984 National Playwrights Conference at the Eugene O'Neill Memorial Theatre Center. In September 1985, it was produced by the Double Image Theatre (Max D. Mayer, Artistic Director; Leslie Urdang, Managing Director) in New York City, where it was directed by Mark Linn-Baker; the sets were by Adrianne Lobel; the costumes were by Debra Tennenbaum; the lights were by Stephen Strawbridge; the production stage managers were Ruth Kreshka and William H. Lang.

The cast, in order of appearance, was as follows:

Murk	Randle Mell
April White	Jayne Haynes
Denise Savage	Deborah Hedwall
Linda Rotunda	Mary McDonnell
Tony Aronica	Larry Joshua

This play is dedicated to all those good assassins
who contributed to the death of my former self.

CHARACTERS

Murk: A big man, red-haired and baby-faced. He has no sense of humor. He does not pour drinks; he produces them from nowhere. He has a wooden foot.

April White: A beat-up, tired, vulnerable woman with beautiful, damaged eyes. She can go from serenity to hysteria without showing a seam.

Denise Savage: She's small, wild-haired, strong, belligerent, determined, dissatisfied, and scared. She is in pain, paranoid, and full of hunger. She has hungry ears.

Linda Rotunda: A done-up, attractive, overripe Italian woman. She pronounces the name Anthony as "Antony," and the word virgin as "version." She is physically very womanly and very strong.

Tony Aronica: A streamlined Italian stud with a streak of self-doubt and a yearning sweetness.

All of the characters are thirty-two years old.

The play is informed by the occasional paranoid silence.

All characters enter through the audience.

The interior of Scales, a Bronx bar. Two dead plants provide the only decoration. There are no bottles visible. There are no mirrors. Downstage, a goodly distance apart, are two small rectangular tables. One chair per table. The bar is unclean, the tables vaguely dirty, the air stale.

The floor, which is shaped like a trapezoid with the narrow end Upstage, is green and white linoleum that's coming up in places. There's a blackened rectangular mark, Down Right, where a jukebox used to be. The floor has about it a live performance feel, for the concert which is about to take place. The place is lit too, too brightly, a powerful incandescent light which permits no lies.

From the opening of the house, Murk and April are onstage. When Murk is in his usual state, he is still. He's wearing a presentable shirt and tie, khaki trousers and a web belt, and black oxford workshoes. He's regarding April. April is sitting on the only stool, at the end of the bar, Left. She's sleeping, her head resting in her arms. Murk decides to wake her.

Murk: April. April. April. April.

April: What?

Murk: You were asleep.

April: On the bar?

Murk: Yeah.

April: No.

Murk: Yeah, you were.

April: Okay if you say so. Top me off, Murk. I'm losing my head.

Murk: Where's your money?

April: I don't got no money.

Murk: You got no money, I don't serve you.

He serves her a shot, in a delicate little glass. She sips it. Enter Denise Savage. She stomps in and looks around. She's dissatisfied with all she sees. She's wearing a rather limp navy blue dress and black pumps. She carries a black bag, not too big, that she seems to want to throw, but she doesn't know what to throw it at.

Savage: What time is it?

Murk: Seven-thirty.

Savage: Where is everybody? Where is somebody? Where is

94

any fuckin body?

Murk: It's Monday night.

Savage: I wanna have a good time.

Murk: Come on, Savage. It's Monday night.

Savage: As if that made a difference. Why don't you put some fuckin nuts on the bar for Chrissake?

Murk: We don't have any nuts.

Savage: Then somethin. Cheese doodles. Make a fuckin attempt.

Murk: You hungry?

Savage: No.

Murk: Why don't you sit down?

Savage: I don't wanna.

Murk: Alright. Stand up.

Savage: I've got energy. Do you understand what I'm saying? I'm young. I'm strong. I just ate two Cornish game hens and a buncha broccoli. It's only seven-thirty. I don't feel like watching television once more for the rest of my life and I can't sit in that apartment that smells like a catbox with my mother who looks like a dead walrus for one more second or I will die. I will. So I put on a dress and my black pumps and I got lotsa cash and here I am. What's happening?

Murk: Why don't you try Cotter's?

Savage: Cotter's is dead.

Murk: Then the P.C.?

Savage: The P.C. is totally beat.

Murk: So sit down. It's Monday night all over.

Savage: Wait a minute. Oh no, man. Don't tell me this. Where's the jukebox?

Murk: It broke. It started to smell like burning, and they took it out. We'll get another one in a couple of days.

Savage: No jukebox?

Murk: Not tonight.

Savage: I gotta feeling like something's chasing me.

Murk: That's not my problem.

Savage: I gotta feeling like the house is on fire.

Murk: Uh-huh. *(Overwhelmed, Savage goes to the down left table and sits. She takes a worn pack of cards from her bag, and starts setting up for solitaire.)* What are you drinking?

Savage: Nothing.

Murk: You gotta have something.

Savage: Why?

Murk: Rules.

Savage: White wine.

Murk: Alright. It's a dollar. I ain't serving you over there, and you gotta pay as you go.

Savage: Why?

Murk: Rules.

Savage: Alright. *(She goes, pays, takes wine back to her table.)* Murk?

Murk: What?

Savage: You wanna shoot a game of pool?

Murk: No.

> *Murk produces a watering can and comes out from behind the bar. He limps. He waters the two plants.*

Savage: Murk, why you water those plants? They're dead.

Murk: They don't know that. *(Enter Linda Rotunda, a done-up, attractive, overripe Italian girl. She comes in, sits down, and starts crying.)* What are you having?

Savage: Hey. Are you blind? Give her a minute.

Murk: Alright.

Savage: Linda?

Linda: Denise?

Savage: Hi.

Linda: Hi.

Savage: Do you want me not to notice that you're crying?

Linda: I don't care who knows.

Murk: What are you having?

Linda: A rusty nail. No ice.

Murk: Alright.

Linda: I gotta situation here, but I don't know you good enough to talk about this.

Savage: Comon. We went to school together.

Linda: Grammar school only.

Savage: So we're not friends. Cry by yourself.

Linda: No. Hey. I can't go home It's too early. My mother would know something is wrong. She'd be in my face inna minute.

Savage: You wanna shoot a game of pool?

Linda: No.

Murk: Your drink's here. Two dollars.

Linda: Oh.

Savage: Let it sit up there a minute. It drives him crazy. Why you crying?

Linda: It's my boyfriend Anthony. Something's gone wrong with him.

Savage: That's Tony Aronica, right?

Linda: Yeah.

Savage: The one who wears leather pants.

Linda: Sometimes he does.

Savage: Incredibly good-looking.

Linda: Yeah, that's him.

Savage: He knocked you up last year.

Linda: Where'd you hear that?

Savage: I heard it.

Linda: Nobody knocked me up.

Savage: Now that's pushin it, Linda. You're a neighborhood joke. You get knocked up every time you stop walking. It's stupid to lie about it. Everybody knows. You're sloppy and you're fertile.

Linda: Are you bein nasty to me?

Savage: No. That's the way I am. Comes a bein lonely. That's why I never hadda a boyfriend like Tony Aronica. At least that's one a the reasons.

Murk: Hey. Pick up your drink.

Savage: See? It drives him nuts. It preys on his mind. Let him wait.

Murk: You can leave it here all night for what I care. But it's pay-as-you-go. Two dollars. I'm waiting.

Linda goes, pays, takes drink back to table.

Savage: He's never grown up. He still thinks he's playin Simon Says in the playground.

Murk: I never played Simon Says.

Savage: Well, whatever.

Murk: I played War.

Savage: Bang, bang.

Murk: Shut up, Savage.

Savage: You can't take no back and forth at all, can you?

Murk: I said shut up.

Savage: Okay, don't get shook up. *(To Linda.)* So, what's wrong with you? What's the story? Did you get knocked up again?

Linda: No. It's Anthony. He's gone crazy.

Savage: Is he hittin you?

Linda: No.

Savage: What's he doin?

Linda: He wants to see other women.

Savage: What?

Linda: He wants to see other women.

Savage: And for this you think he's crazy, huh? You are a pisser.

Linda: You don't understand.

Savage: I understand that. That's very common.

Linda: No, no. You don't understand.

Savage: Have it your own way.

Linda: He wants to see ugly women.

Savage: They may look that way to you, honey, but I guess he sees 'em different.

Linda: You don't understand. He told me. He says, Linda, I wanna see ugly girls.

Savage: He said that?

Linda: Yes.

Savage: Well, what did he mean?

Linda: He meant what he said.

Savage: But that's not possible. Men don't go after women they think are ugly. If they end up with an ugly woman, it's because they made a mistake and they think she's good-lookin. Alright a drunk, a crazy guy, or a loser. But a guy like Tony? A guy like Tony Aronica would never end up with an ugly woman. You know why? He's just got too much dog in 'em. He thinks like a dog.

Linda: What are you tellin me? You're tellin me nothin. I tell you what's goin on, and you tell me it ain't goin on. It's goin on. Anthony wants to see ugly girls cause I don't know why, but that's the fuckin news and don't tell me otherwise. Every Monday night I go to his place and we spend time together, and this night I go and he's got this look in his eye. Like he knows some-

thin, and like he never seen me before. I got a scared feelin right
away. I touch him but he puts my hand away. He says he wants
to talk. What's he wanna talk about before we go to bed? What's
there to talk about? When a woman wants to talk to a man, it's
cause she wants the man to see her better. When it's the other
way, when the man stops you from touchin to talk, what's there
to talk about? It's gotta be bad. I tried to keep him from talkin. I
turned myself on. But there was somethin in his mind. Even my
mother sees what Anthony's got. Even my mother. She'd like a
taste. She knows where I'm goin on Monday nights. I don't come
home till late, the mornin sometimes, but she don't say anything.
Any other time she would. But she knows where I go, and she
wants it for me. Once I was goin, and she whispered to me so's
my father wouldn't hear, Take it, Linda. That's all. Take it, Linda.
And I did. And now he don't wanna see me cause he wants to see
ugly women. I said I'd be ugly for him, but he said no. It didn't
work that way. I'm so ashamed. I feel ugly. I feel fat. Anthony
don't want me no more.
Savage: You're not fat. You're almost fat. But you're not fat.
You wanna play some cards?
Linda: No.
Savage: These cards are disgusting anyway. I left'em near the
humidifier one night and they got all spongy. I got the humidifier
cause my mother was dryin out. She never goes anywhere, she
can't, and we got so much heat in that fuckin apartment - I looked
at her one day and she looked like a dead plant. So I went out and
I got the humidifier and I run it every night. She still looks like
freeze-dried shit, but I feel better cause I did somethin. I didn't
just take it. I didn't just fuckin accept it. I believe in action. Anyway, between the humidity and my sloppy ways, these cards are
real crappy. Some of these Sister Rosita's, you know, these
witchtellers, they're supposed to be able to see your future inna
pack a cards. I look at these cards, I never see anything about my
future. I just see my fuckin life. I'm gonna go insane.
Linda: What are you talkin about?
Savage: I'm talkin about tension. I'm talkin about somethin
snappin at your heels, but you can't get away. Bein apart from
everybody else. Bein alone. There's a wall there. Like you're inna

glass box, a bee inna jar, dreamin about flowers, smellin your own ... death. People look at you, it's through somethin. You touch somebody, there's somethin over your hand.

Linda: I don't get you.

Savage: I'm tryin to tell you somethin, but it's not easy.

Linda: So tell me anyway.

Savage: I'm a virgin.

Linda: What?

Savage: You heard me. You're just astounded. I'm a virgin.

Linda: Why you tellin me a lie?

Savage: In the beginnin, it was just bad luck. I'm not like you, and I got a big mouth, and well, it's easy not to lose it at first. You're scared, they're scared, somebody says: Boo, and everybody runs away. At least that's the way it was for me. To start with. But then it became a thing. Most everybody I knew lost it, you know, over a certain period a time, and there I was, still in the wrapper. It woulda been easy to lose it then. But it became a thing, you know? I felt different. I felt like I was holdin out for somethin. Not some guy, not just some guy. I felt like I was holdin out for somethin, sayin no, no, I'm not takin that life just cause it was the first one I was offered. So here I am. I'm thirty-two. And I'm still sayin no, no. And I still only got offered the one life, and I still don't want that one.

Linda: You're a virgin?

Savage: Yeah.

Linda: Wow.

Savage: Say somethin.

Linda: What's it like?

Savage: It's like holdin your breath, only you never have to let go. No, that's not what it's like...

Linda: I never knew anybody grown up who never, you know...I feel like you know somethin I don't know.

Savage: Well, I know you know somethin I don't know.

Linda: Yeah, but everybody I know knows what I know. Except you. It's like common knowledge. But what you know, it's like a secret. How does it feel?

Savage: I feel strong. Like I'm wearin chains and I could snap 'em any time. I feel ready. I go to work and I feel like I could take over the company, but I just type. I go home and I see my mother in her chair and I feel like I could pick her up with one hand and chuck her out the window and roll up the rug and throw a big party. Everybody's invited. I go to the library and I wanna take the books down off the shelves and open all the books on the tables and argue with everybody about ideas. I wanna think out loud. I wanna think out loud with other people. You know what's wrong with everybody? Too smart. I know it sounds crazy. I know. But it's true. Everybody's too smart. It's like everybody knows everything and everybody argued everything and everything got hashed out and settled the day before I was born. It's not fair. They know about gravity so nobody talks about gravity. It's a dead issue. Look at me. My feet are stuck to the fuckin floor. Fantastic. But no. That's gravity. Forget it. It's been done it's been said it's been thought, so fuck it. It's not fair. I've been shut outta everything that mighta been good by a smartness around that won't let me think not one new thing. And it's been like that with love, too. You're a little girl and you see the movies and maybe you talk to your mother and you definitely talk to your friends and then you know, right? So you go ahead and you do love. And somethin a what somebody told ya inna movie or in your ear is what love is. And where the fuck are you then, that's what I wanna know? Where the fuck are you when you've done love, and you can point to love, and you can name it, and love is the same as gravity the same as everything else, and everything else is a totally dead fuckin issue?

Linda: That's what it's like to be a virgin?

Savage: That's part of it. Maybe that's the good part.

Linda: You wanna be my friend?

Savage: I don't know how.

Linda: Me neither.

Savage: Why you want me?

Linda: Cause I gotta make a change, and you're different.

Savage: What are you gonna do?

Linda: Things have got to where I got to make a change.

Murk: Hey, keep it down.

Savage: Back off.

Linda: All I had was Monday. I just marked time till Monday. I ain't got Monday no more so I gotta make a change. Everything's doin shit on me an changin on me an lookin different than it was before and now there ain't no Monday and I'm thirty-two and my mother's gonna be on my case again my sucky life and I'll be fucking guys under staircases and I gotta make a change for myself this time no matter how much it hurts, I don't want to, scared, or it's goodbye Linda for sure. You gotta help me.

Savage: How?

Linda: Don't ask me that. That's the question. I don't know. But I gotta change.

Savage: I gotta ask cause so do I, too.

Linda: What are we gonna do?

Savage: I don't know.

Linda: I'm scared. I feel so scared.

Savage: Why?

Linda: I gotta move outta my whole house.

Savage: So move.

Linda: Why ain't you moved outta your house? *(No answer.)* Why ain't you moved outta your house?

Savage: I can't do that.

Linda: Why not?

Savage: My mother's a shut-in. She's trapped. I can't leave her.

Linda: Ain't we shut-in's, too?

Savage: I gotta good room. I got books there that I read. And I gotta refill the humidifier all the time. My mother, she can only walk on canes. I figured it out. Without me, she'd die in three days.

Linda: You're scared, too.

Savage: No, I'm not.

Linda: Yeah, you are.

Savage: Yeah.

Linda: I thought you weren't.

Savage: I'm scared of everything. I see what could go wrong with everything so I don't do nothin. I got this one thing in me that I hate. I'm a coward.

Linda: We gotta be friends.

Savage: Alright.

Linda: I ain't never been friends with a girl. I guess this is it.

Savage: I ain't never been friends with nobody. I ain't had the time. I got my mother. I got the job. I just talk at people, which is lonely. I honestly could just fall down from loneliness.

Linda: Maybe ... Maybe we should do somethin together.

Savage: For instance what?

Linda: I don't know. Maybe we should go dancin together or somethin.

Savage: Dancin?

Linda: Somethin.

Savage: I don't dance.

Linda: Somethin.

Savage: Maybe we should, I don't know, getta apartment. Together.

Linda: Yeah? That'd be a step out, wouldn't it?

Savage: It's an idea.

Linda: So we're like girlfriends now, right? We're girlfriends, talkin to each other about bein roommates.

April: Who wants a friend? I'll be somebody's friend.

Murk: Be quiet.

April: No. I mean it. I'll be friends with anybody who wants to be friends.

Murk: Go to sleep.

April: I can't go to sleep, Murk, even though I'm real tired. If I go to sleep, you'll throw me out. That's the rules and that's justice. Who wants a friend? Do I know you?

Savage: Sure you know us. We all went to Saint Anthony's together.

April: Okay, Saint Anthony's. What's your name?

Savage: Denise Savage.

April: And you?

Linda: Linda Rotunda.

April: And what's my name?

Linda: I don't remember her.

Savage: Your name is April. April White.

April: That's right.

Linda: You're April White?

April: That's right.

Linda: Oh my God.

April: Pretty bad, huh?

Linda: You look different.

April: Pretty bad.

Murk: You look outstanding.

April: Thanks.

Linda: You're April White. I'm sorry. I didn't mean to ... You were supposed to be a nun.

April: Was I? Oops.

Linda: You were supposed to become a nun, and work with sick people in India. You made a little speech in front of the class. About becoming a Maryknoll nun. You shook. I thought you were beautiful.

April: I was.

Savage: Yeah, she was.

Murk: She is still.

April: You got pregnant. I remember. You disappeared in the middle of the eighth. Sister Theresa said you'd swallowed a pin. Then the girls started whispering. I didn't like that. That whispering number. It was slimey. It was a slimey way to act. But I remember. You got pregnant.

Linda: You got a big mouth.

April: Sorry. I was just placing you.

Murk: Here. Take a drink.

April: What? Is the haze goin off me? Murk keeps me inna special haze and I keep him company. I didn't become a nun causa Father Rogan. Father Rogan was this priest he was cute he had premature grey hair and he useta tell me about becomin a nun in India. But then one day in the Sixties he got tired a bein a premature grey priest he quit. But he stayed in the neighborhood. He went out he stood onna streetcorner in civilian clothes and hung out. He got fat he liked to drink beer quart bottles of beer. He didn't shave that much. Nobody would talk to him cause the whole thing was just too fuckin awful. But he didn't seem to mind and he wouldn't leave and he wouldn't disguise himself or somethin. He just stood there and stood there. Like a lighthouse.

Murk: Everybody knows this.

April: Everybody forgets everything all the time, which is good maybe. But I remember. Until finally, everybody just got so demoralized by the sight a this bum priest standin there, that a

buncha guys got together and chased him out. The posse. They
ran Father Rogan outta town and into the arms a who knows
what. Not me. So I didn't become a nun. I missed the logic there,
but that's why I didn't go to India in black and white. Help me.
Help me.

Murk: April.

April: No. Help me. I've been in trouble for a long time, and it
didn't make a fuck to me, but, my life's too long. I'm only thirty-
two. I've got too much time to kill. I could live thirty, forty more
years just starin at the meter runnin. I can't knock myself out
enough. And too, I drink and things come outta me. The way I
really am. The animal. The animal gets bigger all the time. She
don't hardly fit in the fuckin haze no more. It's me and my animal. And I'm tryin to stay in and she's tryin to get out. That's
when people go crazy.

Murk: April.

April: No. When they can't stay the way they are no matter
how they hit themselves in the head, and the teeth and the hair
come rippin through everything dead that was walkin around.
Like with the drinking. You drink and you drink. And the more
you drink, the more it only goes through this one part of you, just
this one part of you. And the more it goes through, the more it
kills this part till that part's dead. So in the end or the middle I
don't know where you're walkin around in this fuckin force field,
you know, LIFE, and in there is this corpse and this animal fightin all the time, till the animal pushes off the dead weight and gets
out, and that's when they take you away.

Murk: You gotta shut up.

April: I don't wanna be the crazy one they take away.

Savage: You gotta pull yourself together.

April: Tell me somethin I don't know.

Murk: I'll take care of April.

Savage: Sure you will. Give her another drink why don't you?

Murk: Get outta here if you're gonna talk that way.

Savage: I got my drink here. I'm a payin customer. I'll talk till
my mouth gets tired. April?

April: What?

Savage: We gotta get an apartment.

Linda: Who?

Savage: The me, you, the three of us.

Linda: Oh, her now, too? You ain't serious now.

Savage: Think about it. I'm scared and you're scared. But she's fuckin beyond. To help her we'll be able to do all the shit we're afraid a doin. We're no better off. But we can see her and see there what we can't see in the mirror. When it's too hard to do straight out, we'll say we're doin it for her.

April: That's nice.

Linda: I don't wanna live with a woman like that.

Savage: Wake up, Linda. We're a boxed set. Look at her. That's you. That's you.

Linda: Alright. Let's find a place.

April: Will I have my own room?

Savage: Sure.

April: That's nice, too.

> *Tony Aronica has appeared in the audience aisle. He's a stream-lined Italian guy, open collar, thin gold chain at the neck, leather pants. He brings off the look very well, but he seems tentative, uncertain.*

Savage: Tony Aronica.

Tony: I know my name.

> *He enters the stage.*

Linda: Anthony.

Tony: Hey, you think it was easy kissin off a fox like you? You don't know nothin.

Savage: If you just blew in to run her down why don't you get lost?

Tony: Get outta my business. *(To Linda.)* You don't know nothin. That ain't right. That ain't what I meant. I gotta say what I mean. I feel like I'm just learnin to talk. It's hard. I saw somethin. That's why I tracked you down, Rotunda. What I said whadn't enough to say. You been nice. We had a nice little thing.

Linda: Yeah, it was good.

Tony: I can smell the heat off you, you know that? The fire's never all the way out with you.

Linda: Tony.

Tony: But that ain't what I came to say.

Linda: What you want from me?

Tony: I was in my car outside this place over the weekend. I hadda a couple a drinks and I was a little fuzzy, so I was waitin till I cleared. It was dark. I was sittin there. And this unknown girl got in. She just got in the car. And she started talkin to me. She started rappin to me about the Soviet Union. Yeah. 'Bout their economy. Housin. How they feel about China bein right there. Everything. Everything about the Soviet Union. She musta talked for two hours. Russian paranoia. Tass. The Gulag. I'm sittin there an I'm takin this in. The Trans-Siberian Railroad. What kinda tanks they got in Eastern Europe. Why they need American wheat. And then she was finished. She'd told me everything she knew. So I took her in the back seat and I banged her. And do you know something? It was the best. It was the best I ever had. And it whadn't cause she knew a lotta tricks or like that. It was cause she'd told me about the Soviet Union. And then she left. Now here's the thing. She was very ugly. I don't even wanna talk about how she looked. Mucho ugly. I didn't think I could ever be with a woman like that. But it came about outta whatever, happenstance, and I was. And it turned out to be better than what I went after. Do you see what I mean? Do you see what I'm comin towards? I always went for the girl like you. And what finally fuckin come to me, what finally fuckin penetrated the wall here, was there was somethin else. Somethin I never even thought about, didn't have a clue about. When I talked to you, I called it ugly girls. I don't know what to call it. There's other people. Like in science fiction. Another dimension right there but you can't see it. I got into it for a minute by accident. Through a crack. I caught a flash. The dimension a ugly girls. I'm like one a those guys inna factory and they bring in all new machines. That's what I feel like. Like I gotta retrain or I'm gonna lose my place. Some girls you look at some girls you don't. I wanna see the things I didn't see before an let the stuff I was lookin at go by. I've done the fuckin thing we're in, Linda. I've been with you, I talked to you. I know what that is. That's what I meant when I said you didn't know nothin, but I whadn't sayin it right. You look at what I look at. You know what I know. I wanna look at somethin else. I wanna know somethin else. I'm thirty-two years old. I wanna change.

Linda: Now you're makin me mad.

Tony: I knew you wouldn't get it.

Linda: I get it.

Tony: Like hell you do.

Linda: What pisses me off is you think you know me. You don't know me.

Tony: Gimme a break, Linda. I know you like a book.

Linda: You seen what I let you see, jerk. Nothin else. You seen what I thought you could handle. What I thought you wanted to see. That's all. You don't know me.

Tony: What are you tellin me? You mean you knew about the Soviet Union?

Linda: No, Einstein, that's not what I'm tellin you.

Tony: Then what?

Linda: I feel like a ghost. I'm there and nobody sees me. I talk and nobody hears me.

April: I hear you.

Savage: Me too. Maybe they're the ghosts.

Murk: Boo.

Tony: Boo who? What the fuck are you, the abominable snowman? You know what's the matter with you people? All of you? You're not brave enough. That's right. Like in the old flicks when the guy stands up outta the ditch in the middle of the bombs blowin and flames and machine guns all over and just starts fightin back. Fuck it, right? You only live once. Is it gonna be on your knees? Stand up. You gotta be brave for yourself cause nobody else can be brave for you and nobody else cares. What the fuck, did you think you were gonna live forever? You're not. Stand up. It's pissin away. Your life. I know what I'm talkin about here so hear me good. Waste. It's like I wish they froze me inna block a ice till it was time and I was ready to make my move so I didn't waste anything. Waste, right? You clowns know about waste. I know about waste. I fuckin invented waste. I got this routine down with the girl the car and the bed, the girl the car and the bed, the girl the car and the bed, and I do it with this one part a my brain it's about this big, it's about the size of a piece of gum, and the rest of me I forgot to put away, right? I forgot to put it inna the refrigerator and it's startin to smell. What's that smell? Oh, that's Tony Aronica. HE'S TURNIN FUCKIN GREEN.

Linda: Well, smell Linda. Cause Linda's turnin fuckin green, too. I got news for you, chump. When you use this much a your brain on Linda, how much a Linda do you think you get? Huh? Figure it out. So that chick gave you the scoop on the Soviet Union. That's what the chick brought with her, shithead. What'd she leave with? What'd you give her? The same thing you gave me. A good bounce on the bed. Cause that's all you got in your pocket to give. A good bounce. Ugly girls. Seriously, Anthony. You kill me.

Tony: You don't sound like yourself.

Linda: Listen to you. I think you got about a five-watt bulb burnin in there. It's a miracle to me you can make your way around.

Tony: No, you are. You're talkin different.

Linda: That's cause you're hitting me with a different level a stupidity than I'm used to. You sound like some mad doctor in some shitty movie. You're gonna steal ugly girl brains cause they don't got ugly girl brains on your planet.

Savage: Lay off him.

Linda: What?

Savage: Don't you see the good thing? He's not thinkin like a dog. Do you know what it is for a guy like him to think with somethin asides his pecker? I didn't even think it was possible.

Tony: Hey, don't talk about me.

April: I think you're cute. I'm not gonna do anything about it, but I think you're cute.

Murk: He's a type.

Linda: Don't have too much to drink, April. You might get ugly. Then Tony'd be compulsed to put the make on you. And you're wrong, Savage. He is completely thinking with his pecker. His whole inspiration for this nutty fuckin idea was a good bounce in the back seat of his car and how he can get more of the same. (*To Tony.*) You're a moron. When you're not in bed, you're a moron.

April: He doesn't look that stupid to me.

Tony: You don't wanna understand. I'm sorry I even tried to be straight with you. You're just as dumb as I thought you were. Just inna different way than I thought is all. You just want your Monday night workout, and then you don't wanna know from nothin. You probably wish I couldn't talk. You probably wish I was some kinda animal an ape a bull does what I do for you an then goes to sleep under a tree or some shit where I'm no bother. Well, that ain't me, the me I'm gonna be anyhow. You're a real cow, Linda. You're a real milker. An I'm not what's just good for some barnyard yahoo bullshit. No way. You're right. I don't know you. I thought you were a cow because you were a cow. Now I see you're a cow cause that's what you wanna be.

Linda: Why don't you just fuckin die?

Tony: Cause I'm not in the mood, alright? I'm not in the mood to lay the fuck down an die.

Linda: Well, what are you gonna do?

Tony: I'm gonna change.

Linda: What?

Tony: From the ground. I'm gonna become a different person.

Linda: You ain't got it in you.

Tony: I got tons in me.

Savage: But how you get it out? Where you put it? Who's it for? You can't change. You can't do it. It's like puttin your hands on your own waist an tryin to pick yourself off the ground.

Tony: I am gonna do it, bitch. And you'd best not be in my way. I'm gonna go against my life with everything I got. I'm gonna attack my fuckin self as I am. I'm gonna kick ass and take names. And I am majorly majorly gonna change.

Savage: What are you gonna change to?

Tony: I don't know. I'm gonna get new clothes. *(Indicating Murk.)* Maybe like his.

Linda: What's wrong with your clothes?

Tony: They're mine.

Linda: Changing clothes ain't gonna get you noplace.

Tony: You don't know that.

Linda: You can change your clothes from now to New Year's, it ain't gonna do you dip. What you gotta do, Anthony sweetheart, is you gotta do your laundry. It ain't the new clothes that make the man. It's what he does with his dirty things. Do you hear what I'm sayin to you? You got yourself a shitload a laundry. You can walk away from that, but it'll still be there.

Tony: What are you talkin about? What laundry?

Linda: Me, for instance.

Savage: Linda. Why you pullin him back?

Linda: Pullin him back from what? Where's he goin?

Savage: I don't know. Outta some circle where he's been chokin. Hey, I got an idea. Maybe Tony could live with us, too.

Tony: Live with who?

Savage: With me and April and Linda. We're gonna get a place, an apartment, an start a new life.

Linda: And what exactly would be the arrangement, Denise?

Savage: What d'you mean?

Tony: Three women?

Linda: Don't even bother to get excited, Stud. *(To Savage.)* What the fuck you think this is, Manhattan?

Savage: Don't be so quick, Linda. It's an idea. Think about it a minute.

Linda: April, you, me, and him. In one apartment.

Savage: Where do you live now, Tony?

Tony: In a garage. My uncle's gotta two-car garage and no car. So I keep my car in there, and a bed. A ... I don't think I like this idea.

Savage: Why not?

Tony: It sounds very nerve-wracking.

Savage: So what?

Tony: It'd be like living in a fuckin hen house.

Linda: I ain't doin it.

Savage: Don't be so quick.

Linda: My mother would swallow her tongue.

Savage: Your mother wouldn't be livin with us.

Linda: I won't share him.

Tony: I don't belong to you.

Linda: Me more than them.

Tony: I don't belong to nobody.

Linda: I won't share him.

Savage: Alright. Alright then. You're out of it.

Linda: What do you mean, I'm out of it?

Savage: Tony, what I said before? About not bein able to change? I meant, not by yourself. I've thought about it a lot. It ain't possible.

Linda: What do you mean, I'm out of it?

April: Uh-oh.

Savage: And you know it, too. That's why you're after some other kinda people to be with. I'm gonna tell you somethin, Tony. Somethin I can prove.

Linda: Hey, Denise, what track you on?

April: There are monkeys in this drink.

Murk: *(Instantly replacing her drink.)* No, there aren't.

Savage: I never started the part of my life you always been in, Tony. And I've been readin books an thinkin an usin all the other parts a me you ain't been. I'm different than you.

Tony: You are?

Savage: In every particle a me I'm different. Can't you feel it, Tony? Can't you feel the lack of chemistry between us?

Tony: I don't feel nothin.

Savage: Exactly. I'm what you don't naturally want, so I am what you want if you want to change.

Tony: Whoa. I gotta think about that.

Linda: Savage, what are you doin?

Savage: I'm tryin to take him.

Linda: What?

Savage: You heard me. I'm tryin to take him away from you.

Linda: You fuckin dirtbag.

Savage: I told you I was waitin for somethin.

Linda: You didn't say it was my boyfriend.

Savage: You won't go along with me, Linda, I still gotta go.

April: These monkeys have pitchforks and they're doin the LINDY .

Savage: SNAP OUT OF IT, APRIL.

April: I can't.

Murk: Leave her alone.

April: Does this mean we're not gettin an apartment?

Linda: Yeah, what about the apartment? You were gonna be my goddamn roommate girlfriend.

Savage: I'm changin my plans.

Linda: You never meant ta be my friend.

Savage: Yes, I did, but it's gotta lead somewhere. If it's just another way not out then I gotta go for somethin else. Opportunity knocks like almost fuckin never. Tony.

Linda: You are in physical danger, honey.

Savage: I don't care.

Linda: You will when you're missin a piece a your face.

Savage: It's better than what I'm missing now. Tony, I'm a virgin.

Tony: What? What? Don't. Neither of you. This is interference. I don't know what I'm doin but I got my determination. You talk to me, it's like two bad angels pullin me down. Don't pull me down. I hadda friend Jimmy Rina, he blew up his sister with a nail bomb. So they locked him up for seven years. He got out last week. I saw him at a party. He was sittin inna chair. Some broad was ticklin his chin. But I could see. He was still in jail. They put you inna cage for seven years, the cage is in your heart. No matter where you are. An I gotta cage in my heart, too. Solid steel this life has put in me. I'm lookin out through bars that come a knowin you an you an bein here an wearin these clothes an breathin this tired air. I want out. Don't make no sense. It's only my mind. What's that? Just a blob a bloody shit in my skull. I don't wanna be Tony Aronica no more. So neither a you got nothin ta say to me cause you don't even know who I am.

Savage: You think you know who I am?

Tony: Oh, you too, huh? I don't care who you are, alright? I don't give a rusty fuck who you are. I got my own problems.

Linda: I know who you are, darlin.

Savage: Who?

Linda: Another jive-ass man-grabbin broad who thinks every time she gets an ache it's another guy she needs.

Savage: That's the worst description of me I ever heard.

Linda: It'll do for now.

Savage: But that's not how I am at all.

Linda: I don't care. I don't gotta be fair with you. You're tryin ta grab my fuckin guy.

Tony: WOMEN.

Linda: What's that supposed to mean?

Tony: I know. God fuckin forbid I should know something about women an say what it is. You got a hole in you. I didn't put it there. Remember that. It used to be such a goof playin with girls, too. Back on Archer Street. Back when you went to church or some fuckin place for what you come to me for now.

Linda: You fuckin hypocrite motherfucker.

Tony: What?

Linda: Did you or did you not sing me a fuckin song about ugly women who you are lookin to for a turnaround?

Tony: Yeah, but I'm not...

Linda: So ain't you lookin to get from women just the same what I'm lookin to get from you?

Tony: Yeah maybe, but I'm...

Linda: Then you're just a peg lookin for a hole same as the other way around is with me.

Tony: It's like I'm a ghost.

Murk: Oh, now you're a ghost, too.

Tony: That's right. Am I wrong? Don't nobody listen to nobody except listenin for the trigger that sets them off on their thing. I mean when the fuck do we run out?

Linda: Run outta what?

Tony: Run outta sayin ... Run outta bein who I am.

Linda: Never.

Savage: Maybe very soon.

Linda: Why you say shit outta the blue like that?

Savage: We could run each other outta whatever, Tony, outta town?

Tony: My head hurts, man. I feel like my eyes are gonna cross.

Murk: HEY. *(To Tony.)* What are you drinkin?

Tony: Nothin.

Murk: Then get out.

Savage: Hey, I'm talkin to him.

Linda: No, I'm talkin to him.

Murk: Nobody stays in this bar without having a drink.

Savage: He whadn't drinkin nothin before this.

Murk: That was the grace period.

Savage: Then I'll buy him a drink. What are you drinkin?

Tony: I don't want nothin.

Linda: Good.

Savage: I'll buy him one anyway. Just put it on the bar.

Linda: Don't you buy him no drink.

Savage: I'll do what I damn well please.

Linda: You put your hand in that bag, you're gonna get a fist in your face.

Savage: You don't wanna do that, Linda.

Linda: That's exactly what I want to do. Anybody buys Anthony a drink, it'll be me.

Tony: I don't want a drink.

Linda: Who the fuck asked you? *(To Murk.)* Give him a Brandy Alexander.

April: That's a beautiful drink.

Tony: I don't want it.

Savage: He don't want your stupid Brandy Alexander.

April: A really beautiful drink. A Christmas drink.

Murk: A Brandy Alexander is three dollars.

Linda: I don't care if it's the jackpot in the Jersey lottery. Put the fuckin drink on the bar INSTANTLY. Here. *(Pays.)* You know what I think? I think you can't trust the stars in the sky anymore. You can't trust anything anymore.

   Starts to cry.

Murk: Hey. Hey, don't cry.

April: Murk hates cryin. It reminds him of his mother's tears over him.

Savage: Hey Linda, I'm sorry. I didn't mean to … be the way I am.

Tony: She cries easy.

Linda: *(Pauses from crying.)* You don't know me. *(Resumes.)*

Tony: Alright, I don't know you. You seem to cry easy. Hey, don't let it get to you, baby. Things ain't so bad.

Savage: Yeah. Cheer up.

Linda: Oh, I hate that.

Savage: What?

Linda: People tryin to cheer me up. Who asked you? I feel bad. I got a good reason to feel bad. Everybody's fuckin me over an lyin to me. My life eats it. I got no friends. I got nobody who loves me. My future looks like shit. I'm gettin fat. In ten years I'm gonna look like a rhino. You're tellin me to feel better. What are you, crazy? Get serious. I got nada to feel better about. What I got is a reason to cry. Don't try to take away what I got even if it stinks to give me nothin? My life sucks. Your life sucks. Your life sucks. Don't you tell me to stop cryin. You should start cryin. That's what should happen. You should all start cryin and banging your heads against the wall and permanently get off my fuckin case. Miserable buncha two-faced Doris Days.

Tony: Alright, so cry.

Linda: *(Stops crying.)* Don't tell me what to do.

Linda picks up the Brandy Alexander and drains it.

Murk: *(To Tony.)* This drink is empty. What are you drinking?

Tony: I don't want anything.

Murk: Then get out.

Linda: *(To Murk.)* You should work for the city.

Savage: Let me buy him one now. Don't make a big deal out of it. What are you drinkin?

Tony: Nothin.

Linda: He's drinkin Brandy Alexanders.

April: My mother drank four of those one Christmas, and she died.

Savage: Alright, give him a Brandy Alexander.

April: She drank four of 'em, and then she started breathin out. Ssss. And she never breathed in again. She exhaled and expired.

April quietly sings 'O Little Town Of Bethlehem' under the following.

Murk: Now I'm mad. You've upset April. She's gone Christmas. She always goes Christmas when she's upset. April. April. April.

Savage: Hey. I'm a payin customer. Make the drink.

Murk: You can wait a minute. It's on order. Go to your table.

Murk puts on little rectangular glasses and applies red rouge to his cheeks.

Tony: What's he doin?

Linda: I don't know.

Savage: Murk?

Murk dons a while heard, and puts on the jacket and hat of a

Santa suit.

Murk: The problem with people is they think they're alone. They think what they say don't do nothin. So they say every stupid thing that goes through their gourd, and they do shit they don't even know why. Which leads to what? The world looks like homemade refried shit. Jingle bells jingle bells, jingle all the way...

April: Is that you, Santa?

Murk: Ho ho ho. It's me, April.

April: It's good to see you.

Murk: It's good to see you, too, April.

April: Did you get my letter?

Murk: Yes.

April: I didn't know how to address it.

Murk: I got it.

April: I thought you might pass me right by. I've been bad.

Murk: I forgive you.

April: You do?

Murk: Yes.

April: Really?

Murk: Yes. I've brought you something.

April: You have?

Murk: *(Taking a nicely wrapped Christmas present from a refrigerator underneath the bar.)* A present. I brought it all the way from the North Pole.

April: I don't deserve a present.

Murk: Yes, you do. You're a good girl, April.

April: Am I?

Murk: You're a good girl in a good world. And because you are, my helpers and I worked very hard and made you this. The box may feel a little cold. I just brought it from the North Pole.

April: Thank you. It does feel cold.

She unwraps the present. It's a music box. She opens it. It plays.

Murk: Merry Christmas, April.

April: Merry Christmas.

Murk: Do you like it?

April: More than anything.

Murk: Now promise me you'll be a good girl.

April: I promise.

Murk: And you'll say your prayers?

April: Yes.

Murk: And you won't go crazy?

April: No.

Murk: Alright then. *(Takes music box and puts it away.)* Jingle bells jingle bells, jingle all the way ... *(To himself, as he gets out of the Santa attire.)* Everybody's doin it to everybody, and everybody's saying they don't know why it's happening. It's happening because they're doin it. It's a matter a cause and effect. It's a matter a responsibility. People gotta take responsibility for what they do. *(To Savage.)* Now, that was a Brandy Alexander, right?

Savage: Right.

April: Hey Murk, top me off a little, okay? I'm losin my head.

Murk: I'll be with you inna minute, April.

April: Okay.

Tony: What did I just see?

Murk: Don't make a big thing out of it.

Tony: But what was that? You were bein Santa Claus.

Murk: Don't make a big thing, I said.

April: Murk don't like that. When you talk about how he is.

Murk: It's no good. You can kill a thing like that.

Linda: You were nice to her.

Murk: Talk about somethin else.

Savage: You made like you were Saint Nick. You got the clothes an everything.

Murk: TONY. Do something for once in your life. Talk about somethin else.

Tony: What?

Murk: I don't care. Somethin that don't have me in it.

Tony: Okay. I can't think a nothin.

Linda: This does not surprise me.

Savage: That's why you need me, Tony. Cause you don't know nothin but the girl the car and the bed.

Tony: And the Soviet Union.

Savage: Oh yeah? Talk to me about the Soviet Union.

Tony: They need our wheat.

Savage: Why?

Tony: I can't.

Savage: Why not?

Tony: I'm forgettin what it was.

Savage: You know why? Cause it was never yours. The ugly girl brought you somethin and then she took it away. You never had it to keep. Now I see my mistake. If I offer you my virginity and you take it, you're right back where you were. And that's where you'd take me, too.

Tony: Hey look, I didn't ask you to figure out my whole ...

Savage: If I offer you my virginity, and you take it, then that'd really just be me takin Linda's place.

Linda: Who'd want my place?

Savage: Right. We'd just be ruttin in the same rut you was ruttin in before.

Tony: I don't get you.

Savage: That's right. You don't. I went another way. I'm sealed up like a jug a wine's been layin in the ocean since the Romans. I'm a find. You want me, Tony, I'm found.

Tony: Maybe. Maybe there is somethin in you for me.

Savage: Maybe.

Linda: Ain't I got things in me same as her?

Savage: You're a pig. You gave it away. You just gave it away.

Linda: *(Makes for Savage; stops.)* I don't wanna kill. I wanna win. I spare you.

Savage: This is my offer. My virginity. It's a place. On the map if you know what I mean. You can't go there cause a where you been but I am there and I can take you there. You say you wanna break outta this prison life that's got you tied up in some cage but you don't know how. Here's how. Live with me. Inna room. With no bed.

Tony: With no bed. With no bed? Meaning no ... *(Gestures.)*

Savage: That's right.

Tony: That's a new one. That's a brand new wrinkle. It's got about as much appeal for me as cancer, but it's new. You know, I'm depressed. I'm fucked up and depressed.

Linda: Tony, you were right. I was a cow for you. But I don't have to be no cow. It's cause I thought that's what you wanted. A good bounce and goodbye, right? So I was wrong. Shoot me. But

I wasn't wrong, was I? It was what you wanted till lately, ain't it? So now you're changin. So? Can't I change, too? Don't you see how I wanna change? Can it make any fuckin sense in any way to keep startin from zero every time it's time to make a move? Take me with you. Anthony, we'll go somewhere. Do you really wanna live your whole life leavin people, tryin ta keep up with yourself? Ain't you afraid a gettin lonely? Ain't you? It can be all there is, baby. Think your thoughts and get outrageous, but just remember, you could end up alone. It's how a lotta people end up. Look around. I don't haveta tell you nothin. Open your eyes it's there to see. Like dead leaves floatin in the water. (*To Savage.*) So you're a virgin. The only thing you never used was your body. But up there. In there's your tired old pig brain ain't been off its back since the Flood. Probably reeks in there like dirty sheets an last month's rag. What's so sweet about that? I'm hungry. I wanna bite somethin. *(Takes the newly made drink and downs it.)* Very tasty.

April: That's two she's had. Two more an she's gone.

Tony: I'm leavin.

Tony exits into the audience.

Savage: Where you goin?

Tony: I don't know.

Linda: You goin back to your place?

Savage: Stay.

Tony is in the audience aisle. He turns and faces the stage.

Tony: What? In a room with no bed? With you? Doin what?

Linda: I gotta suggestion. Marry me.

Tony: What?

April: Oh my God. A proposal.

Linda: Marry me.

Savage: What's this?

Linda: Action.

Savage: That's not what I meant.

Linda: I don't care what you meant. You wanna marry me, Tony? You wanna marry me, we could get married. You want different? It'd be different. It'd be a trip.

Savage: That is so tired. That is so old.

Linda: Ain't nobody in this room's ever done it.

Savage: That don't make it new.

Linda: I ain't tryin to be original.

Savage: Maybe that's your problem.

Linda: And maybe your problem is you're tryin to invent the wheel.

Savage: I'M TRYIN. What am I tryin? To rise up. People who died a minute an came back, they say they saw … They rose up outta an saw themselves. An what a relief. What am I tryin? I had this dream. It haunts me. It fuckin haunts me. I was lookin inna mirror. An I noticed a bit of the skin on my cheek was peelin so I pulled it off. Then I saw a bigger piece was peelin an I pulled that off, too. An inna few minutes I'd pulled off my whole face like it was tissues. An I looked in the mirror, and all that was there was a piece of flat grey cardboard where my face had been. An I was glad. I was glad my face was gone. An somebody said to me, God, you've got beautiful eyes. An that was what was left I saw. Just my eyes and the rest blank. An I said, they were always there an they were always beautiful, but now you can really see them cause there's nothing else. I'm not gonna ask you to marry me, Tony. Linda is offerin one thing and I am offerin you somethin else. I'm tryin to pull off my face so you can see my eyes. Do you wanna see my eyes?

Tony: What the fuck are you talkin about? I feel like they're offerin me some choice from the moon. This one says I gotta do my laundry, an this one's gonna rip off her face.

Linda: Who do you want, me or her?

Tony: I don't know what to say to you.

Linda: She's a virgin. She's thirty-two and she's a virgin. That's just sad if you know what I mean. She ain't never done no lovin and now she's startin to get desperate. Is that what you need? Some desperate broad ain't gonna save you from nothin.

Savage: I hate you.

Linda: I can live with that.

Savage: You hit me where it's easiest.

Linda: That's where it makes sense to hit.

April: I got somethin to say.

Murk: April.

April: Tony, will you marry me?

Tony: Are you talkin to me?

April: Why don't you marry me? I don't take up much room.

Murk: Well Tony, are you gonna marry her?

Tony: No.

Murk: Good.

April: I'm a little disappointed, Tony. I thought we mighta hadda real future.

Savage: Oh man, the future. Is the future really in these fuckin old cards?

Linda: Fuck the future. Tony, you walk outta here without me where you goin? You're not takin a step. You're nowhere. I'm nowhere. I'm bein serious with you, Aronica.

Tony: Man, this is hard. I didn't know things was this hard.

Savage: You coulda stayed asleep till you were dead. What's worse? Tony, I do believe there is another kinda livin that don't have deadness in it. I'm offerin you somethin here, somethin unknown, somethin yet to come. Somethin the smartness hasn't gotten at with its names.

Tony steps back on stage.

Tony: *(Gently)* What are you doin?

Savage: I'm tryin to start somethin... new.

Tony: It don't work.

Linda: I'll show you what works.

Linda goes to Tony, kisses him. They get very hot together. Then she stops, turns him around and turns around herself, so they're back to back. She puts her arms through his arms, and picks him up off the ground, stretching him. Then she throws him off, and steps away.

Tony: That was definitely good.

April: I'm a little jealous.

Linda: Ain't nobody gonna make it happen for you like me.

Murk: April?

April: What?

Murk: Will you marry me?

April: I think I'm losin my head, Murk.

Murk: I'll marry you if you promise that we'll go on just exactly like now. No changes of any kind.

Savage: Then why would you wanna get married at all?

Murk: To keep things the same. I'm thirty-two years old. Well?

April: Well … No.

Murk: Oh.

April: I like bein foot loose an fancy free.

Murk: Uh-huh.

April: I like havin my options open.

Murk: Uh-huh.

April: I like it that if we got somethin goin it's cause we choose to have somethin goin, an it's not outta feelin we should or somethin weird like that. Do you understand what I mean?

Murk: Yeah. You're cut off. No more credit, no more drinks.

April: I accept your proposal.

Murk: Thank you. You've made me a happy man.

Linda: If you're so happy, why don't you go on an crack a smile?

Murk: No, I don't think I'll do that. April, I'll buy you a drink. Since you're my intended.

April: I'll have a Brandy Alexander, in one of the large glasses, served on a white doily.

Murk: Alright.

April: As I have told you all, this is the very drink that killed my mother. My father died of nothin at all, which is maybe the saddest thing a person can pass on from. But my mother, who was the only one ever stupid enough to love me, my mother died from this drink that Murk is making me now. I have always taken consolation where I could find it, even when it caused me grief.

Murk: *(Serving the drink on the doily.)* Here.

Linda: You know, I put the fuckin question to you, Anthony, an you got me hangin.

Savage: Me too.

Linda: I can't even take you seriously, Denise. With you it's just an idea in your mind. An not a very clear idea. With me, it's my life.

Savage: Don't you think it's my life, too? Cause it is.

Linda: Then your life is just an unclear idea in your mind cause you ain't livin that I can see . What are you waitin for, anyway? Bein a virgin at your age. Get serious. What kinda silly shit is that? I've had three kids. One of'em my aunt took. The other two went to nobody I know. Which broke my heart. But I've had three kids. An I didn't hang no shit on nobody when I got in the family way because this is my life, understand? This is my life, my circus, my boat to row. I'll do what I do an take what comes. One a those kids was yours.

Tony: WHAT?

Linda: That's right, Mr. Wizard. About time you knew. An did I come to you? I take my shit alone. You've got a son. He lives with my aunt. His name is Alphonse.

April: Congratulations.

Tony: Shut up.

April: Sorry.

Linda: What? You as bad as her? You been dreamin your life'd start when you said go? It's on, man. The movie has been on for a while. An look what you been missin outta your stupidity. You missed the birth of your own son. But you see now I'm tired. I've carried so many boys. (*To Savage.*) What have you carried? Some lock on your heart. Runnin around yellin in your stainless steel panties.

Savage: Don't.

Linda: I don't mean to be mean. But you come against me, I gotta hold my own. *(To Tony.)* An I'll tell you somethin else, Lancelot. I am currently in the family way with another Aronica offspring.

Tony: You ain't serious now.

Linda: I gotta laugh at you. You gotta forgive me. But you ain't got a clue. You ain't flipped the knob on your box inna long time, have you? There are people out here, chum. There are other stories than the one you're in. You're so sure you're the sun, an the moon an the stars spin around you, an God made you an the rest of us is just decoration, right? Like if the flood comes, you'll be Noah, huh? I do doubt it. Not that it's an issue with me. I could care less.

Tony: What's the kid look like?

Linda: He's fuckin repulsive, alright?

Tony: Okay, I deserved that.

Murk: This drink is empty. Tony, what are you drinking?

Savage: Oh, would you get off that kick?

Murk: You have to have a drink you're drinking. If you're finished, you leave.

Savage: Who made up that rule?

Murk: I did.

Savage: Well, the drink's been empty for twenty minutes. Why you enforcin it now?

Murk: It's not empty till I say it's empty.

Savage: Why'd you dress up like Santa Claus?

Murk: Shut up, Savage.

Savage: I feel like I can never get past the goddamn thing here. There's the thing, and then there's what you think about it. But around here, there's just the thing.

Linda: You talk for everybody. Maybe you should just talk for yourself.

Murk: (*To Tony.*) This drink is empty. What are you drinking?

Savage: You can't just keep fillin 'em up an we empty 'em and the night goes by and it's the next day and it's the same thing. That's death. That's death. We gotta get past the thing. We gotta break the sameness. Murk?

Murk: I don't see that. You think a bomb in the works is better than going on the same?

Savage: I believe in action.

Murk: You wanna run around till you're tired, go for it. Knock yourself out. *(To Tony.)* This drink is empty. What are you drinking?

Savage: He's not drinking nothin. How can you keep it up? What's the fuckin point? I mean if this is all you're gonna do for the rest of your life and you know it, why bother to play it out? If you seen the fuckin cards an the future's there an the future's this an nothin more, like a book where every page's the same, why not drop a rock on yourself an die? If every time a glass is empty you're gonna say What are you drinkin, no matter how you feel no matter who it is, then you could be anybody nobody, a machine jerkin when you smack the button, a wall kids bounce balls off, the rope I hang myself with. What's the point? What's the point? (*To Tony.*) What was my crime that I got life?

Tony: Anyone knows the answer to that one, it'd be you. I don't know how to be in your shoes. I don't even know how to be in mine. I don't even wanna be in mine. But here I am. The shoe fits an I'm wearin it. And there's a lot that goes with that. Live with that a minute. I have to.

Murk: This drink is empty. What are you drinking?

Tony: Nothin. And you live with that a minute. I have a son?

Linda: Yup.

Tony: His name's Alphonse?

Linda: Yup.

Tony: Who named him that?

Linda: Me.

Tony: And does it like, stick?

Linda: Yeah, it sticks. It's his name.

Tony: Why didn't you tell me?

Linda: Don't make me laugh, alright?

Tony: Alright. Alright.

Linda: Alright what?

Tony: I'm thinkin. Alright.

Linda: Alright what?

Tony: Would you be cool a minute? Where's the baby?

Linda: My aunt's got it.

Tony: Can you get it back?

Linda: Yeah, maybe.

Murk: Get out, Tony.

Tony: YOU KNOW THESE PLANTS ARE DEAD. You oughta throw them out.

Murk: Those plants are very reliable.

Tony: Linda, I don't know you.

Linda: I know you don't. But you know me.

Tony: I wanna do like eight different things.

Linda: Then but do what you want.

Tony: You say yes to one thing, you say no to a lotta the others causa the yes.

Linda: If ya don't make up your mind ta somethin, you'll go bad.

Savage: That's not what action is.

Linda: You know, you're the leadin authority on nothin. I've just about had it with you. You ain't taken a step since I known ya. Why don't you have a couple a drinks an go out an fuck somebody?

A big pause.

Tony: I'll take a Brandy Alexander.

Murk: Alright.

April: I think the thing you don't appreciate, Denise, is routine.

Savage: You know what I think?

April: What?

Savage: I think you should go off your nut.

Murk: Hey.

Savage: Why don't you just go ahead an fuckin lose it?

April: You really don't know what you're sayin.

Savage: You put yourself in the nuthouse, babe. That's what I think. You put on a fresh straightjacket every mornin before you take your first twitch.

Murk: Lay off her.

Savage: Like there's somebody on April's case. There's never anybody on April's case.

Murk: I'm serious, Savage. Shut up.

Savage: And you're the gatekeeper around here, ain't you? You're the one keeps the spooks in the cemetery.

Linda: You know, you're crazy. You're all over the place.

Savage: You think so?

Linda: Yeah, I do. I come in here cryin, you tell me we should be friends an getta apartment. And April, too. Then my boyfriend comes in and you start hittin on him, and forget me, right? Now you tell April she should go crazy. Which is a bad idea. How am I supposed to think about you, Denise?

Savage: I don't care. I don't care how you think about me. What d'you want? You want me to act like somebody on T.V.? This one got this one way an that's how they are? I don't know how I am, who I am. I don't know what I believe. I don't know where to go to find out. I don't know what to do to be the one person that somewhere inside I wanna be. I don't know nothin but the one thing: I gotta move. And you, too. This whole world I'm in's gotta break up an move.

Murk: Get out.

Savage: I gotta drink in fronta me I ain't finished. We're on the cliff. We were born here. Well, do you wanna die on the cliff ? Do you wanna die in bed? Do you think you're gonna live forever? They told us if you jump off the cliff, you die. And you probably do, but fuck it. Fuck it. We don't know that. You don't know nothin you ain't done, an nobody can tell you nothin. Ain't you tired a livin if this is all livin is? And you know it's not. I may be an asshole and I may not know what to do, but you hear what I'm sayin to you, dammit you do. In your heart you do. This is not life. This is not life. This is not life. Ugly women, right Tony? Somethin else. I don't care what. God, gimme somethin else cause this is definitely not it. New eyes new ears new hands. Gimme back my soul from where you took it, gimme back my friends, gimme back my priests an my father, and take this goddamn virginity from off my life. HUNGER HUNGER HUNGER. If somebody don't gimme somethin, I'm gonna die. I wanna play pool. *(Picks up the pool cue and uses it as a spear or a wand.)* Somebody play pool with me. *(No one moves.)* I come in here a lotta nights, a lotta nights, an I play pool by myself. I like the game. You hit the white ball, and that ball hits another, and it goes somewhere. When I first started, I didn't mind playin alone. But you get tired of it. The balls don't do nothin unless you make'em do it. It's all you. They're just like stones. It's like I'm some woman lives inna cave and plays with stones. Somebody play pool with me. You be the cue ball. Hit me and I'll fly. You don't wanna jump yourself, push me off. You can't keep up your courage alone, playin with stones.

Murk: What d'you want, Savage?

Savage: I don't want you inna red suit, takin me back where I can't go.

Tony: Come on. You want me to play pool with you, I'll play pool with you.

Savage: No.

April: You want me to be a nun and go to India?

Savage: No.

Linda: Do you wanna be friends?

Savage: I don't know how.

Linda: Alright. Goodbye. *(To Tony.)* Will you marry me or what?

Tony: Hey, gimme room.

Linda: I gave you room, but I didn't hear nothin comin forth.

Tony: Well, gimme room now. I feel like I'm under the gun here. But maybe, I don't know, maybe that's the way things really are. Alright. We'll get a place.

Linda: A place?

Tony: Yeah, a place.

Linda: Will we be married in this place?

Tony: Absofuckinlutely not.

Linda: Why not?

Tony: Because your wish is not my command, Rotunda. You wanna live with me or not?

Linda: I wanna get married.

Tony: I know that. But that is not what I wanna do, so I ain't gonna do that. But I do wanna do somethin. Do you wanna do somethin to change our situation or what? Do you wanna live with me?

Linda: Yeah. I wanna move outta my whole house. I wanna live with you.

Tony: Then we'll get a place an we'll live together seven days the week. You wanna claim that kid or what?

Linda: Yeah, I want the kid.

Tony: Alphonse.

Linda: Alphonse Aronica.

Savage: Linda?

Linda: Yeah?

Savage: Goodbye.

April: *(To Savage.)* You want me to do somethin?

Murk: April?

April: Yeah?

Murk: We're gettin married.

April: Right.

Savage: You said there was an animal.

April: Yes.

Savage: There is. There is. There's one in me, too. Big scary fuckin animal. It's the only thing in me that I love. It wasn't always. It's just that these days, these days, it's the only thing in me, it's the only thing in everybody, that ain't a total fuckin horrible lie. I. AM. ALONE.

Murk: Closing time. Last call. Last call. Last call.

Blackout.

THE END

Women
of
Manhattan

*An Upper West Side
Story*

"WOMEN OF MANHATTAN" was first presented by the Manhattan Theatre Club (Lynne Meadow, Artistic Director; Barry Grove, Managing Director) at the City Center Theatre in New York City on May 13, 1986. It was directed by Ron Lagomarsino; the sets were by Adrianne Lobel; the costumes were by Ann Emonts; the lighting was by James F. Ingalls; the sound was by Stan Metelits; the production stage manager was Tom Aberger.

The cast, in order of appearance, was as follows:

Billie	Nancy Mette
Rhonda	J. Smith-Cameron
Judy	Jayne Haynes
Bob	Keith Szarabajka
Duke	Tom Wright

This play is dedicated to women, women

AND

a guy named Larry Sigman

CHARACTERS

Rhonda Louise: 28, hails from the Deep South, speaks and moves in a very deliberate way, and is slender and slow to react. Her frizzy dark brown hair frames a delicate, sensitive face. She is, by nature, always a trifle weary and a trifle solemn, or very weary and very solemn.

Billie: 30, has a high, melodious voice and a dramatic view of her life. When she broods, she sees and hears nothing but her own inner dialogue. Her honey blond tresses surround her great big eyes in her pretty face. She's an exotic, high-strung bird.

Judy: 30, is an independent Connecticut Yankee who has been overtaken by her own cynicism.

These three women love each other.

SCENE I

> *Rhonda Louise's apartment. The background is a drop depicting Manhattan apartment buildings at night, all of their windows lit, a la the old The Late Show. Up Right, suspended in the air of an imaginary sidewall, are some lace curtains establishing a window. Down Left is a white doorframe in an imaginary sidewall.*
>
> *Down Right is a white dining table. On the table are the remains of dinner and a bottle of ruby red wine.*
>
> *Up Center is a white pine bench with a polyurethane finish. On one end of the bench is a single black pillow. To the bench's front is a coffee table with brass legs and a glass top. On the table is a large glazed kiwi custard pie and a glass of ruby red wine.*
>
> *Left is a straight-backed chair with a white lacquer finish. Down Center are a pair of large red sneakers sitting on the floor; they are beat-up and the laces are awry.*
>
> *At Rise, Judy lies on the bench, pillow under her head, eyes closed. Her steady breathing suggests sleep. She is wearing a white, man-tailored dinner jacket, a white blouse with a red bow tie, black trousers, white socks and black oxfords.*
>
> *Rhonda Louise and Billie sit at the dining table, each holding a glass of ruby red wine. Rhonda Louise is wearing a jade green blouse, a black patent leather belt, a white pleated skirt, and black patent leather high heels. Her earrings are red plastic. Billie wears a tight golden blouse with a revealing neckline, a tight black skirt with a slit, white high heels, a silver and topaz bangle, and long and glittering rhinestone earrings. Billie is in her cups. Rhonda Louise is bathing her in a fiery attention.*

Billie: We are all, all of us, doing very well.

Rhonda: Yes. That is true.

Billie: And terrible. At the same time we are doing terrible.

Rhonda: Wait. I wouldn't say we're …

Billie: We're doing terrible. The moneys good. I mean, we've all got money.

Rhonda: I wouldn't say I'm rich.

Billie: None of us are rich yet.

Rhonda: You're close.

Billie: But none of us are starving to death.

Rhonda: No. We're doing great.

Billie: And terrible! Look at this place. It's beautiful.

Rhonda: Thanks.

Billie: It's like a fucking palace.

Rhonda: Well. I put some sweat into it.

Billie: It's like oysters.

Rhonda: Come again?

Billie: You know how really good oysters are just presented like...The yellow lemon, the red sauce, the bed of ice. The presentation. It's like a Chagall - poor Chagall, fare thee well! It's like a Chagall with these spaces left in it for these salty shiny little creatures. Your apartment is like that. Like a wonderful wonderful painting with spaces left in it for us.

Rhonda: Good.

Billie: You know what's so interesting about you?

Rhonda: What?

Billie: You're really kind of European.

Rhonda: I don't think so.

Billie: You have a something. You have an Other quality.

Rhonda: Maybe it's that I'm not wholly integrated into New York.

Billie: Who is?

Rhonda: You seem to be.

Billie: Me? I do the illusion.

Rhonda: In Europe, I read in this book, the way they advertise American movies is Kiss, Kiss, Bang Bang.

Billie: That's reductive.

Rhonda: Well. It's advertising.

Billie: Don't we look great?

Rhonda: You look beautiful.

Billie: You look beautiful! You look like a firefly in a nightclub. What does that mean?

Rhonda: It was your remark.

Billie: It was a compliment of some kind, Rhonda Louise. Trust me. But here we are. And I'm stumped, sister, stumped, I really truly am. Cause you are stunning and I am stunning, and this room is just ideal to show how stunning we really are ...

Rhonda: Like the oysters.

Billie: Exactly! But where are the men?

Rhonda: You told me not to invite any men.

Billie: I know. I know I did that. But where are the men?

Rhonda: That was the whole point.

Billie: I know. But where are they?

Rhonda: The three of us would just deck out and look great for each other and fuck the men.

Billie: I know, I know, but don't you feel we're wasting our gorgeousness on each other?

Rhonda: No.

Billie: Just a little?

Rhonda: No.

Billie: I understand why you're saying that, but come on.

Rhonda: Wait. I know what you're hinting at. That ain't what's going on. Anyway, you're married.

Billie: So what?

Rhonda: So you're here without a man cause your husband's out building buildings somewhere.

Billie: So what? You're here alone, I mean, without a man, because you threw Jerry out.

Rhonda: Stop. Right there. That's a black lie. I'm here alone tonight cause you knew your husband whadn't gonna be around tonight and you don't cheat so you suggested this girls' night which is fine with me, but don't you then turn around and tell me I don't have a date cause I threw this one guy outta my life. That's just a detail.

Billie: Sorry.

Rhonda: If I wanted a guy here tonight there'd be a guy here tonight. I'm dressed up cause you wanted me to dress up. I'll tell you why you're cryin out Where's the men? It's cause we're dressed for men. These clothes evolved outta a situation where observations were made about which kinda garments are effective to wear to attract the male of the species. It's really like female fashion's premier designer is Mister Charles Darwin. The point is these kinda clothes are bait. We're wearin bait. These clothes are just like worms only there's no fish to bite.

Billie: Worms!

Rhonda: Bait.

Billie: It's weird to think of my clothes as a worm.

Rhonda: And you yourself as a hook.

Billie: Especially when I've already landed my fish. Bob. Bob the big-mouthed bass.

Rhonda: Well, that's cause you gotta keep in shape.

Billie: What do you mean?

Rhonda: You gotta know, if it came to that extreme, that you could catch another gentleman. My father use to practice fly-fishing in the living room. He'd be casting this fly in and about a sewing hoop to the consternation of my mother. He was practicing outwitting the trout. It's the comparable same thing to happily married women who flirt. They're casting flies in the living room.

Billie: Is that what you think of me, Rhonda Louise?

Rhonda: Well. Billie. You are one of the worst flirts I know.

Billie: Do you honestly think I flirt to keep in shape in case Bob leaves me?

Rhonda: Yes. Fear! I think that's one of the reasons. But I think you do it too cause you'd like to screw the socks off the lot of'em.

Billie: Is that what …

Rhonda: Yes! Horniness! Definitely! And I think you do it too as a sorta check you run to make sure you still exist. That's the most existential reason. I flirt therefore I am. And I think you do it too to …

Billie: I'M GOING TO TELL YOU WHY I FLIRT.

Rhonda: Why?

Billie: Habit.

Rhonda: Oh.

Billie: There was probably a dozen reasons why, at one time, but they're all dead now. Still standing up but dead. Like stuffed birds in the Museum of Natural History. Like me.

Billie starts to cry.

Rhonda: What's the matter, Billie?

Billie: I feel dead. I feel dead.

Rhonda: You're not dead, honey.

Billie: Yes, I am.

Rhonda: No, you're not. You just feel dead.

Billie: The other night, Bob asked me to marry him.

Rhonda: But … you are married to him.

Billie: He forgot!

Rhonda: He what?

Billie: Oh, it was sweet, really. We had this dinner and we drank some champagne and he'd brought me these pink pink roses, and the moment was just so … He got carried away and proposed.

Rhonda: But that's just so dear.

Billie: Oh, it was precious, it really really was. But it was also just exactly what it is about my marriage that drives me insane. I mean, I could kill!

Rhonda: I don't get it.

Billie: It's the courtship. He can't give it up. We can't give it up. It's been three years and we're still on the balcony, if you know what I mean. I thought that marriage was supposed to lead somewhere, not just be some frozen terrific moment. I thought it was supposed to be this great adventure. Like death.

Rhonda: It's hard for me to sympathize, Billie.

Billie: Oh, I'm sure it is. Nobody ever sympathizes with me. Their troubles are always worse.

Rhonda: Well. You've always done well that I could see.

Billie: And terrible!

Rhonda: You've always had money.

Billie: Yes, I have.

Rhonda: And some guy that adored you.

Billie: Almost always.

Rhonda: And you're good-looking and you have nice clothes and you've always lived in some place that was great …

Billie: But it's always been like photographs! And I want to be in a movie! An adventure movie where half my clothes are torn off by a gorilla and I marry the chief and I'm thrown in a volcano but I survive and become a Hollywood star and give it up and become a nun in an insane asylum in France and learn about being silent and unknown, and I invent something … useful and good … that the government and the corporations want to steal and twist for evil …

Rhonda: Billie! Billie! Billie!

Billie: What?

Rhonda: What are you talking about?

Billie: I just wish that my existence was more … picaresque.

Rhonda: And for this you want my sympathy?

Billie: No, not for that, Rhonda Louise. I want your sympathy for an ache in me that knows no name.

Rhonda: Alright. For that you have got my sympathy. Ready for dessert?

Billie: What is it?

Rhonda: Kiwi custard pie.

Billie: Did you make it?

Rhonda: No. I got it at The Eclair. It's on the coffee table if you want to look.

Billie: I must, I must look at all desserts. Oh, it's so pretty.

Rhonda: Wanna slice?

Billie: Not yet.

Rhonda: Me neither. I'd just like to be baked into a pie, some pie like that. Sleep down in the custard like deep in a downy downy bed of feathers, under a comforter of kiwi slices, sit outside the conversation with not a thing to say, the last best thing, the thing that's saved to be relished, the dessert.

Judy: Sorry, but that's me.

Rhonda: I thought you were asleep.

Judy: No. I'm just stretched out with the peepers shut. Breathing.

Judy sits up.

Billie: What do you mean, you're the dessert?

Judy: I identify with the pie is all. Maybe because everybody admires it but nobody wants a piece.

Rhonda: You know, Judy, you are a terrible guest.

Judy: Sorry. I just like listening to you and Billie. It's funny the things that become apparent when your eyes are closed that you might not notice if you had 'em open.

Rhonda: Such as?

Judy: Such as: When you two have a talk, Billie spills her guts and then when it's your turn, Billie spills her guts again.

Billie: That doesn't sound very attractive.

Judy: Oh, whatever you do, it's attractive, Billie. You're just an attractive person. But Rhonda Louise, what is going on in your mind? Do tell us.

Rhonda: A truly terrible guest.

Billie: God, Judy, I wish I could be like you.

Judy: Those big red sneakers for instance. What are those big red sneakers doing shambling around on your nice neat floor? Might those be Jerry's shoes?

Rhonda: Yes. They are Jerry's shoes.

Judy: But doesn't Jerry not live here anymore? Was he not shown the door some time since?

Rhonda: I threw him out. Which you know.

Judy: I knew you'd thrown him out of the apartment and your life and so on, but I had no idea that you'd thrown him right out of his red sneakers!

Rhonda: Don't be smart.

Judy: I wouldn't know how.

Rhonda: He left the sneakers. Or they fell out of a bag. I don't know which. But there they are.

Billie: Do you really think I spill my guts?

Judy: Yes, but hold on to them for a minute. *(To Rhonda.)* I came to dinner. I ate dinner. It was passable. A little fatty for my taste, but I don't think it's right for a guest to speak out.

Rhonda: You could've fooled me.

Judy: I saw the sneakers when I walked in. Said nothing. The soul of whatever. You've said not a word. I know you're troubled about this character Jerry. That you loved him or were enslaved to something about him or something. I've been patient. I've lain here like a monk on a cot waiting for you to speak. But all I've really gotten is that Billie wants to be in some movie with an awful plot. We're getting to the shank of the evening. When are you going to unveil your pain?

A long pause.

Billie: All I meant by the movie thing ...

Judy: Billie! Hush!

Billie complies. A long pause.

Rhonda: I miss him.

Judy: That's it?

Rhonda: I miss his smell.

Judy: He had a smell?

Rhonda: Yes.

Judy: Do his sneakers contain this smell? Is that why the little devils are still here?

Rhonda: I don't know. Maybe. I hate those sneakers.

Judy: Then why don't you send them back to him?

Rhonda: I don't know where he is.

Judy: Why don't you throw them out?

Rhonda: I don't know. They're too nice to throw out.

Judy: They're too nice? Please.

Rhonda: I know what you think this is, but it's not. I don't keep the sneakers because I love him.

Judy: Uh-huh.

Rhonda: I didn't love him. Not in a way that led anywhere. I mean, I loved him but it was like trying to hug a wall. How do you hug a wall?

Judy: I don't know.

Rhonda: I guess my big mistake was I revealed myself to him. That's where I really went wrong. You know, that thing that most people can't do? That thing that's supposed to be like the hardest thing to get to with another person? It took me time, but I struggled and strove and succeeded at last in revealing my innermost, my most personal soul to him.

Billie: And what is that?

Rhonda: Never you mind.

Judy: And what did he do?

Rhonda: Nothing. Zip. Nothing. He just sat there with a coke in his hand like he was watching television, waiting for the next thing. Like that was a nice stop on the way to WHAT I CAN'T IMAGINE! The whole thing with him was such a letdown. But why am I surprised? You know? I mean, here I was congratulating myself on being able to show myself, show my naked self to a man. But what's the achievement? I chose to show myself to a wall. Right? That's why I was able to do it. He was a wall and I was really alone, showing myself to nobody at all. How much courage does that take? Even when I got it together to throw him out, and I made this speech at him and got all pink in the face and noble as shit. He just said alright and left. What did I delude myself into thinking was going on between us if that's how he could take it ending? "Alright. Just lemme get my tools together, Rhonda Louise, and I'll get on to the next thing." You know how in that one school a thought you're the only thing real in the world, and everything else is just a dream? All these people and things, the stars in the sky, are just sparks and smoke from your own lonely fire in a big, big night. I always thought what a lotta intellectual nonsense that was until Jerry. I mean, to tell you the naked truth, I'm not even sure there was a Jerry. It seems impossible to me that there was. Sometimes I think I just got overheated, worked myself into a passion and fell in love with that wall right there. It must've been! It must've been that wall and me, crazy, loving it cause I needed to love. And not a human man. I couldn't have poured everything out to a really truly human man, and him just stand there, and take it, and give nothing back. It's not possible. But when I get too far gone in that direction of thinking— and alone here some nights I do — at those times it does me good to look and see these sneakers there sitting on the floor. His sneakers. He was here. It happened.

Billie: If that had been me, I would've doubted that I existed.

Rhonda: Well, Billie, maybe that's the difference between us.

Judy: If that had happened to me, I think I would've been glad.

Rhonda: How do you come to that?

Judy: At least something would've happened for me to brood over.

Rhonda: You wanna brood?

Judy: Oh, I brood. But I'd enjoy brooding about something new.

Billie: What do you brood about now?

Judy: We're not doing me now, we're doing Rhonda Louise.

Rhonda: Forget that. With me you're done. What do you brood about?

Judy: Sex.

Billie: Me too!

Judy: But you're married.

Billie: All the more!

Judy: Oh, I'm sure. But what I mean is, since you're married, correct me if I'm wrong, you have sex.

Billie: Well, yes I do.

Judy: Well, I don't. Or anyway I haven't in a goodly while. So the way I brood about sex is different. It's a darker, more perverse, Scandinavian kind of deep deep festering stew.

Billie: God.

Judy: It's not really sex at all. It's too black for that. It's more like a kind of exquisite exasperation. A sullen, slow, galling exasperation having to do with men.

Rhonda: Why you mad at men?

Judy: Because they're all gay.

Billie: They are not!

Judy: They're all faggots!

Rhonda: Maybe the men you meet.

Judy: Definitely the men I meet! The men I meet are all faggots! Some of them know they're faggots, and they're bad enough. But a lot of them aren't sure, so they go out with me for clarification. We go back to my place. Maybe we even get to bed before he bursts into tears and starts telling me about his Confusion. He's all mixed up. I'm like his sister. He's like my sister! These fucking sensitive guys out there sniffing flowers in their designer sweaters, I could just spit! And there's only so much you can accomplish alone. At least me. I have a real problem with my ability to fantasize. Because I can only imagine sexual encounters that I feel are plausible. You know, I have to have at least experienced some small bubble of chemistry between me and the guy in order to imagine the rest. These days that limits me to guys I ran into so long ago that they're too young for me to get really excited about. I lie in bed with my eyes clamped shut trying desperately to age some eighteen year old with a skin problem up to the requisite thirty. And then I see myself lying there in the bed, my face all scrunched up like some numbskull telepath trying to communicate with a dolphin, and I think: The faggots have done this to me! This, anyway, is the course that my brooding sometimes takes.

Billie: Well. Hmm. Well, it's your own fault, Judy.

Judy: How do you figure that?

Rhonda: Uh-huh.

Billie: I meet straight guys all the time.

Rhonda: Me too.

Billie: You're asking for it.

Judy: I'm asking for fags to come home with me and reveal their fagginess to me?

Billie: Basically, yes, that's what you're doing.

Rhonda: I agree. In fact, I really agree.

Judy: I'll take a piece of pie now.

Rhonda: That's my pie. Not yet. Billie's saying something.

Billie: What are you wearing?

Judy: You can see what I'm wearing.

Billie: That jacket.

Judy: What's wrong with my jacket?

Billie: It's MAN-tailored.

Judy: That's right.

Rhonda: And those shoes. E.G. Marshall could be in those shoes.

Judy: Well, what are you getting at?

Rhonda: Go on, tell her.

Billie: Alright. I will. Because I'm her friend. You're a Fag Hag, Judy! That's right! You march around with that efficient priss, and you wear a woman's version of a man's clothes, and you're arch... as an arch. Do you think that turns straight guys on?

Rhonda: It makes them nervous.

Billie: If you wanna get in a straight man's pants you've gotta make him think he's getting into yours. I've seen how you deal with straight guys. You look them over like you wanna give them an enema!

Judy: How can you talk to me this way? I'm not a stone! I have feelings!

Judy cries.

Billie: I'm sorry. I forgot. But you see? That's how it is. You get treated like you ask to be treated. And you ask to be treated like, I don't know ...

Rhonda: Like a fag.

Judy: What?

Billie: I don't know. No, I know. I just know I'm on thin ice with you with this. The only people who treat you nice are fags cause they think you're one of them.

Judy: What about you?

Billie: And Rhonda and me treat you nice because we love you. We see through you like you see through us and that's love.

Judy: I don't want to talk about this.

Billie: Talk about it.

Judy: I don't want to.

Rhonda: Maybe that's why you should.

Judy: Oh. I'm so lonely!

Rhonda: Me too.

Judy: But you miss Jerry. With me it's not even that. I'm not lonely for anyone, I'm just lonely in myself. I wish I could meet some nice guy, get involved with some nice guy.

Rhonda: There are no nice guys.

Judy: Then somebody who was screwed up in a way that complemented what's wrong with me. I wanna be an active heterosexual again! Sounds like volcanoes. "Watch out, Judy's active. Better evacuate the village."

Billie: It's not so great.

Judy: That's easy for you to say.

Billie: Oh, you have to have it, I'm not saying that. All I'm saying is it doesn't undo the big problem.

Rhonda: What's the big problem, Billie?

Billie: Oh, you know. It's like food. Appetite. I mean, people who have a problem with food will always have a problem with food. You can't throw food out of your life. Appetite. I don't know. If you aren't getting sex, you hunger for sex. If you do get sex, you hunger for different sex. Or a good book. Or combat. Or stardom. Do you know what I mean? It's the appetite that's under everything, that's inside everything. Whatever you're doing that's good, inside it is the little appetite mouse with his big big teeth hollowing it out. Making whatever dreams you've managed to happen seem silly and empty and nothing. That's the big problem, I think. That appetite that's under just everything. Ruining it.

Rhonda: You think that's the big problem?

Billie: Don't you?

Rhonda: No.

Billie: What do you think the big problem is?

Rhonda: Self-esteem. True self-esteem.

Judy: Can I say something?

Rhonda: Sure.

Judy: We were talking about me.

Rhonda: That's right. Sorry. So go on.

Judy: Now I feel self-conscious.

Billie: Listen, Judy. We love you. We're sitting here. Just spill it!

Judy: Alright. I feel so strong and everything's out of my reach which makes me feel deluded about my strength, which makes me feel paranoid about my ability to divine what the fuck is really going on!

Billie: So what are you saying?

Judy: Just that I'm really stuck.

Billie: But what's sticking you?

Judy: It's hard to say!

Billie: Jump off Judy, say it, say it!

Judy: ALRIGHT. I'M PROUD OF BEING AN ASSHOLE.

Rhonda: Oh.

Judy: There. I said it.

Billie: Yes, you did.

Judy: I can feel this puss on my face. My mother's puss. This face is her hatchet. I'm proud of being an asshole. I loathe myself.

Rhonda: I think you're good.

Judy: What good does being good do?

Billie: Would you like me to help you, Judy? I can help you if you want.

Judy: I didn't ask for help.

Rhonda: You coulda fooled me.

Judy: Oh, screw it anyway. Sure! Help! You think you can help me, help me. I need help, who am I kidding?

Billie: Listen to me carefully, Judy. I can only help you if you let me help you.

Judy: What exactly are you talking about?

Billie: This isn't going to be easy. There's a few things you don't know, I think …

Judy: And you do?

Billie: That's right.

Judy: For instance what?

Billie: There's a few things about you that you don't know.

Judy: You know things about me that I don't know.

Billie: That's right.

Judy: Well, I know tons about you that you don't know.

Billie: I'm sure you do. That's my point, really. Because I'm not you, because I'm out here, I can see things.

Judy: Well, of course.

Billie: I know we're all intelligent enough to admit that other people know things about us that we can't see ourselves, but, I think very often we don't really believe it.

Judy: What are you driving at?

Billie: You must've had the experience, at a party or something, of seeing somebody, maybe even a total stranger, and thinking that you knew something about that person. Something they didn't even know themselves.

Judy: Sure.

Billie: And you probably didn't tell them. The thing. Because you knew they wouldn't hear you. Not really hear you.

Judy: Why don't you just tell me, Billie?

Rhonda: You are dragging it out.

Billie: Some things have to have a certain extent to take hold. There's a very basic thing that has to happen before I can say something to you, Judy.

Judy: I'm listening.

Billie: I was listening to you. I'm your true friend. I love you. I don't want anything from you except your friendship. Do you believe me?

Judy: Sure.

Billie: Before I can say the thing I have to say to you, you have to stop being proud of being an asshole. *(A long pause.)* Can you do that?

Judy: I thought I could say some things to you without having it thrown back in my face.

Billie: That's not what I'm doing. And you know that. You're just afraid.

Judy: I'm not afraid! Say what you have to say!

Billie: You're afraid of being a humble asshole. Sometimes you think I'm stupid, don't you? Don't you?

Judy: Yes.

Billie: Maybe you thought I didn't know that. I knew that. And that hasn't stopped me from being your friend. Do you know why?

Judy: No.

Billie: Because I'm grateful.

Judy: Why are you doing this?

Billie: I'm returning the favor. One humble asshole to another. Will you please, please, please accept my help?

Judy: Alright. I'll try.

Billie: I want to arrange a date for you.

Judy: What? No. Don't repeat it.

Billie: I want to arrange a date for you.

Judy: With who?

Billie: Someone you don't know.

Judy: A blind date?

Billie: Yes.

Judy: A blind date and I'm thirty years old.

Billie: I know. We're the same age.

Judy: A blind date. I haven't been on a blind date since I was sixteen.

Billie: That has nothing to do with it.

Judy: It was a catastrophe! He was a Mormon.

Rhonda: I feel like I've taken a fistful of L.S.D.

Billie: Judy, what could be more of a catastrophe than your life as it is right now? Judy, I love you.

Judy: I know that! But I do feel like just like punching you.

Billie: Why?

Judy: Because a blind date is humiliating!

Billie: I don't disagree. But think about it. To be humiliated is like being detoxed. Humiliation is the road you've got to travel to become humble. If it's your pride that's crippling you, humiliation is how you get rid of pride. I get humiliated all the time.

Judy: But you deserve to!

Billie: And you don't? If you're proud of being an asshole, and you're the one that told me that's what you are, then you should be humiliated! It's just what the doctor ordered. But watch out! Don't make that the thing I'm offering you. Your pride is just what's stopping you from even trying something new. It's the new thing that I want you to try.

Judy: What new thing?

Billie: This guy I have in mind.

Judy: What's he like? No, don't tell me!

Billie: I'm not going to tell you.

Judy: You're not going to tell me anything?

Billie: No.

Rhonda: In my life, this may be my favorite insane moment.

Billie: This is my proposition. I will arrange this date for you. It will take place within the next few days at a spot I pick. All I ask is, when you meet this guy, that you're as open with him, with your heart and your mind, as you know how to be. That's all. Seriously, Judy, what have you got to lose? Will you do it?

Judy: No. Yes. Alright.

Rhonda: Now, wait a minute! I've gotta hear how this turns out or I'll go mad! You've both gotta promise me... Listen! We'll have brunch! Next Sunday! I invite you both. I'll make something just incredibly good! And then you'll tell the tale. Okay?

Judy: Okay.

Billie: Okay.

Rhonda: Then it's a pact.

Judy: Now that I'm compliant and completely humiliated, now can I have a slice of that pie?

Rhonda: Absolutely! But be careful how you cut it. I got this idea that I'm sleeping in there.

The lights go down.

SCENE 2

Bob and Billie are sitting in two beach chairs, separated by their Hibachi. On the Hibachi are two hamburgers. It's nighttime. They are sitting on their co-op's balcony, which is decorated with little electric plastic Chinese lanterns. They are sipping Tom Collins out of witty glasses.

Bob is wearing a good but wilted white shirt, a neo-expressionist tie, tan pants, and sandals.

Billie's wearing a peach silk blouse, tight white jeans, and tennis sneakers without socks.

Bob and Billie are looking out over the city, which is the audience.

Bob: You know, Billie. You know I'm so happy I'm almost suffering. It's like ... exquisite. I've always felt the word exquisite like had a little sliver of pain in it. Exquisite. Exquisite.

Billie: Bob. Darling. You're the sweetest man I've ever known. But I don't exactly comprehend your ... drift.

Bob: I'm feeling happy. How 'bout you?

Billie: How long till the hamburgers are ready?

Bob: About thirty-five minutes.

Billie: Isn't that an awfully long time to cook a hamburger?

Bob: It's this way I've always wanted to do 'em up. I let the coals go past the height of their heat. I got this chopped sirloin I watched the guy grind it not a flake a fat. It's the fat dripping on to the coals that makes 'em flare up so's the temperature's all over the place. I don't want that for the coals in my barbecue. So I lit 'em, and I let 'em burn at their own pace, and when I put the burgers over 'em to cook, the burgers have no fat to drip down and upset the ecology. The heat is what it is, the burgers are what they are. The meat cooks, the coals smolder and die their steady death. At the moment that the coals are through with the subject of fire, the meat is cooked. That's what I'm after. And it should take about thirty-five minutes.

Billie: Wow. When did you think all that out?

Bob: I've been thinking about this for a while, and now I'm doing it. There are these things in life, these few basic things. Eating. Sleeping. Walking. And I've always been thinking about something else when I was doing them. So I never was doing what I was doing. When I was a kid, my brother Marty was a sleepwalker. I found him in the hall one time doing this motion with his hands. I said, What are you doing, Marty? And he said, I'm playing basketball. He thought he was playing basketball. He's standing there in his pajamas in this hallway in the dark, and he thinks he's playing basketball. I think I've been like that a lot. I think I'm playing basketball or something, but I'm really in the dark. Sleeping. Standing up. They say that people who sleepwalk are really upset about something.

Billie: Are you upset about something?

Bob: No, I'm happy. But that's what this whole elaborate dance is I'm doing with the hamburgers. I'm trying to think about what I'm doing more. Appreciate it more while it's going on. Make something out of it. It's the process of doing—that's life. It's not just eating the thing, stuffing it in your mouth and swallowing it. What's that? That's just missing this freakin point of life, walking around in a dream with your arms out so you don't bump into things like, like Frankenstein's poor dumb monster. This thing made outta eighteen different kinds of death. This sleepwalker who isn't truly sleeping and isn't truly walking. I mean, Billie, don't you wish sometimes, I mean think sometimes — or have you ever had this experience, some other time in your life — that you're asleep or drugged. In some kind of dream you can't get out of. Don't you sometimes feel like this hostage or addict or victim—or have you ever, maybe in the past sometime—felt or thought, even for a second—won't somebody, somebody free me, slap me, save me from this sleep. I'm stuck in. While my life's still lit?

Billie: Are you criticizing me, sweetheart?

Bob: No! No. Don't misunderstand me, baby. This is really about me. It isn't even really about me. It's about cooking the hamburgers and I got off on a tangent.

Billie: Is everything alright at the office?

Bob: Oh yeah. Business is booming. I gotta desk fulla contracts and people waiting to see me. But there's an interesting thing.

Billie: What?

Bob: When things were rough, when things were really rough, when there were no contracts on the desk and I was waiting to see people who didn't want to see me, you know I was really worried.

Billie: Me too.

Bob: I know. I know you were. We were worried. And we hadda good reason to be worried. I was reaching like a madman but I couldn't get the work. I couldn't get to the work. And I knew I could do great with the contracts if I could only get my hands on 'em, but I was swipin' at the air. There was this network of work, and I wasn't in it, and I couldn't get into it, and I was clawin', man. I was clawin' at the freakin' wall cause how the hell was I gonna support you—and I wanted to do that! And have a decent place to live. And I only consider this a decent place to live. I mean, a two-bedroom apartment with a rinkydink balcony is nice and it's enough, but it is not, to my mind, a house. Like my father's house was a house.

Billie: This cost four times what your parents' place did.

Bob: Money don't fool me. Money don't fool me one bit.

Billie: You really are a Victorian.

Bob: I come from Victorian stock. But what am I going to make of myself? What kind of stock am I going to buy into? I think I might like to end up a certain kind of ancient Greek. Only modern. I don't wanna wear a toga. But to go on. I was worried back then. That's my point. I was worried cause it looked like I might completely fail and not make a living and not be able to live someplace decent. I was really worried. But then I solved that problem, that problem got solved. Business is good now. But this is the interesting thing. I'm still worried. I worry all the time. It eats me up. Only now I don't have anything to worry about. So when I lie down, or I eat, or whatever, I guess outta habit, I summon the usual goblins and I invite them to torment me with their little worryforks. I worry about money and I have enough money. I worry about the business and the business is fine. And I worry about you, and we're still like on our honeymoon.

Billie: Oh, Bob.

Bob: I don't wanna live like this. Where I'm worried about stupid shit and miss my whole life. That's why I'm trying to make a ballet outta cooking the hamburgers. I figure it will make me pay attention to what's going on in front of me, and stop with this stupid sleepwalking Frankenstein ... That was the really tragic thing about the monster. Little children playing, nice people having dinner, a wedding, wherever he showed up, wherever he went, that place became a scene in a horror picture. Cause even when he didn't know it, even when he was trying to be a nice guy, he was carrying around this nightmare of who he was. And that infected everything and made it a horror picture. It's a beautiful night. I feel good. I love you very much.

Billie: I love you, too, Bob. I really do. You always turn out to be more...complicated. I think you're more complicated than I am.

Bob: I don't. I think you're a real maze. I'm not gonna lie to you. I'm attracted to other women. I see a nice ass, I turn around and look. But I never play around. I've thought about it, but I would never do it.

Billie: Never say never.

Bob: I would never do it!

Billie: Okay.

Bob: You believe me?

Billie: Yes. Oh, sweetheart, what would I do without you? I don't feel courage. I feel courage in you, but not in me. This may sound crazy, but I don't think I could even be pretty without you to see me and make me pretty.

Bob: Well, that's stupid. Even if I died, you'd be pretty.

Billie: No, I don't think so. Why do you keep talking about death? What, do you think you're going to die or something?

Bob: Well, yeah I'm gonna die. That's a given.

Billie: Don't talk like that. I'm going to die before you and you're going to have to bury me.

Bob: I hope not.

Billie: That's what I want. And I want a closed coffin. I don't want people seeing me dead. I mean that. I don't think anybody looks good when they're dead. And I don't want to outlive you because then I would just wither up and die of depression, and I can't even live with the little depressions I get now.

Bob: You get depressed?

Billie: Sometimes.

Bob: Why?

Billie: Maybe I fantasize you dead sometimes, and get depressed over it now, and start to wither and die. In advance. I'm so afraid of losing me, I mean, you. I mean you. Do you ever fantasize me dead?

Bob: No.

Billie: Good. And I get depressed sometimes maybe because I feel cut off from my body a little bit. Sometimes. Maybe because I have so many clothes. I have so many clothes. It makes me feel like a dummy. It makes me feel like Barbie Doll. And sometimes I do too much shopping, you know? I just shop and shop and shop and shop, and it makes me feel great that I can do that. I feel strong. It almost gets me high. But then sooner or later I like collapse. And I feel so bad. Ashamed. Like I've sinned. And like nothing. Like I was nothing. And I'm in bed. And you're out there working somewhere. Working at a big fat job. And I just feel so weak from that idea that I can't get up. I have to call somebody on the phone. I have to call everybody I've ever known on the phone. From my bed. Like I was a little spider weaving a web out of telephone wires. Just to stand up and walk.

Bob: I didn't know you got depressed.

Billie: Just a little bit. And just sometimes.

Bob: Maybe we're doing something wrong.

Billie: What do you mean?

Bob: I know we're basically really pretty happy, but it sounds like there's something wrong.

Billie: What?

Bob: I don't know. I know I've been selfish. Wanting to do everything. Like my Dad. Be the hero of the marriage. Maybe you should get a job? Or have a baby?

Billie: I'm not ready to have a baby.

Bob: Okay.

Billie: I'm not finished understanding myself. Enough. Ahm. Are you ... I don't even want to ask that.

Bob: What?

Billie: There's some things you don't know about me. You probably don't know how superstitious I am. I read astrology books, you know.

Bob: No, I didn't know that.

Billie: I read them on the sly. And then I quit reading them. When I read them, I believe everything they say. And then I have to quit reading them because I believe them so totally that it isn't right. I was just going to ask you something, but I'm so superstitious that I believe if I say something out loud, that could make it happen.

Bob: Say what out loud?

Billie: Are you losing interest in me?

Bob: No.

Billie: Are you sure?

Bob: Yeah.

Billie: Okay.

Bob: I love you.

Billie: I believe you.

Bob: I really do love you, Billie. But I am beginning to think that you're not showing me everything.

Billie: I feel so scared.

Bob: Why?

Billie: Cause I said it out loud.

Bob: Don't be scared.

Billie: I'm not really. It's just this superstitious thing I do. It'll pass in a minute. Bob?

Bob: Yeah?

Billie: I'm going to try to let go. I'm going to try to show you everything.

Bob: That's good enough for me.

Billie: Bob?

Bob: Yeah?

Billie: I know it's important to you. And I hesitate to even say anything about it. But it must be time to at least turn over those hamburgers.

Bob looks at Billie, and then looks down on the hamburgers, to appraise them. The lights fade.

SCENE 3

The backdrop remains the same, except now just a few of the windows in the buildings are lit, and Mister Quarter Moon has appeared in the sky; he has a smile and a broad wink.

The only pieces of furniture are a round table, Center, covered with a red-and-white checkered tablecloth, and two wooden chairs which bracket the table.

Downstage is a lit sign suspended aloft; the legend reads: MARIA'S CIN CIN HOME OF THE PURPLE MARTINI. (Pronounced: Chin Chin.)

At Rjise, Duke is discovered at the table. He's dressed in a dark and elegant suit. He's very handsome and he's black. On the table is a bottle of dark red wine, two glasses, and a lit candle. Duke's glass is full; the other is empty. He's gazing off Left, smoking a pipe, steeping in a cool tranquility. In the distance, romantic Italian accordion music plays. A moment passes.

Judy enters from Right. She's dressed in a breathtaking, fairytale-blue evening gown. Duke rises. They're both slightly taken aback by the other. Judy because he's black. Duke because of her gown. Both are secretly pleased by what they didn't expect.

Duke: Hello?

Judy: Hello?

Duke: Judy?

Judy: Duke?

Duke: Isn't this funny? Please. *(He pulls out her chair. She sits.)*

Judy: Thank you.

Duke: May I pour you a glass of wine?

Judy: Thank you. I didn't know this place, Maria's Cin Cin, huh?

Duke: Known as the home of the purple martini. *(He pours her a glass.)*

Judy: Quite a handle for a … Well, it seems straightforward spaghetti and meatballs.

Duke: I do hope you aren't hungry? They tell me the kitchen's already closed.

Judy: I always eat well before midnight.

Duke: I do, too. In fact, I'm often in bed well before midnight. But I couldn't resist.

Judy: What?

Duke: I don't know. The mystery of it all, I haven't been on a blind date since I was sixteen.

Judy: Me either!

Duke: I didn't expect you to look like you do.

Judy: I didn't expect you to look like you. Look.

Duke: You mean black?

Judy: Yeah!

Duke: Does it bother you?

Judy: No!

Duke: Frankly, it's not that you're white that threw me.

Judy: It wasn't?

Duke: No.

Judy: Then what was it?

Duke: The way you're dressed.

Judy: Oh, this? I know it's like really inappropriate …

Duke: It's stunning! You're completely beautiful. When you walked in, it actually knocked the wind out of me. It's as if you walked out of one of the storybooks I was addicted to as a boy, the princess I dreamed of saving from heaven knows what. You know, in my whole life no woman has ever walked in and made an impression on me like that. I have to congratulate you. And thank you.

Judy: You're welcome.

Duke: Do you always dress like that?

Judy: Never. I mean, I had this conversation with some friends … Oh, well one of them was Billie.

Duke: How do you know Billie?

Judy: College. How do you know Billie?

Duke: We had an affair.

Judy: Really!

Duke: But you were in the middle of saying something.

Judy: Oh. Yes. Anyway, my friends got on me for the way I dressed, they said I was too tailored or something. Anyway, this outfit is my overreaction to what they said. You had an affair with Billie?

Duke: Yes.

Judy: When? Oh, I'm sorry, I'm being so rude!

Duke: A few months ago.

Judy: A few months ago? But Billie was married a few months ago.

Duke: I think she's been married for about three years.

Judy: I know that. What I mean … Billie had an affair with a black named Duke … You a… She never said a word to me!

Duke: Well, maybe this date's her way of telling you?

Judy: I guess it is. I can't believe that you a, I don't know, that you've confided in me so quickly. I mean, does her husband know?

Duke: I don't think so.

Judy: Well, why did you tell me? I'm a total stranger.

Duke: That has to do with a rather extraordinary conversation I had with Billie a couple of days ago.

Judy: I had an extraordinary conversation with Billie, too!

Duke: She got me to agree that when I met you for this date I would be completely candid with you.

Judy: I agreed to the same thing! Are you still having an affair with Billie?

Duke: No, it's been over for some time.

Judy: How did it end?

Duke: We got bored with each other. Sexually.

Judy: Really!

Duke: Is that so unusual?

Judy: No. But this conversation is making me feel so exhilarated!

Duke: Why?

Judy: I guess because you're a man and you're not lying to me!

Duke: Sounds like you have a pretty low opinion of men.

Judy: No, not really. YES! For the most part I have just the lowest opinion of men! Oh, that felt good to say! Listen, let me ask you something. Are you straight?

Duke: You mean, am I a heterosexual?

Judy: That's what I mean.

Duke: I just told you I had an affair with Billie.

Judy: Right, right. But are you a complete, unadulterated heterosexual?

Duke: Yes.

Judy: What would you do if a guy like put his hand on your leg and gave it a squeeze?

Duke: Well, frankly, I'd probably punch him in the mouth.

Judy: Really?

Duke: Yes.

Judy: I like you, Duke!

Duke: Well, I like you, too, Judy, even though I don't know you very well. Yet.

Judy: What do you mean?

Duke: Well, we just met a few minutes ago.

Judy: No. I mean, what did you mean by that 'Yet'?

Duke: I don't know.

Judy: Did you mean that later on you think we'll sleep together?

Duke: I didn't say that.

Judy: Forget what you said. Is that what you were thinking?

Duke: Well, maybe we will. What do you think?

Judy: I don't know if I'm up to this.

Duke: What?

Judy: This telling the truth. It's not important to me. Other things are more important to me than whether we sleep together or not. There's conversations I want to have with a man.

Duke: So let's talk.

Judy: Alright. What should we talk about?

Duke: I guess we should have these conversations you want to have with a man.

Judy: Right. God, I feel like such an American!

Duke: What do you mean?

Judy: You know. No Zen. No indirectness. Do you think that some things cannot be gotten to by looking right at them, walking right to them? I do. I think the times when I fail the most are when I try to grab a mystery by the neck, and ask it some good stiff Yankee questions. You are very attractive.

Duke: Thank you.

Judy: And what you said about the way I looked when I walked in, that may well be the nicest thing that any man's ever said to me.

Duke: I meant it.

Judy: Thanks. I don't trust you.

Duke: I don't trust you, either.

Judy: You don't?

Duke: No.

Judy: Why?

Duke: I don't know. You seem a little artificial to me.

Judy: I do? Oh, I'm so hurt.

Duke: Now you don't.

Judy: That's because you hurt me.

Duke: Is that the only way I can get the real you? By hurting you?

Judy: I don't know.

Duke: Maybe that's why you don't like men.

Judy: Why?

Duke: Because you only reward them when they're nasty to you.

Judy: You're very insightful.

Duke: Thank you.

Judy: I don't trust you at all.

Duke: Why not?

Judy: First of all, you smoke a pipe. All men who smoke pipes are hiding something. It's a real phoney baloney thing to do. Second of all, you're black but you talk like Robert Wagner.

Duke: You don't like the way I talk?

Judy: Did your parents talk like that?

Duke: No.

Judy: Then why do you talk like that?

Duke: Because I'm better educated than they were.

Judy: I smell smoke.

Duke: Alright. I talk this way because I made a conscious effort to learn to talk differently than my parents and my friends.

Judy: Why?

Duke: Because nobody in my storybooks talked like them.

Judy: Storybooks again. What was with you and these story-books?

Duke: I don't know, you know it was some silly thing.

Judy: Tell me.

Duke: Well, I guess it was my name. Duke. I saw that dukes were in these stories, so I figured I should be in them, too. That's why I like this whole thing. Meeting at midnight. A mysterious woman. Strange conditions imposed. And the way you're dressed. I guess what I'm saying is I'm a black guy who talks like Robert Wagner and smokes a pipe, which means there's no really comfortable place for me in the world. Except in some situation like this. But even here, it seems, I'm not trusted. Too bad.

Judy: Do you go through a lot of women?

Duke: Like a hot knife through butter. Do you go through a lot of men?

Judy: No.

Duke: I think you're very sweet.

Judy: I wish I knew how to do this.

Duke: What?

Judy: I don't know. I'm lonely. I think you're lonely, too. We're sitting here together. Maybe I should have one of those purple martinis.

Duke: Don't do it. It'll kill you.

Judy: You've had one?

Duke: Yes.

Judy: Then you've been here before?

Duke: Yes, I have.

Judy: With Billie?

Duke: Among others.

Judy: Oh. So this is like your den. I didn't realize I was sitting here among the bones of your previous meals.

Duke: Are you going to start a fight with me?

Judy: Maybe.

Duke: Have I done something to offend you?

Judy: Maybe I'm just sensing if I really knew you I'd hate your guts.

Duke: If you really knew me. If you really knew me, Judy—and I'm not sure that's possible—but if you really could, I think you'd like me.

Judy: This seems like a very weird date to me.

Duke: Listen! Maybe I'm not doing a very good job, but I am trying to talk to you!

Judy: Okay.

Duke: This is very hard for me! I've been going from woman to woman for the last two years. I sleep with them, I get bored with them, I go on! Do you know what that's like?

Judy: No.

Duke: It's like if they dusted my body it'd just be nothing but fingerprints! If they dusted my soul, well, that's when the women wore gloves. There's a bitterness in my mouth. I'm trying not to let it make me talk bitterly. To you. Because it is true what you say. I am lonely. But I wonder if you know what that means. When I say I am lonely. That is peculiar and special to me. My loneliness is not your loneliness. Do you understand?

Judy: Yes.

Duke: I have this personal world. I live in there. It's not much, but it's all I have. I have to be sure, if I let you in, that you're not going to wreck it! You seem very angry to me.

Judy: You seem pretty angry to me.

Duke: I am angry. You're angry. We walked in like that. From other situations. I don't know what to do about that. God, I'm so nervous. I'm sorry. I don't know what you must think of me. I've really been having a great time. In my life. It's just, at the moment...

Judy: I understand.

Duke: No, you don't! Oh, I'm sorry. Boy, what brought this on?

Judy: Maybe I've done something wrong?

Duke: No, I don't think so. It's just ...

Judy: Can I do something?

Duke: What?

Judy: *(Taking a hankie from her sleeve.)* There's this little white mark on your face. I think it's a little powder or something. Can I wipe it off?

Duke: Sure.

She touches the hankie to her tongue, and reaches across to him.

Judy: I don't know why I want to do this so much.

She takes a lot of time and tenderness removing the invisible mark. He's awkward and cooperative.

Duke: Is it coming off?

She doesn't remove her hand.

Judy: It's gone.

He takes her hand gently.

Duke: I think maybe you just removed one of those finger-prints I was talking about. Nice hand.

Judy: Thank you.

Duke: I'm starting to feel romantic.

Judy: This is a romantic place.

Duke: I wonder what would happen if we actually both relaxed?

Judy: I don't know.

Duke: We'd probably stop talking.

Judy: Oh, no. At least, I don't think I would. There's these conversations I would just love to have with a man. And I think if I were really relaxed maybe I could have them.

Duke: What the hell are these conversations?

Judy: Well, this is probably one of them. I guess. I don't know. I've never had these conversations so I don't know what exactly they would be.

Duke: Would they be about love?

Judy: Oh yeah.

Duke: Sex?

Judy: Oh yeah, definitely sex. And they wouldn't be about my family.

Duke: No?

Judy: No, I'd like to leave that behind. Everything about my family. I'd like to finally leave that behind.

Duke: Sounds good to me.

Judy: There are certain things that a man needs to know, though, sort've as a basis. Like that family stuff. My personal almanac. But I'd like him to get it from, I don't know, my doctor or something. Like when you go to certain countries, you've got to get inoculated. Like you go to my doctor and say, I'm going to have a conversation with Judy, so you'd better give me that Judy's Almanac Shot. Then we could just leap over that stuff when we talk. Like conversational moon gravity. Wouldn't that be great?

Duke: Yeah.

Judy: And maybe if we talked long enough, we could stop being afraid and we could talk about just anything at all. Would that be love then?

Duke: No.

Judy: What would it be?

Duke: I don't know. Sympathy?

Judy: That's right. We'd be in sympathy.

A long pause.

Duke: Well. I know what I think.

Judy: What?

Duke: I think we should sleep together.

Judy: Why?

Duke: Because I can't think of anything else, left, that comes before.

Judy: You can't? I can. I can think of loads of things.

Duke: Such as?

Judy: Such as why would you want to?

Duke: I find you very attractive.

Judy: Why? Because of my dress? My hair? My face? What about me do you find attractive enough ... No! So compelling that you would want to have me naked in your arms and physically pass within my walls, broach me, that you would want to possess me, be possessed, lose yourself?

Duke: If you think it'll be that good we should definitely get to it.

Judy: No, I don't think it would be that good. You approach the whole thing too casually.

Duke: Maybe you approach it a little too seriously.

Judy: I don't think so.

Duke: How long's it been since you last shared your favors?

Judy: That's none of your business.

Duke: That long.

Judy: Maybe you're halfway right. I think we may have something to teach each other. Maybe you sell too cheap and I sell too dear. You know what my friends tell me my problem's been?

Duke: What?

Judy: They say I'm a fag hag. One of those women who ...

Duke: I know what a fag hag is.

Judy: I don't want to be that sexually stupid anymore. I want to move on.

Duke: Make some mistakes.

Judy: That's right.

Duke: So, comon, make one with me.

Judy: No! I mean, don't you be so American either. My doctor doesn't have a shot to give you. There are some things that you should know about me, that I should know about you before ... Before.

Duke: Why before?

Judy: Because that does not come first in my mind.

Duke: Even if it doesn't come first, why should things happen in order? Real life doesn't happen in order. Don't be so American yourself.

Judy: You're right. But we shouldn't do it that way anyway because it'd just be more of the same rut you're in.

Duke: But what about you? Not doing it is just more of you being in the same rut you're in. Why do you put my problem ahead of your problem? The way I understand it, that'd be love, and I know we're not in love yet. As far as I can make out, we're not even in sympathy yet!

Judy: Then we shouldn't sleep together!

Duke: I don't even know why I'm arguing with you! I don't even want to go to bed with you!

Judy: Yet!

Duke: What do you mean, yet?

Judy: If you knew me better, you'd kill to sleep with me!

Duke: Dream on, Judy!

Judy: I will! I will dream on. Because that is exactly what I am talking about. My dreams. Which you do not know. And which you don't think are important enough to know. Do you think this body is something? What a joke! Any great poet the last three thousand years will tell you what a joke that is! This stuff, this flesh, this heavy breathing ... We have this aptitude in our hearts and brains and souls to arrive at something so rich and inflamed and unspeakable and sacred and New! Not this tired shit you want to foist on me. That's not what I want. I won't give up my standards! I know what I know. If I tried to live on the kind of thing you're offering me, I'd starve to death. You've got to dig for treasure, Duke! Not settle for the stuff just lying out on the ground. You could sleep with me if you weren't so god damn lazy and narcissistic and were willing to exert yourself a little and show some interest in the actual core of another human being! But you will not sleep with me because I will not perform a stupid mechanical pantomime, like I was trying and failing to remember something fine, something from a better world, something alien and beautiful and lost! What, you look vacant, don't you get it? I'll give it to you in a nutshell. I'll give it to you in basic modern American: I'm not interested in the hardware without the software. Look, let's just let this fall apart, okay? Don't hang around for the sake of neatness. I'll get the check. It was worth that much to me to have my say.

Duke: Hey, this is just you and me talking. This isn't *Inherit The Wind.*

Judy: What do you mean?

Duke: I mean, you're running on a little bigger than life.

Judy: Maybe your life.

Duke: You're like a genius at not getting laid.

Judy: Don't be vulgar.

Duke: Did you have a bad experience or something?

Judy: I've had a lot of bad experiences.

Duke: So have I. Have you wondered why Billie fixed us up? She must've been thinking of something.

Judy: I guess so.

Duke: I mean, I don't know about you, but I feel like we're natural enemies.

Judy: Do you really?

Duke: Yeah. Like the mongoose and the cobra.

Judy: Which one are you?

Duke: Take your pick.

Judy: I figure you for the snake.

Duke: I find you very attractive.

Judy: Wait a minute! Wait a minute! What did I miss? I thought we were natural enemies?

Duke: That's exactly what I find so hot!

Judy: That's sick!

Duke: Call it what you want!

Judy: You're like a wall!

Duke: That's right, Judy! Like the Great Wall A China. You can't get by me. Lean forward.

Judy: Why?

Duke: I'm going to kiss you.

Judy: I really don't understand how we got to this point.

Duke: People don't end up in bed by logic.

Judy: Are we going to bed?

Duke: Lean forward!

She leans forward. They kiss. She gets caught up in the kiss. It ends. She leans back, looking at him. She's surprised.

Judy: That was good.

The lights go down as Duke smiles wolfishly.

SCENE 4

We're back in Rhonda Louise's apartment. It's the following Sunday, in the early afternoon. The backdrop now shows the apartment buildings flooded with sunlight, and Old Sol smiling in a blue sky.

On the dining table are the remains of brunch.

At Rise, Rhonda Louise and Judy sit at the dining table, each holding a bloody mary garnished with a wedge of lemon and a large stick of celery. Rhonda Louise is in a white cotton nightgown and a maroon silk robe. Judy's in jeans and an orange sweatshirt.

Rhonda Louise is bathing Judy in a fiery attention.

Rhonda: So? What happened then?

Judy: About twenty-six hours of very primitive, passionate lovemaking.

Rhonda: You're kidding!

Judy: We went at it like the primordial forms. There were plateaus, upheavals, ditches. We got so deep into this bed it was like dinosaurs wrestling in a tarpit. At one point my tongue had a spasm that made me squawk like a parrot being electrocuted.

Rhonda: Did you have an orgasm?

Judy: I think so.

Rhonda: Good.

Judy: So where the hell is Billie?

Rhonda: I can't imagine. I'd call again, but I just keep getting that machine.

Judy: You'd think she'd be dying to know how it came out.

Rhonda: Maybe she found out from Duke?

Judy: Can you believe that? Billie cheating on Bob with some black guy named Duke?

Rhonda: I know! What an image! And then you end up shackin with the same guy!

Judy: Yeah.

Rhonda: It's almost Gothic! And it was kind of — is this the right word? — generous of Billie.

Judy: I don't know if I'd call it generous. I don't know what I'd call it. I'm all mixed up.

Rhonda: If you ask me, you're all stirred up. Look at you.

Judy: I wish Billie would get here. I'd like to quiz her about a thing or two. Do you assume that this whole saga I told you, that this was a happy story?

Rhonda: Well. It's news.

Judy: I don't know how I feel about it. Something hurts. I gave something up!

Judy cries.

Rhonda: Hey. What's this?

Judy: I had this idea. Of who I was. Of what I believed. This guy, he wasn't … He didn't love me!

Rhonda: Of course he didn't, honey. He just met you.

Judy: I made these speeches. Told him that I wouldn't sleep with him because I had standards. Hardware, software. He even admitted, said, we were enemies! And then he told me to lean forward, and I did!

Rhonda: You leaned forward?

Judy: Yes!

Rhonda: Well, that doesn't seem so bad.

Judy: I just went right against everything that's supposed to be me. And he knew I would! He knew it!

Rhonda: What did he know?

Judy: That I was a big liar, even though I was supposed to be telling the truth! I don't know how to tell the truth! I don't know how to be a humble asshole! I'm so humiliated!

Rhonda: Why?

Judy: Because I'm an animal! No, worse! I can't even admit what I am. He had me pegged right off. I don't want a nice guy. Nice guys bore me to tears! I wanted some stranger to see through me and be mean to me and just tell me what to do! You! Slut! Lie down and get ready!

Rhonda: Judy, Judy, Judy, Judy. You are some case.

Judy: I know.

Rhonda: Did this guy call you a slut?

Judy: No.

Rhonda: Of course he didn't. If he'd called you a slut, that would've been that. You would've given him the boot.

Judy: You don't know that.

Rhonda: Yes, I do. But hey, you know what it must've been? You must have a thing like that, in your mind? A fantasy.

Judy: I don't know.

Rhonda: Maybe you got a touch of it from this guy? A little whiff. And maybe he picked up on it too, went with it a little bit.

Judy: I don't know.

Rhonda: That's what it sounds like to me. And him! From what you tell me about him, he certainly had that kind of thing happen from you.

Judy: I don't follow.

Rhonda: All that stuff about the storybooks. He had some fantasy, too! You wheeled in in that Cinderella gown, and it got to him.

Judy: You mean we were both just deluded?

Rhonda: A bit. So what?

Judy: That's grotesque.

Rhonda: Oh, what are you talking about? No, it's not. That's how people get started with each other. Anyway, a lot of the time. They make up a lot of stuff to start, and then, as they go on, they replace it with real things. That's how people go from romance to love.

Judy: Then I don't want romance. It's sick.

Rhonda: Now you're just lying and wrong. You want it and that's how it should be. You need the romance. It's like a local anesthetic the heart supplies during the painful beginnings of knowing a man. The trick is to let it wear off in its natural time, and go on and let that open tender place be touched. Don't shrink back every time you feel a little pain. If you do, you'll end up with nothing. (*The doorbell rings.*) Come in! It's open! (*Enter Billie in a white windbreaker, tight green jeans, splendid western boots, and a black turtleneck. She's got a big black eye. She walks in slowly. We see the eye before they do.*) Hey, Billie.

Judy: Billie, where have you been?

Rhonda: Oh my Lord, look at your eye!

Judy: Oh God!

> *Billie starts to cry, lightly at first. Rhonda goes to her and holds her. The sobs get deeper. Rhonda holds her drink to Billie's eye.*

Rhonda: What happened, baby?

> *Billie pulls herself together enough to answer.*

Billie: Bob.

> *Billie goes back to crying.*

Judy: Bob?

Rhonda: Bob? Bob what? Bob did this to you?

Judy: No!

> *Billie pulls herself together.*

Billie: Yes!

> *She goes back to crying.*

Rhonda: But how? Why? I don't understand!

> *Billie pulls herself together.*

Billie: I'm so happy!

> *She goes back to crying.*

Judy: (*To Rhonda.*) She's happy?

Rhonda: That's what she said.

> *Billie pulls herself together, and addresses Rhonda.*

Billie: Don't you understand? The honeymoon's over! The

great adventure has begun!

Rhonda: Oh. I see.

Judy: He hit you?

Billie: Yes!

Judy: And you think this is good news?

Billie: It's what I've been praying for!

Judy: Well, Rhonda Louise advises: Don't shrink back every time you feel a little pain.

Rhonda: I wasn't talking about this kind of thing. Why did he hit you?

Judy: Did he find out about the Duke?

Billie: What do you mean?

Judy: Did he find out that you had an affair with Duke?

Billie: Duke told you?

Judy: Yeah.

Billie: That bastard!

Judy: What are you talking about? You told the guy to be completely truthful.

Billie: I meant about himself! I don't see why he had to drag me into it. Anyway, it's over. It's been over for a while.

Judy: I know. He told me.

Billie: What else did he tell you?

Judy: That you got bored with each other. Sexually.

Billie: Stop!

Rhonda: Why did Bob hit you?

Billie: Is it very black?

Rhonda: Among other colors, it is also black, yes.

Billie: Can I have a sip of your drink?

Rhonda: Here, take it. I don't need liquor anymore. I have you.

Billie: Thanks. *(She takes a drink.)* Bob hit me because I wet the bed.

Judy: You know what I thought you just said?

Rhonda: You didn't.

Billie: I wet the bed.

Judy: What do you mean you wet the bed? You didn't wet the bed.

Billie: Yes, I did.

Judy: How humiliating!

Billie: Oh, I don't feel humiliated.

Judy: Not you, me. I took advice from you?

Billie: Oh, how did that go?

Rhonda: Billie, how did you come to wet the bed?

Billie: Oh, you know how these things are. It's complicated.

Rhonda: Speak to me.

Billie: It came out of an atmosphere.

Judy: You came out of the atmosphere.

Billie: You know, like lightning. There's this long tense sameness in the air. And it just gets more so and more so. Till zap. This big white bolt across the sky.

Rhonda: Be more specific.

Billie: There's a thing that can happen in marriage. It's a kind of incredibly boring endless Mexican standoff over some idiot shit. You're in your trench and he's in his. Years can go by. Nothing changes. It just gets more and more deeply the same. I can't tell you how profoundly this kind of existence bites the big one. Anyway, last night, I was thinking. I was thinking, If I could just let go. If I could just completely let go, what would I look like? Would Bob find that attractive? And while I was thinking this, I came to realize that I was just flooding the bed! I mean, Cats and Dogs. I thought I was dreaming. I saw Bob's face over me, like a big stormcloud. I got very cold. Like Bob was blocking the sun or something, even though it was the middle of the night. I felt very small, like I was shrinking down into a dot. He grabbed me by the shoulders and pulled me up. He said, Listen! I don't give a fuck what you do! You can lie down and die for what I care! But Nobody, Nobody pisses in my bed! And then he punched me right in the eye..I saw stars, just like you're supposed to. And through the stars, I could hear him crying.

Rhonda: I'm having trouble with my reaction to this.

Judy: Did you leave him?

Billie: I just made love to him, and made him breakfast.

Judy: I never saw this side of you before.

Billie: What side?

Judy: The victim.

Billie: Oh comon, lighten up. I'm no victim.

Rhonda: Well, the man did hit you. Don't ignore that.

Billie: Oh, you weren't there. Either of you. Not just for the punch. For the whole thing. Bob and I became brutes. We had to.

We'd gotten to the point where there was no civilized way for us to save ourselves. So I pissed on him, and he punched me in the eye.

Rhonda: Quite a transaction.

Billie: I did bite him, too. But that was more of an afterthought.

Rhonda: Why didn't you just shoot each other?

Billie: It's harder to make up.

Judy: Promise me, Billie. If he ever lays a hand on you again, you'll leave him.

Billie: Why would I make a stupid promise like that? Look, my father didn't hit my mother, and I've never shown any particular hunger for getting hit. I don't think I'm in line to become a battered wife. What's a battered wife, anyway? I mean, you see me, and my husband hit me, so I'm a battered wife? Please. Save that deep thought for a TV movie. I thought that my marriage was dead, or I was dead, or both. Now, somehow, I've got 'em back again, and me, in my personal heart of hearts, I don't give a shit to judge the means good or bad. I just want to understand. It's funny. Here I am, closer to my husband than I've been in a long time, a long long time. But I feel free. I feel like I can do anything I want.

Rhonda: Maybe you can and maybe not.

Billie: I don't really know. I'm just describing how I feel.

Rhonda: But what if you couldn't be violent?

Billie: I don't know. Then you lose, I guess.

Rhonda: Then it's a game?

Billie: Maybe. If it is, it's not one I learned in advance. All I know is when the moment came for me, I did what I had to do. Are you alright?

Rhonda: I think so, sure.

Billie: But, so, Judy, for Godsakes tell me, how'd it go with Duke? Ain't he something?

Judy: I don't want to talk about it.

Rhonda: They spent the night together.

Billie: Bingo!

Judy: Nobody likes a squealer.

Rhonda: It was apparently very explosive.

Billie: Bingo, bingo!

Judy: That guy is a total shit.

Billie: Did you think so?

Judy: Isn't he?

Billie: I don't know, I thought he was adorable.

Judy: But isn't he like a hypocrite?

Billie: Oh, don't be a dildo, Judy! Of course he's a hypocrite. Do you think I would've been crazy enough to fix you up with a nice plain sincere guy? Do I look like a complete incompetent?

Judy: Why wouldn't you fix me up with a nice plain sincere guy?

Billie: Because you would've chewed him to pieces and never gotten any nooky. Why? Because you're a sick chick. Why are you a sick chick? Because you don't get any nooky. How'd you come to be in such a perfectly stupid loop? Who cares? Ancient history. Leave it to the scholars. The point is here and now you needed to get down and be had. A nice guy wouldn't have shaken you up enough to get you to drop your drawers. Are you going to see him again?

Judy: Nnn... ness.

Billie: Ness? What's ness mean?

Judy: It means yes.

Billie: When?

Judy: Tonight.

Rhonda: Wow.

Billie: I'm a genius. And don't think I passed on damaged goods. Duke and I had a short relationship utterly free of sincerity. That's what I wanted at the time, whore that I was.

Rhonda: Did you tell Bob you've been having other guys?

Billie: No. And I don't know if I ever will. I might. How'd you like Maria's Cin Cin?

Judy: I hated it!

Billie: Yeah, it's a great place. God, I love romance!

Rhonda: Do you still?

Billie: Yes! But I absolutely absolutely absolutely hate honeymoons!

Judy: I'm not sure I understand the difference.

Billie: I'm not sure you should.

Rhonda: There's something that I don't get.

Billie: What?

Rhonda: Well. The other night when we had dinner and you told me you were suffering from an ache that knew no name.

Billie: Yeah?

Rhonda: You'd been cheating on Bob.

Billie: Yeah?

Rhonda: You didn't tell me.

Billie: Right.

Rhonda: Then you were lying.

Billie: About what?

Rhonda: Your ache. You knew the name of it.

Billie: I did?

Rhonda: You felt bad cause you were cheating on your husband.

Billie: No.

Rhonda: No? God, I feel like I'm looking at y'all from miles away.

Billie: Why?

Rhonda: I don't know. Kiss, kiss, bang, bang. I listen to what's gone on with you and Judy. Kiss, kiss, bang, bang. Is this it?

Billie: You can't stand outside these things and hope to figure them, Rhonda Louise.

Rhonda: Maybe so. Probably no big thing. Probably just my problem. But now to step onto firm ground. Billie, you are aware you missed my brunch?

Billie: I know. I'm sorry. I turned on the machine, and then I turned on Bob. And then how could I not make the man an omelet?

Rhonda: Well, it's just like I always said. You are a terrible guest.

Billie: I see the sneakers are still here.

Rhonda: Oh yes.

Billie: Maybe you should let me fix you up on a little date?

Rhonda: No.

Billie: No? Just no?

Rhonda: Yes.

Billie: Yes meaning no?

Rhonda: Yes.

Billie: You can't hold off forever.

Rhonda: It hasn't been that long.

Billie: It's been a few months.

Rhonda: Yeah. That's not that long.

Judy: It is harder the longer you wait.

Rhonda: We're different.

Billie: She's still right.

Rhonda: Then it'll just be harder is all.

Judy: You've both given me so much advice. Rhonda, can I give you some?

Rhonda: Sure.

Judy: Sleep with somebody. It really... puts you back in touch.

Rhonda: Trust me. We are different.

Judy: I just want to help.

Rhonda: I know. But I don't want any help.

Judy: Alright then, the hell with you! You're on your own. But it makes me mad!

Rhonda: Don't be mad.

Judy: Why not? Billie gets to fix me up on a date, you tell me how I should feel about my life, it's not fair that I don't get to help you! What am I? Do you think you're better than me?

Rhonda: No.

Judy: I think you do. You're damn right I'm mad! It's a big cheat to give and then turn around and not take when it's your turn. It's arrogant! I had to step on my pride to take something from you and that was hard for me, but I did it because I trusted you!

Rhonda: You needed to!

Judy: Well, what do you need, Rhonda?

Rhonda: Nothing.

Judy: Don't say that, I'm standing here trying to give you something, tell me what you need!

Rhonda: Nothing.

Billie: Oh, comon!

Rhonda: YOU CAN'T HELP ME!

Billie: Hey, take it easy.

Rhonda: How can you help me? What, you think I should go on a date and everything would be hunky dory? Sleep with some man I don't want? Maybe get pasted one to have a spiritual awakening? I don't buy it. It happens to you, okay. Try to deal with it, make sense of it. I'm not in the mood to go out and clobber the world with my idea of how it should be. This guy left me, okay? I feel like shit about it. I feel like I'm not worth thirty-five cents. Now I could run out that door and try to find somebody to plug that hole I feel in me, but I've done that before and I'm not going to do that again. I'd rather shrink down to my natural size, whatever that is, than get pumped up again. What do I need, Judy? Esteem. True self-esteem. Can you give that to me? Billie, can you give that to me?

Billie: No.

Rhonda: Thank you. So I'll wait. I'm not waiting for Jerry to come back. I'm not waiting to die. I'm waiting for me. And I may take awhile. I haven't even thrown out his sneakers yet. You tell me these things about your lives and I try to be a good friend and sympathize and not judge. But I've got to draw the line at mistaking us all for being the same. We're all three of us in different places. Billie's married. You're going into something. I'm coming out of something. There. There. And there. Like three stars in the sky. I don't deny your friendship. I love you. But respect me.

Judy: Okay.

Billie: Okay.

Rhonda: When I was a little girl, and I was having fun, I would yell at my sister, Be like me! I meant I wanted her to play with me, feel the pleasure I was feeling. But she wouldn't. Cause she wasn't me. That was what I found troubling and didn't understand. That I couldn't just open my arms, like the gates of heaven, and let another soul enter my paradise. I need to be alone. I've been alone all my life. I've been alone with a man beside me in my bed. I need to be truly alone now. So I can admit it. And think about it. And, I guess, so I can come up with a better invitation. Be like me ain't gonna get it. That's just an invitation to loneliness.

Judy: You know what Duke said?

Rhonda: What?

Judy: He said my eyes were like water. He said my eyes made him want to go for a swim.

Billie: He never said anything like that to me.

Rhonda: Peace. Peace now. Each to her own.

THE END

**the
dreamer
examines
his
pillow**

This play is dedicated to my family.

"the dreamer examines his pillow" was presented by the Double Image Theatre (Helen Waren Mayer, Founder/Executive Director; Max Mayor, Artistic director; Leslie Urdang, Managing Director) in New York City in October, 1986. It was directed by Max Mayer; the sets were by Adrianne Lobel, the costumes were by Dunya Ramicova; the lights were by James F. Ingalls; the production stage manager was William H. Lang; the assistant lighting designer was Michael Lincoln; and the sound was by Janet Kalas.

The cast, in order of appearance, was as follows:

Tommy	Scott Renderer
Donna	Anne O'Sullivan
Dad	Graham Beckel

"the dreamer examines his pillow" was originally presented as a staged reading at the 1985 National Playwrights Conference at the Eugene O'Neill Memorial Theatre Center.

"the dreamer examines his pillow" was subsequently produced by the Double Image Theatre in association with The Powerhouse Theatre at Vassar College, Poughkeepsie, New York, in 1986.

SCENE I

A rough dirty whitewashed concrete basement room. Only the rear wall is visible. In the wall is a door. On the wall, fixed with four big hurtful nails, is a crude, violent drawing of a man's face. The face has one big eye and one small eye; it's painted with black strokes, and has a drop of red and a faint smudge of green. There are long cracks in the wall, emanating from the nails.

At rise, Tommy is sitting in his busted recliner looking at his dirty refrigerator. He's unshaven. He's drinking a can of beer. He's in dirty white garb.

Tommy: Hail to you, O my refrigerator. Is my self in you? Can this be right? I guess this is something I gotta exist through. Makes sense. It's a tense drag, though. *(A loud knocking at the door.)* Who's that?

Donna: *(From off.)* It's Donna.

Tommy: Donna? Hah. Why do you honor me, Donna?

Donna: (From off.) Open the fuckin door.

Tommy: Alright. Since you put it that way.

He gets up and opens the door. There's Donna, an intense girl inside a black dress with a few white polka dots.

Donna: You.

Tommy: You look great.

Donna: You've got to be fucking kidding me. Get outta my way. I'm comin in. *(She pushes past him and takes the place in.)* What a shithole.

Tommy: I call it "Home."

Donna: You do, huh? How do you think 'em up? You got somethin to drink? Somethin protected? A glass a bottled water or somethin?

Tommy: How 'bout the rest of my beer?

Donna: How 'bout a fresh one, doghead?

Tommy: Charming. Alright.

He goes and opens the refrigerator.

Donna: I hope nothin's livin in there.

Tommy: And me, I hope just about the reverse.

Gives her a beer.

Donna: How long you lived here now?

Tommy: Four months.

Donna: This place got bugs?

Tommy: Yeah.

Donna: Do you got bugs?

Tommy: I don't know.

Donna: You used to be clean, Tommy.

Tommy: Yeah, well. That's the way I used to be. This is the new me.

Donna: What's with you?

Tommy: Nothing.

Donna: What kinda number you doin?

Tommy: I'm not doin nothing.

Donna: Don't gimme that shit, professor. You think I got nothin up above? You think you're dealin with one of your dipshit know nothin chippies at the local disco? I'm hearin shit. I'm seein shit. I'm smellin the smoke somethin's burnin don't you tell me there's no fire. YOU ARE HITTIN ON MY SISTER.

Tommy: So you heard.

Donna: I heard.

Tommy: These things happen.

Donna: Other things happen, too. I forsee your ass with a foot in it. The foot is wearin my shoe.

Tommy: I don't see how you're involved.

Donna: Don't aggravate me, please?

Tommy: You're out of it, right?

Donna: Outta what?

Tommy: My life?

Donna: I thought so.

Tommy: You're not sure?

Donna: You've been sittin here waitin for me, ain't you? Ain't you?

Tommy: I've been sitting here.

Donna: How long you been seein Mona?

Tommy: Who says I've been seein her? I don't even feel like answering you. A month.

Donna: She's sixteen.

Tommy: Just sixteen. I'm twenty-seven. So what? Life's short. Let's have fun.

Donna: We both know what's going on here.

Tommy: A man's gotta do what he's gotta do. You look good.

Donna: You always thought too much.

Tommy: I don't agree.

Donna: Look at this junkyard. What're you doin? This ain't a good lifestyle.

Tommy: So you're right. Which don't make you feel no better. When you comin back?

Donna: I ain't comin back.

Tommy: What're you doin out there without me?

Donna: I'm gettin by.

Tommy: *(Revealing himself.)* WELL HOW 'BOUT ME?

Donna: HOW 'BOUT YOU?

Tommy: I MISS YOU.

Donna: YOU LEFT ME.

Tommy: I LOVE YOU.

Donna: YOU'RE HITTIN ON MY SISTER.

Tommy: What? You expect me to die? I could. I'm tryin to do somethin to keep goin. You're gone. There's nothin … I gotta make my heart pump the blood. Understand? You're gone.

Donna: *You* left *me.*

Tommy: So that was somethin I did.

Donna: I don't know how to react to you. You boggle my fuckin mind. What're you sayin? You want me back?

Tommy: NO. No. That I cannot do. That way's just that fuckin killin pain. I can't … I don't know what to do with you, Donna. But if I don't see you, I'm starvin dyin lost like a a a feelin of a lackluster world but …

Donna: Why are you breathin on my sister?

Tommy: It's all you.

Donna: Mona ain't me even in your demented eyes. She's sixteen.

Tommy: What else could I do? I don't got all that many options.

Donna: You didn't have that option, either. That was just criminal shit you did outside the bounds. What's the picture for?

Tommy: That's a picture a me.

Donna: Who by?

Tommy: Me.

Donna: It's terrible. Why the one eye big and the other small?

Tommy: That's what I look like.

Donna: Oh, it is, huh?

Tommy: You don't think it looks like me?

Donna: No.

Tommy: Then it's like I thought. You know the before but not the after.

Donna: This is what you've changed to?

Tommy: This is what I've always been like, really. Different moods. But this is the basic guy.

Donna: This looks like some monster done outta crayons by an ungifted child. And look how you got it up there. A little scotch tape woulda done the trick. Ain't you got no respect for your walls?

Tommy: No. None.

Donna: Well, you should.

Tommy: The nails holdin it there is part of it. I don't know why I'm tryin to explain. You've always been hostile to anything you didn't understand in the first three seconds. Life just isn't simple enough for your basic approach. Just sayin somethin's over don't make it so. It just puts a lid down so the pressure can build to where everything's bent. There's lightning screwed in a jar in here.

Donna: You were the one ended it.

Tommy: So I fucked up. And I don't know what to do even now. I look bad, don't I?

Donna: You look bad. But you look okay. *(Indicating picture.)* You don't look as bad as that.

Tommy: Yes, I do.

Donna: You are crazy. Listen. Tell me somethin. You been with Mona?

Tommy: I've seen her.

Donna: Have you been with her?

Tommy: Yeah.

Donna: *(In sudden extreme pain.)* How? How could you do that? Do you hate me?

Tommy: No.

Donna: She's my sister and you ... did that?

Tommy: I didn't. Really.

Donna: What? But you just said you did.

Tommy: It happened.

Donna: But Tommy, who happened it?

Tommy: It just did though. Happen.

Donna: Don't gimme that shit. That is the worst. That is my most unfavorite lie.

Tommy: Your sister did it.

Donna: My sister did it. And where were you at the time? Chinatown?

Tommy: I was there, too.

Donna: I want a promise. You won't touch her again.

Tommy: Why do you care so much?

Donna: She's my sister.

Tommy: It's cause a what you feel for me.

Donna: Felt.

Tommy: You still love me.

Donna: Yeah, I love ya. I dote on ya. I hate your fuckin guts. I'm lost how to proceed with you. You're like a nut. You see everything through this slot. It kills me. I thought you loved me.

Tommy: I do.

Donna: I don't get it. How could you love me and drag my family down into this shit?

Tommy: Why do you think I'm sittin in this garbage can? Huh? Cause everything's cool an I'm in good shape? Huh? Look at me. Look at my picture I did. That's me. One eye sees too much one eye can't get big enough to see my way out of how I feel, I'm holdin my face up with nails. Everything's you. I see everything and everything's you.

He grabs her and crushes her. They kiss passionately.

Donna: I'm scared.

Tommy: God.

Donna: I'm shaking.

Tommy: I want you, Donna. I wanna take you right now.

Donna: I can't do this.

Tommy: I know. I'm scared, too. But I can't help myself.

Donna: *(Pulling away.)* No. Maybe you can't help yourself, but I gotta help me. I really can't. I'm gonna go crazy if I get sucked back in with you.

Tommy: Comon. It's what we both want.

Donna: You can't leave me, go to my sister, and then come back to me, too. What am I if I let that happen? I ain't talkin about how it would look. I'm talkin about what it would be. I'd be lost. No life. Just part a whatever you happened to feel. I ain't no figment in your blood and if you don't get off Mona, I'm gonna kill you. I'm gonna give you the gun. Can you hear me through the mud? I'll kill you.

Tommy: Hey. Calm down.

Donna: Why? Why should I?

Tommy: You'll make yourself sick.

Donna: You amaze me. You're amazing. I'm amazed.

Tommy: There's only you. You and only you. Nobody else knows me.

Donna: What about Mona?

Tommy: I never talk about you to her.

Donna: No?

Tommy: No.

Donna: Am I supposed to be grateful?

Tommy: No.

Donna: You can talk about me if you want. I don't give a shit.

Tommy: I don't want to.

Donna: I talked about you to my girlfriend. Judy? Judy thinks your poison. Your picture's in her post office. She spits on the ground when your name is mentioned.

Tommy: What did you tell her?

Donna: The truth.

Tommy: It must've taken a long time to tell.

Donna: Not that long.

Tommy: Then it wasn't the truth. The truth about us is long.

Donna: I kept the story together. I just left out the tears.

Tommy: I'm sorry.

Donna: You said that before and so what? You go right on steppin on my neck. Even now. You're gone and you're still just doin vile shit that affects my life. Screwin my sister. It's like diabolical. I mean, what's wrong with you?

Tommy: I don't know. I really don't.

Donna: You oughta find out, man. That should be your mission.

Tommy: I don't know.

Donna: You're sittin in this place. You got it like the Black Hole a Calcutta. You make this horrible picture of yourself and you put it up and you drink beer and you look at it. You go out in the street. You mess with my sister. You come back here and you wait for me. You want me to think you're crazy? Is that it? I won't do it. I hold you responsible for every single thing you done and I always will. I don't buy this crazy alibi it's been goin around. "I killed her cause I was crazy." I don't give a shit you killed cause you was crazy. All I care was you killed. You killed her. And if you're that crazy it's gonna be the death a you.

Tommy: Killed who?

Donna: I'm tryin ta say something but I'm too upset.

Tommy: Take it easy.

Donna: This whole thing with you from beginning to end has just worn me down. How long's it been now?

Tommy: A year.

Donna: I gotta get some shots or something. Life's too short. Bail me out, Tommy. Leave me alone.

Tommy: You know I can't do that.

Donna: You selfish thing. Then gimme another beer.

Tommy: Alright.

He gets her another.

Donna: How much rent you pay?

Tommy: Two hundred.

Donna: How you pay it?

Tommy: Different ways.

Donna: You robbed your mother.

Tommy: She told?

Donna: She didn't want to, but she thinks I drove you crazy so she bitched to me.

Tommy: You don't understand. Why d'you just keep jumpin right in when you don't understand?

Donna: You don't feel it, do ya? Like the Nazis. I'm talkin to you while you're havin an out-of-body experience somewhere.

Tommy: Are you callin me a Nazi?

Donna: No. I wouldn't do that. But I'm reminded.

Tommy: I didn't do anything with the purpose a hurtin you. Or my Ma. Or anybody. I didn't have any evil intentions.

Donna: I could believe you. It just don't matter.

Tommy: I didn't plan to rob my mother. It just happened.

Donna: Who happened it, Tommy?

Tommy: These things that've taken place, they're not what I woulda done.

Donna: But you done these things.

Tommy: I didn't choose to. I was compulsed.

Donna: By who?

Tommy: By somethin in me that's not me.

Donna: What? You gotta little man livin in there?

Tommy: Yeah. I got a devil.

Donna: *(Trapping him.)* You're the devil.

Tommy: No. I swear to God I'm not.

Donna: You're the devil.

Tommy: You don't understand.

Donna: I see everything.

Tommy: I get … If you get inna car crash. Maybe you're dazed or whatever. You walk around, down a road. You don't choose to walk down the road. You don't know what you're doing.

Donna: So if you walk away, maybe even there's a girl crashed in the car, and cause you're punchy, then it's alright?

Tommy: Well, at least it explains why.

Donna: You hate your boss. You stab him with a knife in the heart. He dies. So? I explained why. You hated him. Does that make it right?

Tommy: What if I saw red and didn't remember a thing? Came to and just found him lyin there, dead on the ground.

Donna: You still killed your boss.

Tommy: I didn't kill my boss. I don't have a boss. This is hypothetical bullshit.

Donna: You're a bum and you're nuts and you broke my heart even though I loved you, and I hold you strictly responsible. No matter how you squirm under the light. Listen. I don't care. You treat me like shit. You rob your mother. You pork my sister. I don't care. Just so long as you would finally finally cop to bein the prick who did that stuff. But this standin above outside like like it happened and ain't that a shame but I don't act that way it musta been somebody else, Mister Crazy Mister Compulsed Mister Explanation Mister Nobody's Home — that line of shit drives me totally insane. In which condition I may cut your throat. But if I do, I did it. Just exactly me. God, I miss you. I'm so lonely for you. I wish you'd wake up. I wish you'd kiss me when you're awake.

Tommy: I am awake.

Donna: Maybe you even believe that.

Tommy: What do you want from me?

Donna: Nothin I can have.

Tommy: What?

Donna: This is sad. This is so sad. Maybe I should go.

Tommy: No.

Donna: There's no point to this. You don't want me back.

Tommy: Yes, I do. I want you back.

Donna: Huh? You just said a minute ago that you didn't.

Tommy: I know.

Donna: And now you do?

Tommy: Yes.

Donna: I don't know how to feel.

Tommy: Don't think about it. Just feel.

Donna: I can't. I'm emotionally confused.

Tommy: I believe in God now.

Donna: Oh no.

Tommy: Things got so bad. I was just rippin up. Everything I was doing, it was just like to get out of a burning house. A crazy jump out the nearest window and you land where you land. One night it all hit me. Everything I lost. You. And the soul ... When I left you, a fuse got lit. I didn't know. The other end was my soul I didn't know I had. And then one night the fuse that got lit all those days before reached my soul. And it just combusted ta fuckin daylights. My ribs swung open like two sets a fingers, like two hands that'd been holdin in the sunlight, the solar system, comets, fire big and old like my share a the beginnin of the universe. My soul fallin out. Like all the crown jewels spillin outta some old suitcase, my body, where nobody knew they were. I was on my knees. All the pain I ducked all my life, I could hear it comin. And I'm here to tell you it's true. There ain't no athletes in foxholes, cause I've been there now and when the bombs go off for real you are weak. I called on God. I called for God, HELP ME GOD. And it helped. At least by the fact that I believed he heard me relieved the pressure of the too much I was feelin. Let my ribs reach out and get back what got out, what was out there that's supposed to be inside, take it back in and close again. But ever since then, even though the pain went back in, I can see it, glowin out through the long red slots between my bones. And it gives me hope to see it. It lets me know I'm alive, not left over. It gives me hope, Donna, that there may be more to me than my brain and its noise. It gives me hope that I have a light in me that I don't understand and maybe can't even claim.

Donna: So you believe in God now?

Tommy: Yeah. Do you?

Donna: No. But you go ahead.

Tommy: I kneel down before I go to bed. And when I get up in the morning.

Donna: And then you go out and rob your mother.

Tommy: That was a cheap shot.

Donna: Oh, I can do better than that. I'm holdin back.

Tommy: I'm tryin to explain somethin to you.

Donna: You got such total unjustified faith in the explanation ta make things okedoke.

Tommy: Well, maybe so, but it works.

Donna: It don't work. Only in your personal hot fever does it work. You know what I hear when you say this shit? Words. Babblin words that don't got the first thing ta do with what you're doin.

Tommy: So I got only words. What do you got?

Donna: Me? I got nothin.

Tommy: I rest my case.

Donna: But I'm survivin. Better than you, maybe. No, that ain't true, neither. I cry all the time. I'm amazed I got more tears. Seems impossible. Anyway, fuck the melodrama. I came here ta get somethin. Which is a promise solid as steel from you that you will leave my sister strictly alone. Are you gonna gimme what I come for or not?

Tommy: No.

Donna: No? Whaddaya mean, no?

Tommy: No. I won't promise.

Donna: Why not?

Tommy: Cause I can't answer for myself at this time. Or maybe what I mean is, I can't answer for the guy I may be later. I can only talk for me now.

Donna: Well, what's the guy-you-are-now gotta say?

Tommy: That Mona ain't here now, so no, I won't touch her.

Donna: That's it?

Tommy: That's it.

Donna: That's the best you can do?

Tommy: That's right.

Donna: What are you?

Tommy: Honest.

Donna: You are not an adult.

Tommy: I'm more the adult now than I ever was. At least I'm not lying.

Donna: You're gonna haveta do better than that. Did you ever hear a law?

Tommy: You don't get what I'm goin through.

Donna: You talk about yourself like you were an isotope or somethin. Unstable to the nines. Today I'm Tommy, tomorrow, who knows? A trained seal. A marachino cherry. IDENTITY. Do you know what I'm talkin about? This is important. Identity. What's yours? You got one. Did you know, or is this news out there on your planet? You are somebody. Tell me who.

Tommy: I don't know.

Donna: Find out.

Tommy: How?

Donna: Law. There's all this stuff that you do and wanna do. And then there's your personal law, that starts and stops you. What's your personal law?

Tommy: I don't have one.

Donna: You're fulla shit. You know what I think's the matter? I think that you got more than one set. You got two or more sets a personal law. One's your goodboy law that you learned sometime a long time since, and one's your real law that comes up outta your pitch-dark soul. You talk about your soul. That's good. That's a start. You mean what's down there in the gloom buried under a thousand mattresses, every bed you ever slept on. But you know what it is down there inside the last Chinese box? It's your Identity. He's a little guy you've never been introduced to. And in his wallet, he's got your real personal law. He's what you're pointing at when you say, that's a devil.

Tommy: No, don't say that.

Donna: Your devil is your soul.

Tommy: Shut up.

Donna: No. Your devil is your soul.

Tommy: That devil's what I gotta get rid of.

Donna: You get ridda that devil you'll be a soulless TV man.

Tommy: I wanna be good.

Donna: Yeah, and you believe in God. Good is bigger and more rotten than you know.

Tommy: Alright then, but you gotta live with that then, too. Cause that's where I nailed your sister from. From there. Where I don't understand. That's where I robbed my mother from. An why I can't talk about what comes next.

Donna: You gotta get down, Tommy.

Tommy: I am down.

Donna: You gotta get down in your identity. You gotta read out from your personal law.

Tommy: And then after I'm down, then what?

Donna: You hear what I'm tellin you, you crazy motherfucker. Know thyself. Then maybe we can talk. And in the meantime, STOP HITTIN ON MY SISTER.

Tommy: Why?

Donna: Cause I am speaking to you from me. My law, which I know, says if you fuck with my sister, you, you are fucking with me. Do you hear me?

Tommy: Yeah, I hear you.

Donna: And take that picture down. It upsets me.

Tommy: I need that.

Donna: This is just somethin for you to wallow in. Somethin ta keep you where you are now, which is really where you were, only you won't let go.

Tommy: I'm tryin to understand myself.

Donna: Your tryin ta nail yourself into a picture that'll drive you crazy cause you are not a picture. I've scoped out these would-be thinkers with the books they're pushin on the mornin shows. Some clown tryin to explain some woman he never met to herself. People oughta know better. Why you tryin ta nail yourself into a picture, Tommy?

Tommy: I'm tryin to understand myself.

Donna: I think you're tryin ta stand still, rot in this room not movin so's your brain can catch up with you.

Tommy: How can I do anything till I understand myself?

Donna: Are you a man or what? Fuck your brain. Did you pork my sister with your brain?

Tommy: I don't know.

Donna: You painted that picture with your brain. Where am I in that picture?

Tommy: I painted that picture to understand myself.

Donna: Do you wanna be a painter?

Tommy: No.

Donna: Are you sure?

Tommy: Yeah.

Donna: I didn't think so. A good thing, too.

Tommy: You're so hard on me.

Donna: I love you.

Tommy: I love you, too.

Donna: No.

Tommy: Why you say no?

Donna: My life's so horrible. How'd my life get so horrible? What'd I do? You're the one that's fucked up. Why am I the one that's bleedin? It's unjust.

Tommy: There's no justice inna relationship.

Donna: What the fuck did you say to me? Relationship? I hate that fuckin word. That's one those TV words that beats it all down inta the same. Don't use words like that on me.

Tommy: Comon, it's the lingo.

Donna: It ain't my lingo.

Tommy: It's English.

Donna: Then English ain't my lingo.

Tommy: What is then?

Donna: What I say is my native tongue, and what I say comes outta thinkin as I go along. Not repeatin words outta somebody else's life that happens to look like mine at the moment causa love. It's cheap. Like cheatin onna test. That ain't how ya learn.

Tommy: You make everything so hard.

Donna: I don't *make it* that way.

Tommy: Listen, Donna, let's just chuck it. Let's just give up chewin this same fuckin bone till we got no teeth left. We're comin from nothin, we're goin ta nothin.

Donna: What are you talkin about?

Tommy: Relief. Let's take a break. You know when you're not here, when I'm alone, I can feel exactly the flesh of your cheek on my lips. I can smell your hair. I can feel the length of your body under me. When I'm not around, can you feel my body that way?

Donna: Yeah.

Tommy: Do you?

Donna: Yeah.

Tommy: Can't you feel it, Donna? The whole thing's spinning and we're in it and we're spinnin, too. There's almost nothin here already. We've busted everything.

Donna: I gotta get outta here.

Tommy: Come here with me.

Donna: No, I tell ya. I'm not gonna get deluded with you no-more. I've been up there in the romantic clouds with you. We always gotta come back down to this shithole room or some other shithole room, and I can't feature that no more. I think what I gotta do is I gotta understand the world outside a us.

Tommy: Why?

Donna: Cause I part a the way feel the reason we fell in such a deep hole is there's so many deep holes around.

Tommy: So what if there are? What are you gonna do about it?

Donna: I think what I gotta do is, I think I gotta go to The Heights. I think I gotta go to The Heights and talk to my father.

Tommy: Your father.

Donna: You never met him. He moved to The Heights a long time ago.

Tommy: What's he gonna do?

Donna: There's some questions I wanna ask him. And there may be somethin I want him to do. To you.

Tommy: To me?

Donna: That's right.

Tommy: What would you want him to do to me?

Donna: I may want him to beat you up.

Tommy: You mean, hurt me?

Donna: Yeah. I beginning to think that I may have to get very basic with you.

Tommy: But why would he wanna hurt me?

Donna: He's my father. And he's Mona's father, too.

Tommy: Is he strong?

Donna: Yeah. He's very strong. And he's very smart. But he's got some faults, too. I gotta a couple a questions I wanna ask him. And then I'm gonna ask him about you.

   Donna walks to the door and exits.

Tommy: Donna? Donna? O my refrigerator. Is my self in you? (*The lights fade quickly to black. And the refrigerator door, of its own volition, slowly opens. A blinding light emanates from it, engulfing Tommy. He stares into the light and has a vision.*) I dive into a lake fulla hot water. It doesn't hurt me. It gives me power. I go down to the bottom. There are caves, large fish, extravagant wrecks, underwater birds. One of the birds is Anger. It's faster than anything else. There's music. The ground under my feet is hot food. It crawls part way up my legs as I walk. Electric bolts and submarines bar my passage. Certain caves beckon to me. Old men and women long dead advise me. Crews of skeletons rig the dead ships with wormy sails and rotten ropes. They sing ... I breathe the water and choke a moment, but then I'm okay. The bird that's Anger lands on my shoulder. My chest becomes larger. I'm wearin less clothes. I was afraid. I am less afraid. I see ahead the possibility of being brave. The caves stand before me. God help me cause that is where my future lies. The caves are mothers and fears and no one will know what will happen to me when I go in there. I have always been before the caves. Gotten my power from them. Gotten my weakness from them. It's time. Enter away from the ordinary extraordinary twilight I have lived in. Don't read the newspapers, be the news. Run no more. Hold yourself away from your own sight no more. Throw people between yourself and yourself no more. Call up the things you have buried. Be free to be hated. Unloved. Alone. Be alone with yourself. In the dark of the mother cave where you have always stood outside. You're not so frightening that you can't be looked on. Call the Being from the tomb you've been carving all your life. You dream of outer space of distant seas of unknown people. What could be further deeper more unknown than your own tongue whispering the unlying truth in your own ear. You fear no one. You have never feared anyone. Except yourself. Yourself you have feared, subjected yourself to, humiliated yourself for all the days of your life. You have given the power to everyone because you cannot bear to have the power yourself. Oh my oh my oh my. God help me I am a free man.

Primal drums start beating simultaneous with a blackout.

SCENE 2

Donna is heard calling for her father through the primal drums.

Donna: DADDY. DADDY. DADDY. Daddy? Daddy? I've gotta talk to you. Daddy?

The lights come up on Dad's Place. The drums cease. Dad's Place is at a physically higher level than Tommy's place. Dad, a powerful, handsome guy, is sitting in a chair. The only chair. He's wrapped in a huge, very soft, old red chamois robe. He's got a big drink in his hand and a bottle of liquor near his slippered foot. Hanging on a redwood wall behind him is a painting of a voluptuous nude woman. It's a good painting with a neo-expressionist feel.

Dad: *(To himself.)* Oh no no no no no no. It's my daughter come to make me a parent. *(To the offstage Donna.)* I hear you. Come in. Come on. Come up. Jesus, I even recognize your voice. It's you. Your dead mother's little girl. Come on in and pull up a chair. Have a drink. How long's it been? Six months anyway. Not that I'm ribbin you to the purpose a bein more periodic. Nothin could

be further from the truth. I'm thrilled I ain't seen you. I hate kids.
Especially my own. At least other kids turn into adults. Eventually. If they live. But your own kids are always your kids. At least
that's the common wisdom. And the other thing about your own
kids, of course, is when they show up, you know, you know that
they want somethin. And also, that they're probably angry.
About somethin. Somethin you did and forgot fifteen years ago.
But not them. Cause they're your kids.

Enter Donna.

Donna: Hi, Dad.

Dad: Hi, Donna. Long time no daughter.

Donna: Yeah, it's been a long time.

Dad: You look like shit.

Donna: And you look like a big piece a red lint. So fucking what?

Dad: So. You're mad at me.

Donna: Maybe I am. I don't really know. It ain't central, anyway. To what brings me up from lower Broadway. Where's all
the paintings?

Dad: I sold some. Some are in storage.

Donna: Getta lotta money for 'em?

Dad: Yeah.

Donna: How much?

Dad: A lot.

Donna: There were so many. Just the one now, huh?

Dad: Yeah, it's the last holdout. It's an old one, too. I did it
what, maybe fifteen years ago. Funny the thing that pops outta
the water when the ship goes down. I wouldn'a picked this one,
but there we are. Here it is. Cheers.

Donna: What ship went down?

Dad: Mine.

Donna: I need to talk to you.

Dad: Oh no you don't.

Donna: Yeah, I do too.

Dad: You're wrong.

Donna: What's that on your finger?

Dad: A ring.

Donna: Whose?

Dad: Mine.

Donna: You never wore one.

Dad: It was your mother's. I stuck it on and I can't get it off. I may have to chop off this finger.

Donna: Mona ain't here, is she?

Dad: No.

Donna: Where is she?

Dad: I don't think she lives here anymore.

Donna: Don't ya know for sure?

Dad: No.

Donna: She's only sixteen, Dad.

Dad: So? When I was sixteen, I was eatin outta garbage cans in Philadelphia.

Donna: That was you. You probably loved it. You get off on squalor. Mona's different. If she ate out of a garbage can, she'd die.

Dad: And a hellava way to go, too. Adios, mi Mona. Shitcanned at sweet sixteen.

Donna: I'm glad to see you.

Dad: I can't think a why.

Donna: Don't be a jerk. You're my father.

Dad: So?

Donna: So? So don't be so freakin smug or I'll jam that drink up your nose.

Dad: You lay a finger on me, I'll break your back. You know I could and you know I would. So just forget the threats, alright?

Donna: Is that the booze talkin?

Dad: Yeah, it's the booze. An several of my primitive ancestors that are jumpin around in my jungle brain.

Donna: Well, just remember. Your ancestors are my ancestors.

Dad: Shh. Drums.

Donna: Oh, you hear drums? It's probably high blood pressure.

Dad: The drums say, Fuck off.

Donna: Why do you hate me?

Dad: I don't hate you.

Donna: Why are you shutting me out?

Dad: Look, I ain't seen you in a very long time, Donna, which is great. It's put me inna great mood. But don't push it.

Donna: I've got questions for you.

Dad: I don't answer questions.

Donna: You'll damn well answer mine.

Dad: Or what?

Donna: Or ... I'll move back in. It could happen, Pops. The prodigal could return. Me an Mona could start up our old cat-fights.

Dad: ALRIGHT. I grant you three questions.

Donna: You grant me three? What is this, a friggin fairytale?

Dad: Call it whatever you want.

Donna: I got more than three questions.

Dad: So take some away with you an work on em yourself. It ain't my job ta unravel every little thing for you.

Donna: It ain't a matter a every little thing. There's hard stuff that I ...

Dad: THREE QUESTIONS. THAT'S MY ONLY FUCKIN OFFER. TAKE IT OR LEAVE IT.

Donna: Alright. I'll take it. I agree. My first question is How do you see women?

Dad: You want an answer to this?

Donna: I want your answer.

Dad: Alright. I see all women bald. It started a long time ago. I found I was bein deceived by hair. I was all the time gettin the wrong impression a this woman or that woman cause their hair created a certain mystique. So I made a resolution one New Year's that whenever I looked atta potential woman, I'd shave her clean as a hardball, in my mind, and then I'd look at her and I'd see what I saw.

Donna: Did it make a difference?

Dad: Shit yeah. In fact, the first woman that I shaved in this way was your mother. And the result was so ... simple, that I got swept away and married her. The terrible thing was, on the honeymoon, in the mornin, when I woke up, she had all this awful hair. What a shock that was. But, this is how we learn. Women who are not bald have hair. I still do though, see all women bald. I guess it's a weakness a mine now, a dream.

Donna: I never saw paintings you did a bald women.

Dad: This is not what I did in my art, this is what I did in my life. I've never managed to be as dumb as an artist as I've been as a man. Close sometimes. Perilously close. But I always managed to keep the bald woman out of the picture.

Donna: Then why don't ya paint no more?

Dad: Oh, I dried up, I got the horrors, I drank myself out of it, I lost interest. I got obsessed with the fact a my own mortality, and every time I looked atta canvas all I saw was my own grave. And then there was the guilt and my nerves and I never got over the death of your mother. And the sight a you and Mona discouraged me, along with the heat an cold. And a tired feelin I got from time to time. And monsters from Jimjam Land. And illness. And fear of failure. And success. And heights. These are some a the reasons I don't paint anymore. Would you like me to go on?

Donna: Shut up. I have two more questions.

Dad: You count funny, but okay. Would you like a drink?

Donna: No.

Dad: You didn't learn ta say no from me. That's a good sign. Shows how much good my neglect a you is doin.

Donna: Second question. What is sex for?

Dad: Alright. Sex is for makin babies. I'll never forget when I figured that one out, I experienced fuckin vertigo. I was thirty years old. Before that I made like I knew, but I was really like one a those primitive tribesman who thinks sex is a gift from the gods and babies come from bugbites. It's when your mother and my girlfriend got pregnant the same week... Somethin about all that news hittin me at once gave me the... Well, it was like the apple for Newton. What a moment that was. The zipper on my pants became like this major responsibility. I felt like I had the *Space Shuttle* in there. That's the first time sex went dead for me. When I found out what it was for. Has sex gone dead for you yet?

Donna: No.

Dad: Don't worry, it will. It's a cycle thing. Somethin happens in your brain, or between you an somebody else, an it just goes dead. It's all shellfish. I got this deveined shrimp, and she's gotta shucked oyster.

Donna: Don't tell me the story a your life an try ta make it pass for wisdom.

Dad: But there's a kicker, see? Cause after it's been dead for a while, an you're sure it's dead, deader than dead, it comes back. Yeah. Like a ghost but flesh an blood. Usually it comes about outta a moment a madness. You go nuts. You figure you can, your sex is dead, what'sit matter you whig out? Maybe you drink too much or you laugh too much. You do somethin ta stoke yourself up. And there's a woman there, usually the wrong woman, just some wrong woman, an suddenly you've got her. In the wrong place. The closet atta party, a bathroom, the storage room where you work at some shitty office job you don't care about an it's the Christmas party. It was dead. It was gone an buried in the cold cold ground, an suddenly you're high an your nailin some teenager like gangbusters against a buncha filing cabinets. Do you know what I'm talkin about? I'm talkin about sex, man. I don't know where it goes when it goes away, but it's a long ways off. But when it comes back, you don't remember what sex is for, you don't remember a goddamn thing except if you don't get it if you don't get to it, your eyeballs 'ill pop out, they'll pop right out the window, an you'll lose your mind. Then after maybe, you remember what it's for. When you're sittin like a bag a shit in some chair with rollers on it, an notice that your heart every once inna while is hittin your ribs like some youngblood boxer sparrin from the inside. An maybe you think, I coulda knocked her up. That coulda been a knockup I just did. But you just don't care. Cause you just found out that you ain't dead. You're just too glad, too glad too glad, to feel bad about anything. So when sex goes dead for you, and it will. That I promise you. Just remember. It comes back. It resurrects.

Donna: Dad. Somethin's happened to me. It's made me have a lotta ideas. And I'm very upset. About it. And it's got to do with you.

Dad: How?

Donna: Well, inna couple a ways. There's this guy. His name is Tommy. I'm in love with him.

Dad: So go kiss him or somethin.

Donna: He's hurtin me. A lot.

Dad: So then go talk to him.

Donna: I just did that. Listen. He … Well, he's been foolin with

Mona, too.

Dad: He's seein you an Mona?

Donna: Yeah.

Dad: My, my, my.

Donna: He's all fucked up. He's stealin now. He looks like shit. But all that I can deal with. Even the Mona thing, I think. But this is the thing. In the whole way that this has come down, I thought I knew what I was doin. The me part of it. Till today. Another like level came into it. I always heard that girls went after guys who reminded em of their fathers. An I guess I kinda believed that idea or was spooked by it at least, so... I've always made double goddamn sure never ta go near any guy I thought was like you, because then I'd like turn into my mother, right? A thought that makes me think a the phrase, Fate Worse Than Death. Anyways, I always steered clear of this certain kinda guy for that reason. Like this guy Tommy. I'm like absolutely sure he's totally different than you. And then today, I go to him, inta this pit where he's livin, and up on the wall is a painting a drawing he did.

Dad: This guy your seein?

Donna: An Mona. A really lousy picture, self-portrait. But it scared me. I think more than anything that's ever happened ta me. I heard the fuckin Twilight Zone music. Cause here I am, goin along, thinkin things are one way, that I'm choosin an goin my own way, an maybe doin a terrible fuckin botch a that, but doin it. An then I see this picture. And I think, Do I really know what's goin on in my life? Or am I just a complete molecule or some shit. If this guy Tommy is turnin into you, then I'm in some kinda car I don't even know I'm in, and some guy inna scary mask is drivin, an he's had the route the map since the doctor smacked my ass. Where am I? I'm in love with this guy Tommy. He's drivin me crazy, yeah. He's tearin my heart out an steppin on it, yes. The whole thing I'm doin looks to be a total fuckup, but I can deal with that I can live with that. But what I wanna know gotta know is IS THIS MY LIFE OR WHAT? Is this my pain? My love? Or is what's goin on here just like history? You treated my mother like shit. You cheated on her. You lied to her. You humiliated her in public. When you had money, you wouldn't give her any. When she had money, you took it. You walked on her face with muddy shoes. When she was in the hospital, you didn't visit her. And then finally she just fuckin died. Now I hate your fuckin guts for that, but I decided a long time since that I wasn't gonna spend my whole life wishin you dead or different, cause I didn't want my life bossed by your life. I even thought, Maybe she deserved it. I knew I didn't know the whole story and never would an what was it my business anyway? But that was before. Today, I saw that picture on Tommy's wall, an it was writin on the wall to me, an the writin said, Watch Out. You could be in the middle of somebody else's life. So that's why I'm here. Because before I thought I didn't have to know about you to do my life, and now I see I better find out a few things. It's like medical history.

Dad: What bullshit.

Donna: That's what you say when I pour out my heart to you?

Dad: I'm sorry. What you're afraid of just cracks me up, that's all.

Donna: I don't understand.

Dad: Alright, you want your father's smarts, I'll give you your father's smarts. What you have are women fears.

Donna: Women fears.

Dad: That's right.

Donna: I hate what I'm hearin.

Dad: Well, tough shit. You got women fears. That's what I know and I'm tellin you. When I talk to a woman, I feel like I'm yellin across the Indian Ocean. That's cause I'm a man. Do you wanna hear this or not?

Donna: Yes.

Dad: Women are very concerned about bein trapped. All women, or virtually, anyway. They worry about it, that's been my experience. So what they do, a lot of em, to feel strong, they trap a man. They trap some guy in their dream. And then they feel trapped cause they gotta guard what they caught. At least let me say, this is what happened with me an your mother. But there's a certain universal here.

Donna: And men don't feel that?

Dad: What happens with men is a little different. I think that men recognize or make up that they are trapped, already, an what they do is, the man feeling is, they long to be free. Of mother, wife, job, art, whatever.

Donna: Do you hear yourself? You sound like a total jerk. This stuff you're sayin can be knocked down by a three-year-old with a feather.

Dad: So what? I'm tryin to tell you somethin to get somewhere, somewhere maybe you'd like to get to. Don't think you can get everywhere by algebra, honey. Things ain't that straight. Life ain't at all like the psychological section in the New York Times three-warning-signs-to-look-for bullshit. Things ain't like that at all. If somebody's willin to talk to you an tell you shit they think is true, don't be so quick to knock it. People don't usually part with the weird shit they personally know because they know how easy it will be to punch holes in. Now I'm tellin you somethin. It's for you to poke through the soup an find the meat. So listen up. There's a level where you fear an want that's a woman level. This shit you just told me about bein afraid you're turnin inta your mother, that's on the woman level, that's a women fear. So my suggestion about that is, you go talk to a woman about that. But there's another place under that place, where men an women can meet an talk, if you know what I mean. It's way down. An it's dark. An it's old as the motherfuckin stars. If you want somethin from me, or if you wanna tell me somethin, that's where we're gonna haveta be.

A long pause.

Donna: Alright. *(A long pause.)* Tommy an me ... When he loves me. In bed. When he puts his arms around me, and I can feel his skin, his heart beating, his breath, and I smell him, it's like Africa. It's like, I get scared because all of my guts shake ... Sometimes I press my hands against myself because I think things are coming loose inside. He just touches me, starts to barely touch me, and I'm so frightened because it's so much, it's so hot, it's so close to losing my mind. It's beyond pleasure. It's ... He takes me over. Like there's a storm, I get caught in this storm with electricity and rain and noise and I'm blind I'm blind. I'm seeing things, but just wild, wild shapes flying by like white flyin rain and black shapes. I feel I feel this this rising thing like a yell a flame. My hair I can feel my hair like slowly going up on its toes on my skull my skull.

Everything goes up through me from my belly and legs and feet
to my head and all these tears come out but it can't get out that
way, so it goes down against my throat swells an through down to
where it can get out GET OUT GET OUT. But it doesn't go out, so
I, I EXPAND. Like to an ocean. To hold the size of it. An then it's
maybe something you could speak of as pleasure, since then somehow I can hold it. I'm this ocean with a thousand moons and
comets reflecting in me. And then I come back. Slowly. Slowly.
From such a long way. And such a different size. And I'm wet. My
body my hair. The bed is just soaked, torn up and soaked. There
ain't a muscle left in me. I'm all eyes. My eyes are the size of like
two black pools of water in the middle of an endless night. And
Tommy's there. And he did it to me. He took me completely. I
wasn't me anymore. I was just a blast a light out in the stars. What
could be better than that? What could be better? It's like gettin to
die, an get past death, to get to the universe, an then come back. In
the world where we talk and fight and he fucks me over, it all just
seems so unimportant after that. I don't understand how he can do
that for me an then turn around an be such a, well, smaller. It is a
small world this world, in comparison to where we go in bed. And
I guess we gotta be smaller in it.

Dad: What are you tryin to tell me, Donna?

Donna: I'm afraid.

Dad: Of what?

Donna: I'm afraid to leave him or that he'll leave me. I'm afraid
to be without the sex we get to. Everything else seems like nothin
next to it. But I can't give up who I am to be his love slave. That's
what I'm afraid of. That I'll lose myself if I stay with him, and that
I'll lose the sex if I get away.

Dad: I've felt that.

Donna: You have?

Dad: Yeah.

Donna: But that seems like a woman thing to me.

Dad: Nope. Men have that too. It's a very down thing. It's very
near the bottom.

Donna: In one way, he don't know a thing about me, not really.
And in another way, what he knows is the key that lets me outta

my life. It's like what he don't know about me is exactly what I
don't care about anyway.

Dad: Yeah.

Donna: You've really had this?

Dad: Oh yeah. I had this with your mother. It's why I always
kept a girlfriend on the side. I hadda keep somethin away from
her, so I didn't lose everything when we went nuts in bed. And
too, because I wanted to protect what we had in bed by havin
somethin else goin that was not that intense. Sort've a comparison, a reminder. Somethin common to underline the extraordinary. Your mother was the love of my life.

Donna: But if that's true, how the fuck could you treat her like
you did?

Dad: That bed was what we had. When I got outta that bed, I
didn't walk, I ran. When I got outta that bed the most important
thing was that my feet hit the ground, found the fuckin ground. Do
you understand? If there was gonna be anything else a me outside
a that bed, it hadda be without her. Otherwise, she woulda taken
me over all the way. I hadda create a second place in me and outta
me where I could work. Do my painting. I got the studio. I got the
girlfriend. WHY DO YOU REMIND ME OF THESE THINGS? It's
so fuckin painful. Your mother's dead. My baby's dead.

Donna: I can't believe this. You mean, you really loved her?

Dad: Shut up shut up. Can't you understand? All I have now is
that little bit I kept from her. That little room. I can't even paint
anymore. Why would I want to? What do I care what I see, why
would I describe it? I hid part a me from her to save somethin
cause I was scared. I'm so sorry. I'm so sorry. I shoulda given her
that, too. If I'd given her everything, then when she died, I woulda died, too, and that woulda been the merciful end of it. Why
did I save something? What for? It wasn't worth it. What I saved
wasn't worth a goddamn thing. If I only known.

Donna: I'm here.

Dad: I can't stand the sight a you. You remind me just enough ta
make it unbearable. At least Mona don't look like her. You. Sometimes, the way you ... Sometimes you could be her. But you're not.
Sure I treated her like shit. I was so angry cause she had so much a

me. I thought it was too much to let somebody have. And when she was dyin in the hospital, sure I didn't go an see her. I couldn't bear it. Don't you get it? I just couldn't bear to watch her leave me. You come here to tell me things you think I don't understand. So maybe you were right. Maybe you are turnin inta your mother. And maybe this guy Tommy is turnin inta me. I don't know. But the big news is you don't know who those people are. I promise you.

Donna: You never told me.

Dad: It just woulda sounded like an apology for abuse.

Donna: All my memories seem wrong now.

Dad: Good. Maybe now then you can remember a few things.

Donna: Who am I?

Dad: Don't worry about it. I think you worry too much.

Donna: I love this guy.

Dad: Come here, baby. I hate the sight a you, but let me hold you in my arms.

He holds her.

Donna: I don't see any future for me.

Dad: Good.

Donna: It's not good.

Dad: You can't see the future anyway. It's a very realistic feelin you're havin.

Donna: Can I move back home?

Dad: No.

Donna: I want to.

Dad: You probably feel like suckin your thumb, too. But there's a time an place, an that time an place called home is gone now.

Donna: What am I gonna do?

Dad: Well, that's a question. You could run away to the circus.

Donna: This is the fuckin circus.

Dad: You wanna grapple an go inna single direction and stick with it, ride it out inna straight line right to heaven, the grave or whatever?

Donna: Yes.

Dad: There's only one thing that goes straight, my baby, and it's not love. It is not love. You can chase that one forever, it won't come to you. It won't bow, it won't serve, it won't do what you want, what it should, it won't be how you thought, or was taught how it was meant ta be. You can't lead it cause it'll be draggin you wherever it wants. If you wanna go inna straight line, give up people. People are what zigzag. I'd rather predict the weather three months in advance, my sweet girl, than try to tell you one thing about the future of the dullest heart.

Donna: I got one more question.

Dad: You mean I ain't answered three questions yet?

Donna: Two.

Dad: Maybe we should call it a day, cause I gotta tell you, I'm startin ta feel pretty bad. You're makin me think about things I honest ta God don't wanna recall.

Donna: Just one more. Why did you stop paintin?

Dad: Don't ask me this.

Donna: Why did you stop?

Dad: Same reason I started.

Donna: And what was that?

Dad: I saw somethin.

Donna: What?

Dad: When I started, it was simple. I saw something, an object, an I saw something about that object. And I set that down. Imperfectly. And when I looked at the thing I'd drawn, and the object I'd drawn it from, the two things started a quarrel. And that quarrel lasted through every painting I ever did.

Donna: But then you stopped.

Dad: I hadda dream. One night. Your mother'd been dead about a year and a half, I'd been drinkin a lot. And then one time I went to bed sober. And I had a bad night. I hadda lotta dreams. And then I had one of those big dreams. I went out for a celebration drive with my girlfriend. We were celebrating your mother's death. It was a great night. The cops stopped us. And while they were checkin us, a guy, a petty thief came from nowhere an grabbed a box or somethin. One of the cops started ta draw his gun. And all I could think was Stop the bullet. So I ran in front of the cop and he accidently shot me. So I was killed. I was dead. I was killed. I was dead. I was killed by a single bullet not even intended for me.

Donna: What did it mean?

Dad: I woke up. My eyes musta lit up the room, that's how it felt. I woke up my girlfriend and I threw her out. That's how we broke up, you know. Right that minute. And after she was out, I went ta the bed, and I looked at the pillow. There was a dent there where my head had been. And I thought, never put your head in that hole again. That's when I stopped paintin.

Donna: I don't understand.

Dad: You think I do? Yeah, I do. That's the night I found I was alone. That's the night I found out there wasn't a person left in the world I had a thing to do with. So I sold the paintings. Most of 'em. Some are inna warehouse somewhere. And I live on the money. And I go inna straight line. An I do not stink up my world with people.

Donna: You've got a broken heart.

Dad: You've asked your three questions, and I've answered em. Now leave me alone.

Donna: It never occurred ta me that you loved her.

Dad: So what? If you'd known, what would you have done?

Donna: I mighta tried ta comfort you. When she died.

Dad: Then it's a mercy on us both that you didn't have the true drift, cause if you'd tried to comfort me I probably woulda knocked your teeth out.

Donna: Big tough guy.

Dad: An you, the big tough girl. This guy you've been seein, it seems clear ta me at least that he's been walkin on you. An that's somethin you've been lettin him do.

Donna: Yeah, I have.

Dad: Big tough girl.

Donna: I want some a the money you got from sellin the paintings.

Dad: Why would I give you money?

Donna: I don't know. I'm just tellin you what I want.

Dad: Alright. I'll give you some money. What will you do with it?

Donna: Maybe I'll go somewhere. Or maybe I'll give it to my sometime boyfriend. Depends on how things go.

Dad: I'll give you money. I won't give Mona any money. Money just makes Mona get more Mona, an that I couldn't take.

Donna: And now there's one last thing.

Dad: What d'you mean?

Donna: One last thing I gotta ask.

Dad: I answered yar goddamn questions, and I'm not gonna answer anymore.

Donna: There's nothin else I wanna ask you about anythin. Now, what I want is, I wanna ask you ta do somethin.

Dad: The answer is fuck no. You're on your own. I'm serious now. What d'you want me ta do?

Donna: I want you ta go an talk to this guy Tommy.

Dad: I won't do it.

Donna: I want you ta go an talk ta him because he's all fucked up, an he's been boffin both your daughters, and because he may be turnin inta you.

Dad: No fuckin way would I do that.

Donna: I want ya ta go an talk to him, an see if he's curable, reasonable, whatever. And he should promise you that he'll stop seein both your daughters, or that'll he'll stop seein Mona only an go on seein me. And if he won't promise ta one a those things, I want you ta beat him up.

Dad: Where the fuck did you come from? You're like a totally medieval bitch.

Donna: An no matter what he promises, if you take him in an see that he's turnin inta you, I want you ta beat him up till his skull is ringing like a church bell. Will you do it for me? Dad? Dad?

Dad: Why would I agree ta do this?

Donna: Because it's a family thing. Cause I'm your daughter who looks like your wife. And becausa pride. This guy Tommy he's treatin me like a dirtbag, like you treated my mother. Now in your own life you couldn't treat my mother better cause the sex power made you crazy. Well, I can't deal with this guy for the same reason, the same reason that drove ya crazy in yar own life. But here's the chance, see? You take care a me, maybe in another life or somethin, I'll take care a you. You hear what I'm sayin? Maybe that's what the family's for. Maybe this is how you get ta face yourself. Maybe this is how you get ta unfuck your life. Hear me, Daddy. And help me. I can't help myself. An for all intents an purposes, if ya don't do this, your life is over anyway.

Dad: Alright. I'm not promisin anything. But I'll go. I'll talk ta the guy.

Donna: Before you go, gimme that ring.

Dad: No, it's mine.

Donna: No it's not. It's on you but it's my mother's ring, and it belongs to me. Give it over.

Dad: I couldn't even if I wanted to. It's stuck.

Donna: I'll get it off.

She twists it off, causing Dad a lot of pain.

Dad: Owwwww! Holy shit, that was painful.

Donna: Yeah, I bet it was.

Dad: You're your old man's daughter.

Donna: Go if you're goin. *(Dad exits. Donna remains. The lights go down. As they go down, Donna thinks.)* So whaddaya know. There is a weird justice. An somebody else can do somethin ta move your life forward. I guess it's what I hoped. I ain't totally alone after all.

Donna takes the ring and pops it in her mouth. Primal drums of greater urgency begin to sound.

SCENE 3

The drums cease. Lights up. Tommy is discovered.

Tommy: Maybe that's it. There's somethin ta be said, after all, for feeling happy. Maybe God's in his heaven after all. That would be a first class goof. I guess I always thought if I was left alone to myself long enough that sooner or later I would have a breakthrough. But can you have a breakthrough without thinking anything new? Just a breakthrough feeling? But fuck, man, there musta been some moment out there in the desert when them wanderin Jews first smelled the milk and honey comin over the hills ahead. Still in the desert, but honey in the air.

A knocking at the door.

Dad: *(From off.)* Anybody home?

Tommy: Come in.

Enter Dad, in a tuxedo.

Dad: Hi.

Tommy: Hi.

Dad: What a shithole.

Tommy: Yeah, ain't it though. I gotta move.

Dad: Yeah, you do.

Tommy: I guess you must be Donna's father.

Dad: That's right. I'm Donna's father. And I'm Mona's father.

Tommy: Both.

Dad: That's right.

Tommy: You come to beat me up?

Dad: Not necessarily.

Tommy: You're younger than I thought you'd be.

Dad: So you've thought about me?

Tommy: Not till lately. You wanna beer?

Dad: Sure, I'd take a beer.

Tommy goes to refrigerator, gets a beer, gives it to Dad.

Tommy: So, you hadda talk with Donna?

Dad: Yeah.

Tommy: She's some girl.

Dad: Yeah.

Tommy: So's Mona.

Dad: No, she's not. Mona ain't in the same league with Donna. Donna's a plum.

Tommy: I know.

Dad: What, are you testing me?

Tommy: Yeah.

Dad: Well, stop it.

Tommy: Alright.

Dad: Close your eyes.

Tommy: Why?

Dad: Because if you keep them open I'm going to suck them out of your face.

Tommy: Okay.

Tommy closes his eyes.

Dad: What do you see in there?

Tommy: Donna's face.

Dad: Uh-huh. Okay, let go a that. What else do you see?

Tommy: Mona's face.

Dad: Good. Now tell that to go away and what else do you see?

Tommy: Donna's face.

Dad: Hey, don't be lazy. Look around in there. It's a big place.

Tommy: I can't see nothin else.

Dad: You may be too close to it. It may be real big. I tell you what. Look up. Look way up. Do you see anything there?

Tommy: Oh. Yeah. I do.

Dad: What is it?

Tommy: It's my ma. She's big as A&P. Whop. There she goes. MA. No, she's gone. I think she was angry. Donna an Mona were angry, too.

Dad: What else?

Tommy: Now I see nothin. Dirt. Pollution. Oh, there's Donna again.

Dad: Oh man, you are a case. Okay, open you eyes.

Tommy: *(Opening his eyes.)* Why'd you want me to do that?

Dad: Never mind.

Tommy: That was interesting.

Dad: *(Looks at picture.)* You do this?

Tommy: Yeah.

Dad: Do you think it's good?

Tommy: No.

Dad: You're right. It's not. It's terrible. If it was strictly infantile it might have a certain charm. It's the adult badness of it that really makes it very bad.

Tommy: You sound like you know about these things.

Dad: She didn't tell you I was a painter?

Tommy: No.

Dad: Well, I'm not. But I was.

Tommy: Why are you wearin a tux?

Dad: Because I am the father of the bride.

Tommy: Oh? And who's the bride?

Dad: Donna is the bride.

Tommy: I didn't know she was getting married.

Dad: Well, if that's what I was tellin you, how would you feel?

Tommy: I'd feel really bad.

Dad: Why?

Tommy: Cause I'm in love with her.

Dad: I understand you been seein my daughter Mona, too.

Tommy: Yeah, well, I have seen her a couple a times. But not really. I mean, it was sort've ... a sick ... a wrong ... a mistake.

Dad: Do you have any doubt at all that I could kick your ass from here to the moon?

Tommy: None.

Dad: Good. Then we're onna a good conversational footing. How old are you?

Tommy: Ahm. Twenty-seven.

Dad: I understand you've been fuckin over anybody whose shadow fell in your food.

Tommy: That's right. I have.

Dad: Why?

Tommy: Because I've been very confused.

Dad: You know about the hitchhiker thing? You're hitchhikin an you get in some dude's car, an you can tell him anything, cause you don't know him. An he can tell you anything. This kinda thing happens all the time. Of course, there's another side to it. I mean, the hitchhiker don't know the driver, an vice-versa. Either one a them could be a homicidal maniac serial killer. After pourin out your heart, it could be goodbye Charlie. Or Tommy. But that's the next step. We don't haveta get to that revelation till we get to it. What I'm sayin is, Tommy, you're not in love with me, and I'm not your father. When I ask you why you've been fuckin everybody over, you can tell me. Now why?

Tommy: Revenge.

Dad: Revenge?

Tommy: I don't know why I said that.

Dad: Don't worry about it.

Tommy: It just came out.

Dad: Well, let it keep comin out. Revenge for what?

Tommy: I don't know. This world.

Dad: Don't fuck with me now.

Tommy: No, I'm serious. I don't know about you but me this world has been comin in at me like chaotic madness. Which has caused me a lotta confusin pain. It's kinda been me against the world. I think everybody starts out that way. You know? You're born alone. And the whole world hits you like a bucket a broken glass chucked in your face and I don't get the joke. It's just cruel, you know, it's just cruelty comin from somewhere. And then somebody comes along and you fall in love. I fell in love. With Donna. And then that's like the point at which you get mixed up with the world. She was my introduction to the outside. Or somethin. But since I've been hurt so much and confused so much all my life by everything that was outside, when I finally came face to face with it in the person of this girl, I think I hadda a hunger in me for revenge. What do you think a that?

Dad: Makes sense.

Tommy: And who gives a shit, right?

Dad: You're still hitchin a free ride.

Tommy: Anyway, I'd hurt her, an then I'd hurt myself as punishment. Back an forth. Mona came into that. I think people like Mona, her age, it's not uncommon they get inta the orbit a somethin that don't truly got a thing to do with them.

Dad: I hadda a girlfriend like that.

Tommy: Did you?

Dad: Yeah. Alright, Tommy. Now I'm gonna ask you the question. What have you learned?

Tommy: Well, I'm still not *to* anything. Donna was here, and she dug way into me, an then she left. But after she left, somethin happened. I hadda vision. I mean, I turned the big lights on myself. I looked at myself an forgot everybody. And a funny thing happened. I could feel myself become harmless. I felt like runnin around to these people. To Donna and Mona, and my mother...

Dad: Women.

Tommy: Yeah, women. I felt like runnin around to the women in my life and saying, I'm harmless to you now. Because I don't want revenge anymore. Because now, now I'm lookin at myself.

Dad: Well, Tom. I really hate to be the one to tell you this. I know you've been through a lot. And I know at the moment, because of this private experience you've recently had, that you're in touch with a certain buoyancy you no doubt feel you've earned, but I'm here to tell you that as a result of all your pain and experience and self-examination you haven't learned zip about dip.

Tommy: What?

Dad: I know it's hard to take. But there it is.

Tommy: But what did you think of this stuff I told you?

Dad: I think you're one hazardous motherfucker.

Tommy: But I just told you…

Dad: I heard you.

Tommy: I'm just like, dealing with myself now.

Dad: Uh-huh.

Tommy: You don't believe me?

Dad: I believe you believe it. Although that's already probably fadin away.

Tommy: What are you sayin?

Dad: That you have two problems. Your first problem is that you are very present tense. I mean, I can just see it in your fuckin eye. You're one a these guys who could say you're sorry a thousand times, and mean it. And go right back an do it again. You're like a too typical, too HUMAN kinda guy. It's impossible for you ta learn anything from the history of your own life. If it hadn't been done before, you woulda invented the New Year's Resolution. And you woulda been the first guy to break it, too.

Tommy: How can you talk about me like this? You just met me.

Dad: Your second problem is you're women-fixed. You don't know who you are cause all you got in your head is women. And you're mad at women cause they're cloggin up your head. The bottom of that problem, which you won't get to for some time to come, is you don't know why you're alive.

Tommy: You just walked in the door. I think you're talkin out your ass.

Dad: I can talk about you cause I was you. At least this part a you I'm talkin about. You're one a these subconscious motherfuckers. Ninety-nine percent a you operates outta some underground control room you don't know about. You got your own Ministry A Propaganda. Your up-above mind only gets dribbled what it needs to know ta get through the day. When I was in this same condition, which was in another time in my life—I see that now—I broke the back of every person who loved me. I never thought I'd come face-to-face with me then.

Tommy: That's a very egotistical way of lookin at it.

Dad: Yeah, so what? The only way I can take everything in is through my body, which makes everything pretty fuckin personal. What we're havin here, Tommy me boy, is a personal conversation.

Tommy: You think I'm like you?

Dad: Yeah.

Tommy: I don't know.

Dad: You don't haveta know. I'm tellin you somethin. Humor me.

Tommy: What are you tellin me?

Dad: You see this picture you did?

Tommy: Yeah?

Dad: This picture's the beginnin of a lotta trouble for you.

Tommy: I don't understand.

Dad: I useta have a subconscious situation like you. Then I started ta put pictures out.

Tommy: I painted this to understand myself, that's all.

Dad: I had the same whim, at least I thought it was a whim. I reached down inta the black water where I couldn't see, and I pulled out the first thing I found. It grabs you cause you don't understand it. It's in you, but it's strange ta you. So you put it out there where you can see it. An then it looks at ya. An you look at it. An ya say ta yourself, What is that? And then that's when the change starts.

Tommy: What change?

Dad: The balance between what you know an what you don't know about what's goin on inside. When ya start reachin across that line, inta the dark, an pullin things out before your conscious mind is ready for em, that's when what's awake an what's asleep ain't fixed down anymore. It's like the difference between Newton an Einstein. Neat an not neat.

Tommy: But it never was neat.

Dad: But you didn't know that.

Tommy: NO. I just lost my footing. I got confused and I didn't understand a lotta things that I useta do fine with. And the whole area a love was not one I was used to. But my ... what I'm gonna do is, I'm gonna find my footing. I'm gonna find the solid ground under me somewhere that I know I know is down there somewhere under me. And I'm gonna walk on firm ground again. I'm gonna be trustworthy again, like I was.

Dad: When you were a kid.

Tommy: Not exactly.

Dad: Yeah, that's what you mean. Once you reach across that divide, inta that black pool where the stuff you don't understand is, the stuff that don't fit, you ain't never gonna walk on firm ground again.

Tommy: You can't know that.

Dad: You gotta get more honest.

Tommy: You gotta get more honest.

Dad: Alright. You're right. I do. I'm glad to see you. Cause you're a lot like the way I was. And I can see, cause you're standin there, that I've changed. I really have changed. I'm not the man I was. So you're a comfort to me. If there was somebody who was like that for you, somebody who was like you the way you used ta be before you were the way you are now, we could probably draw a straight line through the three of us and see where we're goin. But there's only the two of us. Like the object an the paintin of it. The difference between the two an argument. The conversation we're havin now.

Tommy: Why are you wearin a tux?

Dad: You see, I got to the point, I lost the women who were keepin me from askin the question, Why live? That's a long way off from you yet. That may never happen to you at all. When you find yourself alone and when you ask that question of yourself alone, separate from everybody else's needs, it's like pullin the plug on your power, man. It's like lookin into the hole where your art your strength your black water was, an there's nothin there but a dry black dent in a pillow past broken in, past broken down. Cause there is no answer to that question for a man alone. But then Donna came to me today, and she needed somethin from me, somethin that belonged ta her. And she reminded me that she's connected ta me. That things in me belong to other people. That I'm connected. That like it or not I'm not alone and it's not over till it's over. Why Live? Cause it's not neat and the individual life is deceptive and a dream. We spill over into each other, man. We spill blood and breath and come an time over inta each other like shelves inna water wheel.

Tommy: Why are you wearin a tux?

Dad: You said you wanted revenge against the world, but what

216

you're fuckin over is women, women. Your mother, my daughters. It's gotta come to an end, Tommy.

Tommy: It has come to an end. Now I only hurt myself.

Dad: Liar. To yourself a liar, to my daughters a liar, to me a liar.

He tears down the picture, crushes it, and stuffs it in the refrigerator.

Tommy: Hey, I'm tryin ta face myself.

Dad: I believe you. It's just not enough.

Tommy: I can't do any more.

Dad: I believe you. It's just not at all enough.

Enter Donna, in full bridal regalia.

Tommy: Donna.

Donna: *(To Dad.)* Has he promised not to see Mona?

Dad: No.

Donna: Is he like you?

Dad: Yeah, he is.

Donna: Beat the shit outta him.

Tommy: I promise not to see Mona.

Dad: You can say that, but ya can't stick to it.

Tommy: Yes, I can.

Donna: It don't matter if it turns out he's like you. Is he really?

Dad: Yeah.

Donna: Then bang his head till it rings like a fuckin bell.

Tommy: I don't know that I'm like him at all.

Dad: You are alright.

Tommy: How do you know that?

Dad: Cause when I was your age, I painted a picture of myself, and it looked just like that. Except that you have no talent.

Donna: How could I make such a mistake?

Dad: The same way your mother made it.

Donna: How did she make it?

Dad: Her mistake which is your mistake is no mistake at all. You went for the guys like me an him cause that's what you like an who you are. And what you hate and makes you crazy is that it's a mirror and what the mirror tells you. You got this misery built into you.

Donna: Hit him.

Dad: No. Why don't you stop runnin away from yourself, the woman who's turnin inta her mother? Why don't ya go inta yourself?

Donna: Why don't you?

Dad: I did my whole life. I cut an cut inta myself, an then one night I hadda dream, and I hit white bone. An I looked at my pillow, where I'd dreamed that dream, I looked at that hole where my head had been dreamin, and I said No more.

Tommy: No more.

Donna: No more.

Dad: BUT I WAS WRONG.

Donna & Tommy: HUH?

Dad: You can't stop. Once you step off the edge, you're gone. Once your head's been in that place, you can't ever take it out.

Dad takes off his tux jacket and puts it on Tommy.

Tommy: WHY THE FUCK ARE YOU DRESSED LIKE A BRIDE?

Donna: NONE OF YOUR FUCKIN BUSINESS.

Tommy: WHY AM I WEARIN A TUX?

Dad: Figure it out.

Tommy:	**Donna:**
I'm not ready, I'm not ready	Me neither, Me neither,
I'm not ready, I'm not ready …	Me neither, Me neither …

Dad: It's always been this way. It's always been a total fuckin mess. It's never the right time, and it's really horrifyin ta everybody, like a car accident ya see comin. But, there is this problem of time an tide, of mortality, of the woman only havin so many years in which she can conceive — Sex is for makin babies. That picture I kept, that one paintin a mine that I kept. It's of the Wrong Woman. It's called The Wrong Woman In The Wrong Place. That's the non-historical woman that I treasure. That person who wakes you from Death-Too-Soon. You gotta make the big mistakes. Remember that. It makes it easier to bear. But remember, too, that Sex does resurrect. Flyin in the face of the truly great mistakes, there is that consolation. Donna, cough up the ring. *(Donna coughs up ring. Dad takes it and forces Tommy to put it on her finger.)* I now pronounce you Man and Wife.

Donna and Tommy look at each other and scream. Dad laughs.

Tommy: This feels totally wrong.

Donna: *(Looking at Dad.)* It never occurred ta me that he loved her.

Dad: BEGIN. BEGIN. Son. Daughter. Self. Stranger. BEGIN. *(To the audience.)* BEGIN.

THE END

ITALIAN AMERICAN RECONCILIATION was originally presented as a staged reading at the Eugene O'Neill Theatre Center's National Playwrights Conference. It then opened in New York as a full production on October 30, 1988 at Manhattan Theatre Club's City Center Stage II (Artistic Director, Lynne Meadow; Managing Director, Barry Grove.) It was directed by John Patrick Shanley, with sets by Santo Loquasto, costumes by William Ivey Long, lighting by Peter Kaczorowski, sound by John Gromada and the production stage manager was Ruth Kreshka.

The cast, in order of appearance was:

Aldo Scalicki	John Turturro
Huey Maximilian Bonfigliano	John Pankow
Teresa	Laura San Giacomo
Aunt May	Helen Hanft
Janice	Jayne Haynes

> *"What thou lovest well remains,*
> *the rest is dross*
> *What thou lov'st well shall not be reft from thee*
> *What thou lov'st well is thy true heritage"*
> —Ezra Pound
> Canto LXXXI*

CHARACTERS

Aldo Scalicki: An intense Italian guy, about thirty years old. All his life he's lived in Little Italy, in New York.

Huey Maximilian Bonfigliano: Aldo's best friend since childhood. Huey is more obviously vulnerable.

Aunt May: A handsome Italian woman in her middle years.

Teresa: A big striking Italian girl in her late twenties.

Janice: An angular, patrician Italian woman with strawberry blond hair and austere good looks. She's in her thirties.

The time is the present.
The place is three locations in Little Italy, represented by a unit set.

*Ezra Pound; *The Cantos of Ezra Pound*, Copyright 1948 by Ezra Pound. Reprinted by permission of New Directions Publishing Corporation.

ACT I

SCENE I

A unit set representing three locations in Little Italy, in New York City. The three locations are Pop's Soup House, Huey's apartment, and the rear of Janice's house.

Pop's Soup House, which is an Italian diner coffee shop, is indicated by a counter, a couple of stools, a cafe table and a chair. The rear wall, which contains a door with a window in it, is decorated with a mural depicting Roman ruins.

Huey's apartment is represented by an oak table and two chairs. In the rear wall is the front door to the apartment.

Janice's house is a little two-story number, of which we can only see the back; there's a bit of a garden with a white metal patio table. The second story of the house has a petite set of french doors that open on to a little cast-iron balcony. The rear wall, in this case, is a garden wall, and it contains a cast-iron garden gate. High overhead are a few stars.

Something like "O Solo Mio", sung by Pavarotti,* comes on in a big way to open the play.

At rise, Aldo Scalicki enters through the audience. The music sneaks down. He's an intense guy, about thirty years old. He's wearing a well broken-in brown corduroy jacket with patch elbows, a black dress shirt with a yellow tie, black levis, red socks and black shoes. He wears a sweetheart rose. He talks to the audience.

Aldo: How you doin? How's it goin? May I shake your hand? May I shake your *hand*? Let me know afterwards if everything was alright. I'm not just saying that, I wanna know. *(Starts to walk away, comes back.)* Here's a quarter. *(To another person.)* Where'd

* See Special Note on copyright page

you get that shirt? Where? What's it made of? I only wear a blend, fifty-fifty, cotton and polyester, best of both worlds. *(To another guy.)* Is she with you, yes or no? Is she your girlfriend or second wife or what? She's very beautiful. *(To her.)* You're as beautiful as roses. *(Unpins and gives her his lapel flower.)* Smell this and think of me. *(To man.)* Watch her. Watch her like a hawk. A word to the wise, man to man. Hey everybody! My mother's here tonight! Comon, can I get a round of applause for my mother? Comon, I swear to you, she's the greatest woman in the world! I don't want to point her out cause she's shy. Listen, I'm glad you're all here tonight. Not just cause I'm a social person... Excuse me. I just saw someone. Just one moment. There's something I have to deal with here. *(Goes halfway up the aisle, addresses a Young Woman who is seated.)* What are you doing here? Don't look around. There's nobody here gonna help you with your personal doings. Didn't I tell you to leave me alone? You here to shake me up? It's not gonna happen. Okay, let's go. See the guy in the lobby about your money, he'll give it back. *(She gets up and leaves. Aldo starts down the aisle toward the stage.)* Some people don't understand a man when he says a thing the first time. Remember, that ain't the man's fault. *(The Young Woman has quietly reentered the theatre and is on the point of re-taking her seat.)* Hey! Hey! What, d'you think I'm stupid? I see you there. Look, I'm trying to work, I got my mother here, you gotta go. *(She doesn't retake her seat, but she doesn't leave either.)* Listen. I'll meet you. P.J. Clarkes. Eleven-fifteen. Alright? We'll have a talk. *(The Young Woman nods and leaves.)* Can you believe that? I think of myself as an experienced man, but women still amaze me. You know, I'm embarrassed, but I have a slight erection. My own body's a mystery to me sometimes. My mother, God bless her heart, she tried to explain everything to me, but who can explain these little erections? One time I got buried alive at the beach by a bunch of wiseguys, they abandoned me there. All I had was my head out. I'm lookin around. I see this little bird. This little bird looks at me, I look at this little bird. And sonofabitch if I don't get a little erection! How do you figure that? You don't. You don't, that's my answer. There are things that you can figure out and there are things you can't figure out. Now some things I know. In fact, I happen to be very wise. In fact, I am here tonight to teach you something. You wanna think of it that way, you're my class. And what I'm gonna do is, I'm gonna tell you a story. About my friend Huey and me, and what happened to him. And from this story, I'm gonna teach you something. Now my name is Aldo Scalicki, and my best friend... Oh see, who can figure? It's going down now. *(To his crotch.)* Are you through? *(Resuming.)* Anyway, as I was saying, my name is Aldo Scalicki, and my best friend my whole life is Huey Maximilian Bonfigliano. Come on out Huey. . .*(Huey enters from the wing. He's dressed in a very poetic white shirt with billowing sleeves, jodhpurs and embossed royal blue slippers. He has a notebook and a music box. He sits at an oak table. He opens the music box; it plays the theme from "Turandot. " Then he begins writing in the notebook.)* One day, about a month ago, I remembered that I had not seen my friend Huey in some time. I had called him on the phone, but nobody would pick up. So I went over to his apartment.

Aldo exits from the stage. In a moment, a knock is heard at Huey's door.

Huey: Who is it?

Aldo comes in the door.

Aldo: It's Aldo!
Huey: Freakin Scalicki I can't talk to you now.
Aldo: What's the box?
Huey: Music.

Huey closes the box stopping the music.

Aldo: What for?
Huey: Cause I'm workin on somethin.
Aldo: What are you doin?
Huey: I'm writin.
Aldo: Who to?
Huey: I'm not writin nobody. I'm writin.
Aldo: What?
Huey: Somethin.
Aldo: A book?
Huey: No, not a book! I reject that! I reject that book shit!
Aldo: Alright.
Huey: Finished!

Aldo: What'd you finish?
Huey: This.
Aldo: What is it?
Huey: I won't name it. I reject that.
Aldo: Alright.
Huey: You wanna hear it?
Aldo: You wanna read it to me sure I wanna hear it.
Huey: *(Reads.)*

> When I get tired a bein cool
> I slam this bat against the back a my skull
> And curse the stars I see
>
> My heritage is one a rage
> Like a black blindfold
> I can sorta see through
>
> I can see my abductors
> I can count my abductors
> But I cannot identify my abductors
>
> When I attempt to relax
> Close my eyes an picture somethin pleasant
> I fail completely
>
> There is no inner scene I can fall back on
> There is no placid brain picture vacation
> Only something broken, primordial, and mine
>
> If I thought writing this made me a poet
> I'd stick a fork in my eye
> And check out
>
> Poets bite themselves
> I wanna bite You!
>
> What do I mean by Bite?
> Don't try to nail my words
> My words move

If you nail my words they'll die

Then you'll completely understand what I said
Cause what I said will be completely dead.

A long pause.

Aldo: May I sit down?

Huey: Sure.

Aldo: *(Sits.)* Refresh me. What does primordial mean?

Huey: Old. Like a caveman kinda...

He drifts away. Another pause.

Aldo: Alright. Can I speak to you, Huey?

Huey: Sure.

Aldo: You ain't been comin around this last long bit...

Huey: I've had a lot on my mind.

Aldo: I've been callin you...

Huey: I unplugged the phone.

Aldo: And now when I see you, you're dressed in ridiculous clothes, and you are writing this primordial shit.

Huey: GET OUT, GET OUT GET OUT!

Aldo is unfazed.

Aldo: Now I can't help but think that what's goin on with you is just another expression of your usual problem.

Huey: Why don't you leave me alone?

Aldo: How long you been divorced now?

Huey: Three years.

Aldo: Three years. Don't you think it's about time to get over it?

Huey: You understand nothing.

Aldo: Alright. I'm willing to listen. If I don't understand, why don't you take a minute and explain it to me?

Huey: Because I don't understand.

Aldo: What's this appearance?

Huey: Don't talk to me.

Aldo: Tell me about this appearance you're wearing?

Huey: Listen, don't tamper with me while I'm in progress with this thing.

Aldo: You look like a frog.

Huey: I do not!

Aldo: You look like a frog in a pajamma top.

Huey: I have a plan.

Aldo: For what?

Huey: To get her back.

Aldo: Who?

Huey: Janice.

Aldo: You want her back?

Huey: Yeah.

Aldo: It's like you get the Hong Kong Flu, you get rid of it, now you want it back?

Huey: I want her to take me back.

Aldo: She killed your dog.

Huey: I don't care anymore.

Aldo: The woman shot your dog with a zip gun and you want her back?

Huey: Yes.

Aldo: Huey. Huey. Why?

Huey: Love?

Aldo: I'm listening.

Huey: That's all.

Aldo: What are you telling me? Are you telling me you love Janice?

Huey: My life don't mean anything without her.

Aldo: I'm not gonna argue with you there. I don't know whether your life means anything or not. Maybe it doesn't mean anything. Who cares? I mean, why should your life mean anything? My life doesn't mean anything. Maybe that's the good news. Why you want your life to mean something? Okay, with you, your life meant something when you were with Janice. It meant heartache, screaming, bad food, and finally, a dead dog. Is this something to miss? Listen, Huey, a lotta people have an expression of this problem. They had something horrible for a long time, and then they get away from it, and then they miss it. They want the horrible thing back. But only in the very very blindest stupidest way. This is where friends come in. Friends are those people appointed in your life to blow the whistle when you're insane. I didn't see you for awhile. I call you, no answer.

Immediately when I thought about it, I figured you were having some kind of mental episode. So I'm your friend, I'm here to do my job. WAKE UP.

Huey: I gotta good plan to get her back.

Aldo: You know, talking to you is like bein alone.

Huey: But I need your help.

Aldo: You want me to help you get Janice back?

Huey: Yes.

Aldo: Janice hates me.

Huey: I know that.

Aldo: Once when I was a little boy, Janice made me play funeral with her. She made me lie down in a flower box and cross my arms on my chest and be dead. Then she put on a happy birthday hat and blew a party horn. I absolutely believe if I died today she'd show up at my coffin with that hat on.

Huey: You're right. She doesn't like you.

Aldo: She hates me.

Huey: But she likes you better than me. Aldo, let me explain what's been goin on with me. For three years now I've been trying to forget Janice and get on with my life. I moved in by myself, I got a nice girlfriend...

Aldo: Teresa is a wonderful person.

Huey: I know she is.

Aldo: Half the guys in this neighborhood are jealous of you over Teresa.

Huey: I know. I know from out there my life is looking real good. I know that Teresa's great and that she loves me...

Aldo: And she can cook like an angel. She cooks as good as my mother. *(To his mother in the audience.)* I'm not tellin the truth, Ma. That was just a rhetorical fib to make a point with my friend. *(To Huey.)* And, on top a all that, Teresa is easy-goin.

Huey: I know.

Aldo: That's no small thing.

Huey: I know.

Aldo: If I could find an easy-goin girl, I might tie the knot myself.

Huey: You? You're never gonna get married.

Aldo: That's true. But that's not cause there's anything wrong with me. That's because the state of this country has ruined all the girls.

Huey: Aldo, I'm gonna break it off with Teresa and I'm gonna go after Janice.

Aldo: You're doomed. You're like Oedipus. I'm talking to Oedipus.

Huey: I'm doin what a man should do. I've spent a lot of time thinking. Years. Weighing this and this and this. I haven't wanted to be rash. To tell you the truth, the thing that's scared me the most in this whole time in my life is that I would be rash. I haven't been. Nobody could think more about anything than I've thought about this. A man's heart is difficult to know. His own heart. I've spent a lot of time listening to my heart. I've taken out my pictures of Janice and looked at them, and I've put them away again. When I wake up in the morning, I write my dreams down on a piece of paper. I read them over and over and try to understand what they mean. I save them. I have all my dreams in a drawer. I've spent time with Teresa. I love her, I eat with her, I talk to her about what she thinks life is. In my secret mind, I compare her to Janice. In many ways, she's better than Janice. I mean, like, if you were to put them both on television, I think Teresa would get much better ratings than Janice. You know what happened to me one time when I was a kid? I got a crush on this girl. I thought she was great. I followed her all over the place, trying to work myself up to talk to her. I was gonna ask her to this party. Then I told one of the guys from the block what I was thinking. And he laughed at me. He told me I was a fool. Because she wasn't good-lookin. And you know what I did? I dropped my interest in that girl. I never asked her to that party. She was outta my life picture. I dropped her because her ratings were too low. And that was okay. Cause I was a boy. Which means that was the time to be stupid. I'm a man now. I can't worry what my life looks like to other people. You know that guy who told me that girl wasn't good-lookin? I can't even remember his name. I'm gonna break it off with Teresa, and I'm gonna go after Janice.

Aldo: You think Janice is gonna like you better dressed that way than in normal clothes?

Huey: I'm trying to give myself some confidence. I got no confidence that I can straighten out my life.

Aldo: Hey, you alright?

Huey: No.

Aldo: Hey.

Huey: I know I'm a fool, Aldo. Maybe I've always been a fool. I've screwed up every single thing in my life. I feel this pain that makes me weak. The pain is my place in me where I'm hurt from the divorce. I'm a big freakin failure. I gotta find a way to make things right. I tried to go into the future an be new, but it don't work for me. All the ghosts of my old happiness come after me when I stop an be still a minute. I didn't think I could ever be so regretful. I'm a young man, but I feel like everything is over for me unless I go back an fix this broken place. I gotta get back with Janice before I start thinkin about like killin myself.

Aldo: Hey, hey. Listen. Whatever you need. You hear me? I'm your friend whatever you wanna do. You're gonna be alright.

Huey: Aldo, look at me. What happened to me? I was a young man. I never worried about nothin. Now I can't taste my food. The furniture just sits on my floor here. I got no feelin of home. I tried to claim Teresa. I tried to feel my rights with her. She wanted me to. But I don't feel I got that power in me to claim a woman. That strength of knowin what I want. I can't take. I want my power to stand up and be a man and take. I want it back. I think Janice has it. I think she took that power from me, or it's sittin with her. Somethin like that. I'm like Samson and Janice is the woman who cut my hair an broke my strength. I want my strength of being a man back, an I've got to go to Janice for that.

Aldo: It don't sound to me like you love her.

Huey: I don't know whether I love her. I don't care whether I love her or not. Love don't matter to me anymore. I've lost my strength and freedom of being a man, and without that there's a lot more than love I can't do. Without that much longer, I ain't gonna be able to draw breath.

Aldo: Alright then. We'll get that strength back for you. You're my friend, Huey. Listen to me! Life is stupid. I know that, too. You're gonna have these situations which are stupid to live through and yet it has to be done. You need to look like this, go ahead. You need to go back to Janice, go back. We're here now, and we'll be here then. I'm not lettin you go. You let go of a friend a minute, he starts to fly away from you a hundred miles an hour. It's a miracle you ever see him again. I'll hold on to you.

Huey: So you'll help me?

Aldo: Whatever you need.

Huey: I have a good plan.

Aldo: Tell it to me.

Huey: These things gotta be done in a certain order.

Aldo: I'm listenin.

Huey: I gotta break up with Teresa before I can reconcile with Janice.

Aldo: That seems right.

Huey: Teresa should be working the Soup House this afternoon and I must go there and tell her it's over between us.

Aldo: You want me to go with you?

Huey: No. Teresa doesn't like you very much.

Aldo: Why do all the women you like hate me?

Huey: Maybe cause they know you're my friend and they're jealous.

Aldo: I think it's cause they know I won't marry.

Huey: I think women only like the friends you make after you're with them because then they know those friends accept the situation. Old friends wanna take you back to the old days.

Aldo: I think it's cause they know I won't marry. They hate my sanity.

Huey: Anyway, I'm pretty scared to tell Teresa that I don't wanna see her anymore. Just yesterday I told her that I loved her and that I had really gotten over all my mental problems.

Aldo: You told her that yesterday?

Huey: Yeah.

Aldo: How'd you have such a quick change of heart?

Huey: I don't know. Maybe I was lying? I don't know what I was doing. I can't remember yesterday. It really seems like a long time ago.

Aldo: Huey. Maybe you should just hold tight for a few days and wait and see how you're feeling then?

Huey: No. Even though I don't always feel the same way, the way I'm feeling now is the biggest thing. It comes back and back. I never solve it. I think I just get tired of it, and then when I rest it comes back. I really know the solution is in going this way. I don't wanna go, you know. Why you think I ain't done this before this? I was too scared. I don't like to make a move like this. It's too big. I think if I could live the way I wanted, everything would be smaller happenings. But things are big. Love. Marriage. Divorce. Death. Babies. Things are too big for a little guy like me not to be scared. But whether I'm scared or not, I got stuff to do. Things ain't right. I gotta try to make 'em right. And I might as well get on with tryin.

Aldo: I gotta tell you one thing from my side.

Huey: What?

Aldo: I feel this is the moment to say somethin.

Huey: What about?

Aldo: You should know that I don't always know exactly what I'm doing either. I'm gonna tell you somethin it's hard for me to say. I get scared cause a life, too. When my father died and I didn't know him cause he never talked to me seriously, I got hit with the tragic side of being a man. My own father was a stranger to me, Huey. Can you imagine? I can't even imagine that, and it happened to me. My own father never took me to the side and made me feel like his son. And I never grabbed him and made him do that with me. It just didn't happen. Some things just don't happen. The moment goes by. The man is dead now. I can't go back an change that. I got no father. When I had a father, I didn't have a father. And now I never will, no matter how I wish an wish. This is what I'm sayin: It's easy for me never to show the truth to another man. Just like I was taught. That's why sometimes I think I ache for the company of a woman. I know the other reasons, too. But I think it's also because it's harder for me not to show the truth to a woman, sooner or later, if I spend time with them. And then that's why I hate them and love them and need them to the point where I stare at the ones I don't even know.

Huey: Then why don't you get married?

Aldo: Cause it's a sickness that makes me need a woman that way. It's the sickness of bein a man, the stupid son of a stupid father. I got things in me I gotta fix between me an men, before I even get to the women. Huey, we gotta be friends for each other! Or at least I wish an hope we could be friends like me an my father never could be. This is the moment that's gonna tell the tale. I can feel it. We always been close, but we stomp around each other like all the other hotshots. But just now, just now you told me how you felt for real about something, in a way that I thought you only coulda told a woman, an that touches me. That moves me. Maron, I sound like a faggot. No! I just sound like my father never did. And that's how I wanna sound.

Huey: What are you sayin, Aldo?

Aldo: That I love you. And I'm petrified to say that. You're my best friend, and all I ever do is mock and march around and try to look good. Just like my stupid father. And that's dead. I love you, man to man, and I'm here for you. Alright?

Huey: Alright.

Aldo: Tell me what you need from me in this plan.

Huey: I feel like I should say now that I love you, too.

Aldo: You don't haveta say nothin.

Huey: Would you mind if I didn't? I just don't feel up to that.

Aldo: No, I don't mind. Forget it. Tell me the plan and let's get goin.

Huey: Alright. I go to the Soup House and tell Teresa it's over.

Aldo: Right.

Huey: And then once that's done, or undone...

Aldo: Whatever.

Huey: You go, and you pave the way for me with Janice.

Aldo: I have several questions.

Huey: Okay.

Aldo: Why do I get Janice?

Huey: Because if I go without having her prepared, I think she'll just flip out an start yellin, and we'll never really have the conversation. If you talk to her first...

Aldo: She can tear my head off.

Huey: Right. I mean, exactly. I need my head for this one, Aldo, and you don't. If she screams at me too hard, I think I'll get too nervous to talk as good as I could.

Aldo: But why me?

Huey: Because she respects you. She don't like you, but she respects you. And you're a good talker, a good arguer. You're better than me at talkin. And you're not afraid of her. You can take the heat better than me. But most of all, who else but you? Who else could I ask to do this but you?

Aldo: What if she shoots me?

Huey: She ain't gonna shoot you.

Aldo: She shot your dog.

Huey: That was a dog. You're a human being.

Aldo: But does she know that?

Huey: She doesn't even have the gun anymore. It blew up after that.

Aldo: After that?

Huey: It was just a crappy zip gun.

Aldo: When was she usin it after that? What was she shootin at?

Huey: Me.

Aldo: She tried to shoot you.

Huey: That was back when she was drinking. She's dry now.

Aldo: She shot your dog. She tried to shoot you. And now you're sending me to her. Alright. I'll go. I'm paving the way, huh? Son of a bitch.

Huey: Aldo.

Aldo: You know what I think, Huey? I think you should definitely tell me that you love me. If I am doing this, you should say it, you should carve it into a freakin tree.

Huey: I love you.

Aldo: Don't lie to me.

Huey: I do love you, Aldo.

Aldo: I don't know. You're gonna bust up with Teresa, this terrific girl. I'm gonna prepare Janice for you to stage the disaster of your life. All a this in the name of friendship.

Huey: You know what I think of it as?

Aldo: What?

Huey: Like music. *(Music begins to play under and continues to play under rest of scene. Prerecorded concertina music. Aldo and Huey stroll and talk.)* Like a musical movement. I feel this'll be my first music in a long time.

Aldo: Like music, huh? So now you're a composer. Alright, I'm game. I'll be in your first movement. But I'm tellin you. At some point, I'm gonna sit back with my popcorn, Puccini.

This is your show.

Huey: I know that.

Aldo: Just so long as you know that.

Huey: Janice should be home by nine o'clock tonight. She don't work the dinner on Saturday. And I should be all broken up with Teresa by then, so it won't be wrong that way. After you talk Janice to a place where you think I can talk to her, tell her I'll be there at midnight.

Aldo: Ain't that kinda late?

Huey: She'll be tired and maybe it won't be as bad.

Aldo: Right. She'll be tired from takin the pot shots at me.

Huey: The gun blew up.

Aldo: As if that were the only gun to be had.

Huey: If you don't wanna do it, Aldo, just say the word.

Aldo: No, I'll do it.

Huey: Thanks.

Aldo: That's alright.

Huey: We should get goin. I'll go to the Soup House and talk to Teresa.

Aldo: You don't want me to come with you?

Huey: No, I gotta do this.

Aldo: Alright. Huey?

Huey: Yeah?

Aldo: Go easy on Teresa. She's a nice girl and don't deserve your grief.

Huey: I know. I'm scared to tell her.

Aldo: You should be. But don't worry about it.

They exit. Crossfade to Scene 2.

SCENE 2

Lights up on Pop's Soup House. Teresa, dressed in a faded waitress outfit, is discovered on one of the stools. She looks glum. She's a big, striking Italian girl. Enter Aunt May, an Italian woman of middle years.

May: Hi, Teresa.

Teresa: Hi, Aunt May.

May: Why are your eyes red?

Teresa: What are you talkin about?

May: Alright, don't tell me. I'm a widow. I got nothin to do with my life if the people I love shut me out, but that's my problem and I'll get by. Got some soup?

Teresa: Sure.

May: Got that minestrone?

Teresa: Every day.

Teresa sets about serving the soup.

May: I like that minestrone.

Teresa: I used to like minestrone. I used to like walking in the rain. I used to like looking in the mirror. Now all I see there is a moron.

May: You're not a moron, you're a beautiful girl. Why are your eyes red?

Teresa: I've made up my mind. I'm gonna call it quits with Huey.

May: So. That's it. I thought you loved Huey?

Teresa: He's very distracted, Aunt May. I feel this constant thing with him where he's comparing me to his old wife.

May: That's no good. That's bad.

Teresa: Yesterday he told me that he loved me and that he had put all his mental problems behind him.

May: But you didn't believe him. You saw.

Teresa: I could see that he was insane.

May: What's the matter with that boy?

Teresa: He can't get over his divorce.

May: Uh-huh. That's bad.

Teresa: I have been so nice to that man. But that's over. He don't know the difference. His old wife...

May: Janice.

Teresa: Yeah, Janice. She treated him like a dog. Now he looks at all women like they're her. He can't feel when somebody treats him good.

May: I heard she killed his dog.

Teresa: She did that, too.

May: Takes a woman with big feelings to kill a man's dog. A real Bloody Mary.

Teresa: Janice is very terrible. She scares the livin shit outta me. She's like a scourge. She should live on a black mountain and drink out of a skull. The one thing I could never understand was how Huey came to marry her.

May: Maybe she wasn't that way back then. Not that people change. But sometimes somethin small can get emphasized through a bad experience.

Teresa: Like what?

May: I don't know. Maybe like marrying Huey. Who knows? Maybe if you'd married Huey, you woulda gotten to be like Janice.

Teresa: Huh. No way.

May: I don't know.

Teresa: I'm tellin you. No way.

May: And I'm tellin you, I don't know.

Teresa: Well, we're never gonna find out who's right cause I'm gonna break up with him.

May: How you gonna do it?

Teresa: What do you mean?

May: This is important. You gonna point in his face, or are you gonna take the whole blame on yourself?

Teresa: I ain't thought about it.

May: Think about it. You should.

Teresa: What's the difference?

May: If you point the finger at him while he's in front of you, you may not be pointin the finger at him in your sleep.

Teresa: Point the finger in my sleep?

May: That's right.

Teresa: You mean, if I'm not careful, I could get obsessed.

May: That's right. You could get that bug-eyed look.

Teresa: I don't want that. So I'll point in his face and I'll put the whole thing on him. Then he can remember my finger pointing like a knife, and I'll go and sleep good.

May: Yeah. You'll still feel pain.

A pause.

Teresa: Aunt May?

May: Yeah?

Teresa: I feel too weak to break up with Huey. I don't feel I got the strength to just push him away.

May: You're only weak when you try to do somethin you don't wanna.

Teresa: I wanna break up with him.

May: When you do what you want, you're as strong as an ox.

Teresa: I've lost my reasons for us to be together.

May: You're tormented.

Teresa: I am.

May: You wanna break up with him and you don't wanna break up with him.

Teresa: No. I wanna break up with him.

May: You do?

Teresa: Yeah.

May: You're sure?

Teresa: Yeah.

May: Why?

Teresa: I don't like how he's treatin me.

May: You feel bad?

Teresa: Yes.

May: It used to be better?

Teresa: Much better.

May: Then I guess you're right to do somethin to get things movin.

Teresa: In the beginning, he was like this guy who loved me, and he had no past with anybody. It was like he was just starting out to live. Then the past came and got him, threw a bag over him. The man was kidnapped by his own past. He's supposed to come by.

May: Where?

Teresa: Here. He said he'd be by.

May: Then I'd best be on my way.

Teresa: No! I want you to be here.

May: No, you don't. What d'you want me for?

Teresa: I want your moral support.

May: I don't have no morals.

Teresa: I want you here so you can hear what I say and what he says, and tell me afterwards that I don't remember it wrong.

May: I make a bad witness. I don't retain.

Teresa: Just stay, okay? I'm gonna be sad. I don't wanna be alone.

May: Alright. I'll stay. God, you're pretty. I'll never understand why pretty girls always seem to get treated so bad. Or ugly girls either.

Huey appears at the door.

Teresa: Here he comes.

May: Remember. Point the finger. Save your peace of mind.

Enter Huey.

Huey: Hi.

Teresa: Hi.

Huey: Hi, May.

May: You look like the Count of Monte Cristo.

Huey: Thanks.

Teresa: So, how are you today, Huey?

Huey: Good. How are you today?

Teresa: Good.

May: I'm gonna wash my bowl.

Teresa: You look awful.

Huey: You look beautiful.

Teresa: Thank you. *(A pause.)* Huey …

Huey: *(Simultaneously.)* Janice.

Teresa: What did you call me?

Huey: Ja … Teresa?

Teresa: You called me Janice.

May: Oh, boy.

Huey: No, I didn't.

Teresa: You called me Janice. You piece of shit.

Huey: I didn't say that.

Teresa: I knew this was the way your mind was working. I am not your old wife.

Huey: I know that.

Teresa: I feel sick.

Huey: I know who you are. You're Teresa.

Teresa: Oh, very good. Aunt May, ain't that great? He knows my name.

May: I shoulda left when I had the chance.

Teresa: Janice was one person and I'm another person.

Huey: I know that.

Teresa: You treat me like a criminal because this other woman gave you abuse.

Huey: I do not treat you like a criminal.

Teresa: I have been loving you and you have been treating me like you have the right to what I'm giving you. You've been treatin my affection like some kinda torture you've been puttin up with. Like we was in the last days of a bad marriage.

Huey: I have not. You've been misunderstanding everything I have been going through.

Teresa: I understand everything. You louse, you lousy geep. I've got X-ray understanding. You know what the problem with you is? You're spoiled by women. You think you got women love comin to you outta your destiny. You got nothin comin to you. You ain't earned nothin. And, Hey, I've gotta a major bulletin for you, Huey...

She starts to point.

Huey: Listen, Teresa, I don't wanna see you anymore.

Teresa: What?

May: Oh boy..

Huey: I've realized that I have to go back to Janice and I'm really grateful for everything you've given me. Really. But I've come to see it's Janice I need.

May: Point the finger.

Teresa: You're breaking up with me?

Huey: I've come to see it's what I should do. I was tellin Aldo . ..

Teresa: Don't talk to me about Aldo. You're breaking up with me?

Huey: I was hoping you'd see it was the right thing.

Teresa: I feel all switched up.

Huey: I never shoulda left Janice. I know now. I shoulda found a way to work it out with her.

Teresa: I can feel my brain.

May: Forget your brain. Point the finger.

Huey: Are you okay? I know this is hard for you.

Teresa: I.... I... What?

May: Point! J'accuse!

Teresa: Huey, don't leave me.

May: I'm going to the bathroom.

May exits.

Huey: There's no point in making this harder than it has to be.

Teresa: You're numb.

Huey: What do you mean?

Teresa: You can't feel your own face. That woman made you numb. You're like somebody's thumb that got cut off. You're like a cut-off thumb inna glass a water.

Huey: I am not.

Teresa: Huey. Are you talkin about going back to Janice?

Huey: Yeah.

Teresa: Huey. That woman hates you. Why would you break up with a woman who loves you to go to a woman who hates you? It just don't make any sense.

Huey: She doesn't really hate me.

Teresa: Yes, she does.

Huey: She's just mad at me.

Teresa: It's worse than that. I swear to you.

Huey: How could I be with a woman as long as I was with Janice if she hated me?

Teresa: I don't know.

Huey: If that were true, how could I ever trust any woman again?

Teresa: Cause all women ain't her.

Huey: I can't believe Janice hated me. If that were true, then I don't know anything at all and there's no hope for me. I pray to God you're wrong, Teresa.

Teresa: I'm not wrong.

Huey: Cause if she really didn't love me ever then I feel so ugly like I could never never be loved by anyone. If she really didn't love me at all, I think I'll kill myself.

Teresa: No.

Huey: I'll have to. Who am I if I give my love to a woman who hates me?

Teresa: No. Comere.

Huey: No.

Teresa: Why not?

Huey: Cause if you hug me I may get confused and think that I love you, when I already know what I have to do.

Teresa: Okay.

Huey: I've got to go back to Janice. That's the only way outta this trap I'm in.

Teresa: You're not in no trap.

Huey: Yes, I am.

Teresa: You're gonna be alright.

Huey: I don't know.

Teresa: You're just goin through this bad time in your life.

Huey: I hope so.

Teresa: Sure. But be quiet a minute and listen to somethin from me, okay? I need you. I'm not nuts like you are now. I'm in my right mind and I love you and I need you. And I don't want you to leave me.

Huey: Don't.

Teresa: I can't only be watchin out for your feelings, sweetheart. I've got my own feelings to speak. I love you and I need you and I don't want you to leave me. If you get back with Janice, you'll be as sorry as a man can be. She don't love you an she don't mean you good like I do.

Huey: I love you.

Teresa: I know you do.

Huey: But I've got to go back to her.

Teresa: You don't, you know.

Huey: I'm sayin I love you, but I'm like this little crippled man with stumps that can't grab nothin. I gotta go back where I left my hands.

Teresa: Do you love Janice?

Huey: I've got to get her back.

Teresa: Then get outta here.

Huey: Teresa.

Teresa: No! Get out, I said. You can't have it all ways.

Huey goes to the door.

Huey: Let's see what happens next.

Teresa: I ain't gonna wait for you while you're being stupid, you know.

Huey: I know.

Teresa: You don't know nothin. Go on. Go.

ITALIAN AMERICAN RECONCILIATION

Huey exits. Teresa cries. May reenters.

May: All clear?

Teresa: Oh, shut up.

May: I know. It's bad. He is crazy.

Teresa: He is, isn't he?

May: He is very crazy.

Teresa: Why can't he see when he's bein stupid?

May: There's probably somewhere in him where he can.
Men are different than women. Men can get wrapped up in the
past. Women are more that way about the future.

Teresa: Oh God, I feel bad!

May: Yeah. Yes.

Teresa: Do you think Janice will take him back?

May: I don't know. I hope not. Why didn't you break up with
him like you were gonna?

Teresa: I started to.

May: But you backed off.

Teresa: So what?

May: Do you really love him?

Teresa: Yeah. To the best of my knowledge.

May: *(May takes out hand cream and applies it during next.)* I loved
a man like that once. Three years. Precious times. I'll never have
the courage to be that stupid again.

Teresa: What happened?

May: I dropped him.

Teresa: Just like that?

May: I dropped him so hard he was outta sight and gone before
I could wash my hands.

Teresa: How'd you bring yourself to do it?

May: I didn't have to do nothin. The hand on my watch did it
all. Time. I got older by a day. One certain day. I got one day
older than him.

Teresa: I feel older than Huey right now, but that don't make
me let him go.

May: Well, you are not me, as I said. What happened to me is
not gonna be what happens to you. But I do wonder why I've
been through the things I've been through. If all this stuff I
remember is wisdom or just lint. Anything you want me to do for

you?

Teresa: I can't think of anything.

May: Me neither. I never can. There never is anything to do. Makes me feel as useless as I am.

Teresa: You're not useless. I'm glad you're here.

They spend a moment in communion, then Aldo sticks his head in the door.

Aldo: Is Huey here?

May: He left.

Enter Aldo.

Aldo: Has he been talkin to you, Teresa?

Teresa: Yeah?

Aldo: Sorry to butt in, but somehow I'm already involved. Did he break up with you?

Teresa: Yeah, he did.

Aldo: I'm sorry. He's insane.

Teresa: So he's insane. So what?

May: You wanna cuppa soup?

Aldo: Sure. Everybody in this neighborhood thinks you're like totally terrific.

May sets about soup serving.

Teresa: That's great.

Aldo: I do, too.

Teresa: Thanks. Are you asking me for a date?

Aldo: No!

Teresa: That's good. Cause the answer woulda been no.

Aldo: How come all the women with Huey never like me?

Teresa: I can only speak for myself.

Aldo: Fair enough.

Teresa: Cause I don't like Mama's boys.

Aldo: I think it's cause you know I won't marry.

Teresa: Same difference.

Aldo: You're gettin me angry now. I can feel the pulse in my nose.

Teresa: Sorry.

Aldo: I'm here on a serious matter.

Teresa: What?

Aldo: Huey is planning to go back to Janice.

Teresa: He told me.

Aldo: I'm supposed to go an set her up for him.

May: What? What's that mean?

Aldo: He wants me to soften her up for him, you know, take the initial heat, so he can reason with her.

May: Well, you know how to make yourself useful. I should probably take lessons from you.

Aldo: What do you mean?

May: I was just saying to Teresa that I never know how to make myself of use in these situations.

Aldo: You wanna be of use? Lemme tell you something. You can be used. Or you can be of use. To be of use may actually mean not allowing yourself to be used.

May: I don't get you.

Aldo: Don't feel bad. I'm deep. Teresa, listen to me.

Teresa: He wants you to talk to Janice?

Aldo: Yes. Huey is my best friend and he's not himself and he's in a bad way. He's planning the most disastrous thing he could do with his life, and he's got me helping him to do it. I think he should be with you, not Janice. What do you think?

Teresa: I agree.

May: Me too. I think.

Aldo: So I intend to make sure that Huey and Janice do not reconcile.

May: How you gonna do that?

Aldo: I am gonna go to Janice tonight, and I am gonna seduce her.

   May laughs.

May: Ah, I like you! You're crazy!

Aldo: I am crazy!

Teresa: You're gonna put the make on Janice?

Aldo: Yes! I'm gonna make her mine. I'm gonna drive any image of Huey from her thoughts. In this way, I'm going to save my friend.

May: And then what?

Aldo: What do you mean?

May: I mean, if you make Janice yours, then she's yours, right?

Aldo: I can't deal with that problem now.

Teresa: You know, even if you prevent him from going back with Janice, don't think things are gonna be alright between him and me. I have feelings, you know. I've got pride, an a shitload of other stuff, too.

Aldo: I can't deal with that now either. All that will become clear. But one step at a time. What I have tonight is almost like a military objective. Janice is like a hill I gotta take. And I got till twelve midnight to do it.

May: Whatever happens, Aldo, you're a good friend. You're a real good friend. I admire you. When the smoke clears, we're gonna have to have a talk.

Aldo: I'll tell you something. I'm terrified. My stomach is against this. Janice is a very frightening woman and if it wasn't for Huey I would never consider this, not even if I was very drunk. This is a black rendezvous. All I ask of you, Teresa, is that you keep an open mind. Will you promise me that?

Teresa: That's all I promise.

Aldo: That's all I ask. And if you never see me again, and they ask you where I went, tell them I went to a tough place for the sake of a friend.

Exit Aldo.

Teresa: You know, that guy is another example of why I should become a nun.

May: Aw, he's sweet! *(She laughs.)* But him and Janice tonight? What I wouldn't give to be a fly on the wall!

Something like "Papa Loves To Mambo", sung by Perry Como, begins to play as the lights go down.*

---

*See Special Note on copyright page

ACT II

SCENE I

Menacing music from "Turandot" plays as the lights come up.*

The rear of Janice's house; it's night. A lone cricket chirps. A couple of stars twinkle high over head.

Janice is discovered on her balcony. She is an angular, patrician Roman with strawberry blond hair and austere good looks. She's wearing a soft white nightgown which makes her look like a young girl. In her arms she cradles six fat roses. She looks at the sky, full of emotion. Then she tosses the flowers to the ground below. She looks down at the flowers, and bleakly says, "What for?" Then she goes back inside.

Aldo, in a sharp jacket and tie, appears at the garden gate. He tries to open it, fails, and climbs over. He sees the flowers lying on the ground. He calls up in a loud whisper.

Aldo: Janice. Janice. Janice.

Janice reemerges. She's tying a black velvet robe with padded shoulders. The effect is striking, but more adult and severe.

Janice: Who's that?

Aldo: It's Aldo. Scalicki.

Janice: What are you doing in my backyard?

Aldo: I rang the bell about fifty times, but nobody answered.

Janice: It's broken.

Aldo: You should have it fixed.

Janice: Why?

Aldo: So it rings.

Janice: What do I care if it rings? I don't see anybody.

Aldo: Well, you still might get a delivery or something. Flowers or something. Somebody send you flowers?

Janice: Yes.

Aldo: Very nice.

Janice: They're from Huey.

*See special note on copyright page

Aldo: How you know that?

Janice: I know.

Aldo: Well, then, you shouldn't be so confident. You're wrong. I sent the flowers.

Janice: You? Why would you send me flowers?

Aldo: I sent them for Huey.

Janice: Can't even manage to send his own flowers.

Aldo: What d'you mean?

Janice: He's hapless. He's a buffoon.

Aldo: He's my best friend.

Janice: That's your problem.

Aldo: Anyway, it's a shame you destroyed them like this.

Janice: They were dead anyway.

Aldo: Maybe they were dead, but they were expensive. *(He starts to gather them.)* They're not really destroyed. *(He lays them on the table.)*

Janice: Why are you here?

Aldo: Beautiful night.

Janice: I wish it would rain.

Aldo: Beautiful stars.

Janice: Stars make me think of death.

Aldo: I can smell the greenness of the leaves.

Janice: It smells like a cemetery. What are you doing here?

Aldo: Huey asked me to come.

Janice: Why?

Aldo: He wants to patch it up with you.

Janice: Patch up what?

Aldo: What d'you think? The marriage. *(Janice chuckles dryly.)* What's so funny?

Janice: Think about it.

Aldo: You wanna come down?

Janice: No.

   A pause.

Aldo: Janice, Janice, Janice.

Janice: What?

Aldo: We've seen some stuff, huh?

Janice: What are you talking about?

Aldo: Member when we were kids? I'd play Julius Caesar and you'd stab me with the rubber knife and yell Die! Die!

Janice: I remember.

Aldo: You were some nutty little girl.

Janice: You were a jerk.

Aldo: I was very innocent.

Janice: You were a jerk.

Aldo: I was a little kid. I was supposed to be a jerk.

Janice: You did it perfectly.

A pause.

Aldo: Janice, Janice, Janice.

Janice: Why do you keep saying that?

Aldo: We've been around the block a few times.

Janice: Aldo. You are still the same hammerheaded clown you always were. Are you trying to be smooth? You come here outta no place. You send flowers. You say, Janice, Janice, Janice. Am I supposed to be getting the idea? How 'bout just spitting it out?

Aldo: Huey wants to make it up with you.

Janice: Why are you saying this? Where's Huey?

Aldo: He sent me first.

Janice: Oh, I get it. He always was a coward.

Aldo: Huey is not a coward.

Janice: Huey always was a coward, and you always were a stooge. If he wasn't a coward he'd be standing here in his own shoes speaking his own words. If you weren't a stooge, you wouldn't be a standin in somebody else's love scene. Ain't you got no girl of your own?

Aldo: I got girls comin out my ears.

Janice: What a picture.

Aldo: I didn't come here to talk about me.

Janice: That's cause you're a stooge.

Aldo: Stop callin me that! You can be a very difficult woman to talk to, Janice.

Janice: Really?

Aldo: Yes. I mean, if I was here on my own… I mean, if I was the specific guy who was tryin to romance you, I gotta tell you I wouldn't even know where to begin. You are so… nasty.

Janice: I am?

Aldo: Yeah, you're like a fiend. Your eyes look like vampire vulture monster fiend eyes.

Janice: They do?

Aldo: Yes, they do. And you always smile only for the wrong, the most horriblest reason. Sometimes when you smile I expect to see like fangs fall down over your lower lip. I've had the experience when you smile where I wanted to run away down the street cause I was afraid you were gonna bite me.

Janice: Really?

Aldo: You're not angry?

Janice: Why would I be?

Aldo: I thought cause I was telling you the truth that I might be insulting.

Janice: I'm not insulted.

Aldo: Well, good. Cause it feels much more relaxing for me to tell the truth. I expected to have to do a lot of lying tonight.

Janice: Why?

Aldo: You know.

Janice: No, I don't.

Aldo: You know. Romance. Lies.

Janice: I like the truth.

Aldo: So do I. You know, sometimes when I catch sight a you unexpected, my balls jump up in a bunch like I dropped 'em inna glass a ice water. *(Janice laughs heartily.)* You think that's funny?

Janice: Yeah. Don't you?

Aldo: Yeah, but I thought you'd be like the last person in the world to get the joke.

Janice: You don't know me, Aldo.

Aldo: I guess not.

Janice: You always amazed me. Why'd you let me stab you and bury you and treat you like a dog?

Aldo: I don't know.

Janice: You oughta think about these things.

Aldo: I have thought about 'em, and I still don't know.

Janice: I did all that stuff to you to see how much you'd take. I thought, Maybe if I kick him one more time, he'll stand up and take my shoes away.

Aldo: Take your shoes? Why would I take your shoes?

Janice: To take charge of me like a man.

Aldo: What are you saying?

Janice: You still don't get it, do you? I was flirting with you.

Aldo: That was flirting?

Janice: Sure.

Aldo: No, that wasn't flirting. You may have felt flirting, but you weren't doing flirting. You were treating me like I was the snake in the apple tree.

Janice: You just didn't get it.

Aldo: I woulda gotten it if you did it right.

Janice: You would have gotten it if you weren't so stupid.

Aldo: Alright. Anyway, thanks.

Janice: For what?

Aldo: I don't know. For feeling like flirting with me, even if I didn't get it. Listen, I wanna apologize for what I said before. I don't think you're nasty.

Janice: I am, though.

Aldo: No. It's like this what we were just talking about. I've just misunderstood you, so I was afraid of you.

Janice: You've understood me well enough. I've never asked to be understood any better.

Aldo: But you're not this monster I made you out. You don't have evil eyes. You don't have big teeth and you're not gonna bite me.

Janice: I might.

Aldo: Listen, Janice, I think you're okay. You've had your problems just like the rest of us and who am I to pass judgement on you? No matter what I said, you an I go back to the beginning and under everything I'm always gonna have a warm spot for you. The final ultimate drift is I know you're a nice person and I'm gonna make a real effort to remember that from now on.

Janice: Don't bother on my account.

Aldo: I am, though. I'll tell you something. I'm very titillated that you was flirting with me, even in those ancient days. Have you ever... felt like that... since?

Janice: Never.

Aldo: You must have your romantic fantasies here, livin by yourself. Like you're that princess trapped in that castle surrounded by thorny bushes. Waiting for Prince Valiant to happen by. You must have thoughts like that. On occasion.

Janice: Never.

Aldo: The thought of you has crossed my mind from time to time. In an unterrifying way. I have a fantasy life, you know.

Janice: Do you?

Aldo: Oh yes. I have a very full and real fantasy life, and from time to time, you appear there.

Janice: Aldo, are you hitting on me?

Aldo: Maybe I am.

Janice: This is too delicious.

Aldo: What d'you mean?

Janice: You're supposed to be here for Huey.

Aldo: So. Maybe I'm not the stooge you thought. Maybe I got my own agenda of feelings. Janice, I'm gonna be out there with you. I've been thinking about you. The thought of your face and your figure has been eating me up lately. How 'bout it?

Janice: How 'bout what?

Aldo: How 'bout I come up stairs and we rip up the bed a little bit?

Janice: Just like that.

Aldo: That's right. Impulsive.

Janice: Alright. What the hell.

Aldo: Really?

Janice: I'll come down an open the door.

Janice goes in.

Aldo: *(To the audience.)* That was easy.

Janice comes back on the terrace with a zip gun. Aldo has his back to her.

Janice: Aldo.

Aldo turns around and sees the gun.

Aldo: Holy Moly!

Janice fires. The gun, defective, blows up. It burns her fingers. She drops it. Aldo, meanwhile, dives under the table.

Janice: You dunce! You oaf! You slimey sewer rat. Damn it. Look at that. I burned my finger. What do you take me for, you comical boob? Am I not supposed to see through you? You're like cellophane! Let's rip up the bed a little bit. God!

Aldo: Don't shoot me!

Janice: I can't. My gun broke.

Aldo: *(Comes out from under the table.)* You shot a gun at me.

Janice: Don't be obvious.

Aldo: You tried to kill me!

Janice: I burned my finger. That's what I get for usin zip guns. Next time it's Smith and Wesson.

Aldo: Janice. Do you understand what you did? You committed attempted murder on me.

Janice: I was aiming at your kneecaps.

Aldo: I should come up there an give you a spankin!

Janice: Oh yeah? Try it. I'll cut your heart out.

Aldo: Never mind. Janice, I gotta ask you an honest question. Why have you always shown this desire to want me to be dead?

Janice: Because you have never taken me seriously.

Aldo: I take you dead serious.

Janice: No. Why are you here tonight? You came here to talk to me about my marriage? You don't wanna talk to me. Even when you come to me about my marriage, even then you don't wanna talk to me. You just want me to do what you want. You have always been this way. It has always been this way. You want what you want. Lie down. Pull up your dress. Go to sleep. Love me. Don't love me. Marry me. Divorce me. TAKE ME BACK? I have no patience with this stupid arrogant man pride. You come here. When you want something from me. You make your faces and noises and you think I am what? A fool with a heart of soap?

Aldo: Listen, Janice. I don't understand you. I don't understand what you're talking about. Now I'm gonna make you understand why I don't understand you. When I was a little boy, you was always playing at murdering me and watching me be dead. Is that right or not?

Janice: Yes.

Aldo: Now, at that time, Janice, I had not started to do anything to you. We're talking very young here. At that time, no matter what happened later, no matter how I mighta screwed up tonight, at that time, I was perfectly willing to talk with you. I was not a man yet. I was a little boy.

Janice: You were always a man.

Aldo: No, I was not. I started out as a little little boy who didn't know a thing an meant no harm. And this little boy you were already stabbing with a rubber knife. So what I have to say to you Janice is this: You have always been violent and had dark thoughts, and you have always wanted to kill and maim men, and that is not the mens' fault. Do you understand? That is not the mens' fault. That is not my fault. When I was a little boy and we had nothin to do, I wanted to play house. I did not want to play dead. I did not want to lie down in a flowerbox and make believe I was dead so you could wear your party hat an be happy. But you know why I went ahead and played that game with you? I played it with you because I wanted to give you pleasure. That's right. Now you may call that weakness or being a stooge or a fool, and I don't care, cause I know exactly what that is. I was being a human being for you, Janice. On day one, I cared about you, an I showed it by being a human being with you.

Janice: You never cared about me.

Aldo: I cared about you, and I acted like I cared about you. And you, whether you think you were flirtin or what, you had this hatred or violence to me from day one, an you never let up. Not from that day to this. An we're talkin a long time. Our whole lives. Can you blame me, if after years a bein treated like a germ by you, that I stand back, an just deal with you when I have to, an try to get what I want an scram? I am not a fool. I am not a stooge. I am not gonna be affected by your mad attitude towards men into thinkin that I owe you somethin, or I wronged you, or I should be some other way causa your ancient pain. What was it, Janice? Comon, we both know what it hadda be. I didn't know the man, but it was your father, right? Or your grandfather. Or your uncle. Was it your father?

Janice: Yes.

Aldo: Well, I can sympathize, but it's not my fault, alright? What did he do to you?

Janice: Nothing.

Aldo: What did he do?

Janice: He didn't love me.

Aldo: I'm sorry. Honest ta God, I'm sorry. That's terrible. BUT GET OVER IT! I got troubles with my father, too. We never really had love either. He's dead now...

He thinks.

Janice: Mine too.

Aldo: So our fathers are dead. We can't go on tryin ta make our fathers love us or fightin our fathers or tryin ta kill our fathers. What's the point in killin a dead man cause he won't love you? A dead man don't need killin and a dead man can't love you at all. I know you're crazy an just me talkin ain't gonna make you sane. But comon! We're all crazy, that ain't no excuse. You been treatin me bad all my life and enough already. I been nuts, too. I'm tryin to be well, too. Let's drop this shitload, this weight a sorrow, these sandbags on our necks from a million years ago, and try to talk to each other about now. You can't kill me, Janice. You been tryin your whole life, an I just won't die. Even when you fire a gun at me, it explodes in your hand. Even if I die, I'll still be jumpin around inside your head. You know, this distance you are from me, this distance now, if we talk to each other, this could be the least distance there ever has been between us.

Janice: You seem very far away to me.

Aldo: There's somethin I've wanted to say to you for a long time, but I never did. I'm sorry your marriage broke up.

Janice: Thanks. I'm sorry I tried to shoot you.

Aldo: Forget it.

Janice: I think I'm losin my mind in this house.

Aldo: Maybe you should move?

Janice: No.

Aldo: I can feel this sadness between us. Almost like a rope.

Janice: Man, I don't know if I can dog this out.

Aldo: What d'you mean?

Janice: Nothin nothin nothin.

Aldo: Say it. What's the difference?

Janice: Do you suffer from being single?

Aldo: Sometimes. Yeah. It makes me feel like I'm dyin.

Janice: Go on! Get outta here! I don't need this! What for? Flowers! Sending me flowers, flowers! I threw them down. They hurt. Do you think they didn't feel like flames in my arms? God! I feel like I'm tied hand and foot. Why you bein nice and openin the door just for your own intention? Why did you hit on me? It's not me you want but somethin. What? What?

Aldo: I'm ashamed to say. I just wanted to neutralize you.
So you wouldn't take Huey back.

Janice: I see.

Aldo: I'm sorry.

Janice: I like the truth. And I recognize that as the truth. And it
don't matter anyway. I can't be different than the way I am. I am
my castle of thorns.

Aldo: Hey, come down here a minute.

Janice: No. If I get close to you, I'll hate you again.

Aldo: Listen, Janice. I've changed my mind about you. I'm not
just talkin to get you to do what I want. I want to be your friend.

Janice: Forget it.

Aldo: Why?

Janice: I got no attachment to connect.

Aldo: Look. Huey wants to get back with you.

Janice: No, he doesn't. He's just goin through a crazy time.

Aldo: Maybe.

Janice: I should never have married Huey.

Aldo: Why'd you do it?

Janice: I don't remember.

Aldo: Comon, don't gimme that.

Janice: Ain't that weird? I really don't remember. I remember
walkin up the aisle. I remember lookin over and seein him there
and thinkin that he looked like a waiter.

Aldo: Very romantic.

Janice: I remember goin on the honeymoon an bein in this bed
in the Catskills, and him taking me over and over again, and I
didn't know why he kept doin it. I remember him lookin at me,
an knowin he wasn't seein me. Cause if he really saw me, why
would he go on?

Aldo: You're a good-lookin woman.

Janice: That was the biggest trouble with the marriage. After a
while. It started to make me mad he wasn't seein me. So I started
to do things to make him see. Like you pinch somebody to wake
them up. I yelled at him. I gave him bad food to eat. I slapped his
face. Sometimes I locked him out of the bedroom. But still, he
wouldn't open his eyes. He wouldn't see me the way I really was.

It drove me crazy. You can't understand. So. I shot his dog. He loved his dog and I knew that and I killed the dog. Huey came home. He saw what I had done. He looked at me. And there it was. His eyes. He saw me. He saw me. It was a bad time, but I was relieved that at last this lie had been taken away. He looked at me like this for three days. It was a bad time, not like before what other people would've called happy, but a truthful time and I like the truth. But it didn't last. On the fourth day, he began to look at me in the old way again. That was the day I shot the gun at him. So I shot at him with the gun, but it blew up. He left me, though. That at least made him wake up enough to leave me.

Aldo: He's gonna be here soon.

Janice: You mean, tonight?

Aldo: He's coming to reconcile with you.

Janice: I don't wanna see him tonight.

Aldo: Well. He's comin.

Janice: Stop him. Tell him to come tomorrow.

Aldo: He's comin tonight. That's the story. Do you want him back?

Janice: No.

Aldo: Why not?

Janice: We never shoulda been together.

Aldo: I wouldn't know about that. I only saw things from the outside.

Janice: I only married him because he asked me.

Aldo: Why'd he ask you?

Janice: I don't know. I think he just said some things to me, and then he couldn't think of anything else to say, so he asked me to marry him.

Aldo: I don't know. Maybe I'm livin in a fool's paradise, but if there's nothin left to say, this don't strike me as the perfect moment to pop the question.

Janice: We were young.

Aldo: Yeah. It's amazing how much that covers. But if there was nothin, if there was never nothin between you that made sense, how could you a stayed together so long?

Janice: I didn't say there was nothin.

Huey has appeared at the gate.

Huey: I'm glad you said that.

Aldo: Huey, Huey.

Huey opens the gate. Aldo takes this in.

Huey: I tried the bell about a hundred times.

Aldo & Janice: It's broken.

Huey: Well, this is okay. It's a nice night. Hi, Janice.

Janice: Hello.

Huey: You and Aldo been talkin?

Janice: Yeah. We had a talk.

Aldo: *(Whispers.)* She did try to kill me, like I predicted, but everything's okay now.

Huey: *(Whispers.)* She did?

Janice: What are you whispering?

Huey: I was thanking Aldo and sending him home.

Aldo: You sure?

Huey: Yeah. It's like you said, in the end this is my show, right? Right?

Aldo: Right. I hadda whole plan a how this night was gonna go, but it's turnin out to be a different thing. Goodnight, Janice.

Janice: You can stay if you want.

Aldo: No, this is between you an Huey. I mean, ultimately. You gotta do what you think is right. I shouldn't be here. But I wanna say one thing to you, Janice, an I don't usually say this kinda thing, an I say it outta a place a goodness. You should see a therapist. And fa Chrissakes, let the dead bury the dead. *(Whispers.)* Huey, be careful. *(Aldo goes to the gate and tries the handle. It opens.)* This place is like a lotta things. It's a lot easier to get out than it was to get in.

Aldo is gone.

Huey: Well, here we are.

Janice: Yeah.

Huey: Remember this?

Opens music box.

Janice: No.

Huey: You gave me this. Our first Christmas.

Janice: I don't remember.

Huey: O.K. *(Closes music box.)* You look good.

Janice: You're dressed funny.

Huey: Yeah, what are these clothes? These are like a failed thing I did. To buck myself up. I got all these items about myself like these clothes. Ideas I had that never came to nothing, lyin in my head like balls a dust. A lotta ways I started to go that I never went cause I didn't have enough of a base. It's like you haveta have a certain amount a power worked up to go all the way down one road, and I have never gotten together that much power. I mean lately. I mean, since we got divorced. I've been feelin real bad since the divorce. Have you felt bad?

Janice: Yes.

Huey: I'm sorry. It's amazing to me how weak I am since the divorce.

Janice: You always were weak.

Huey: Was I? I don't even remember. How was I weak?

Janice: You let me abuse you.

Huey: You couldn't help yourself.

Janice: So what?

Huey: Maybe you're right. But my feelin about that is I loved you and so I put up with stuff.

Janice: You didn't love me.

Huey: Oh, now wait a minute. Now I'm on firm ground. Yes, I did too love you.

Janice: You were deluded.

Huey: I loved you.

Janice: You needed me. There's a difference.

Huey: I loved you. I didn't need the abuse, I swear to God. I didn't need your lousy meals, I didn't need your cold looks, I didn't need your screaming fits, I didn't need sleepin on the couch, I didn't need any of that on my mother's grave! I loved you and I felt for you, so I put up with that. And I want you back. I don't want all that nonsense back. I want you back.

Janice: What for? *(A long pause. Huey can't speak.)* What for?

Huey: I only wanna say the truth, and I can't think a nothin. I'm a little upset.

Janice: What do you want?

Huey: I want you back.

Janice: No.

Huey: I wanna get remarried, maybe have a baby.

Janice: You don't know what you're sayin.

Huey: I made mistakes in the way I treated you. I know that. We could get new furniture. Go on a vacation someplace warm. I could love you more than I did. Be nicer to you than I was. I could cook the meals. I gotta lotta love in me. I could love you even more than I did, Janice! I'm tellin you the truth. I could just turn it on like bright bright sunlight and it could keep you warm even when you're an old grandmother. You have got to believe me. You gotta listen to me an hear what I'm sayin to you now! All the time we spent together I tried to say this one thing to you a thousand different ways and no matter how I said it, you didn't understand. We broke up. But I don't think you ever really heard me. I'm offerin you my heart an my faith for life! I was, I am. I feel like even now you're not hearing me and you've just got to! Finally. Janice, I could love you!

Janice: No!

Huey: Yes!

Janice: I don't want it!

Huey: What?

Janice: I don't want your love.

Huey: You still don't believe me.

Janice: I believe you. But I don't want it.

Huey: What?

Janice: You've never understood me.

Huey: Then tell me!

Janice: You're so wrapped up in your ideas about how things should be, you've never really looked at me.

Huey: I have too!

Janice: Go home.

Huey: No. Shut up!

Janice: What?

Huey: You heard me. I have too really looked at you. How dare you! I reject that! I mean, really. You know what's the matter with you, Janice? You have never respected meekness as a virtue. And it is a virtue. I just said shut up to you, I don't even like to do that. That's not me. I've looked right at you. I've seen you for what you really are. And I've loved you. Like the dawn comes up and loves the earth, the whole earth. Now you may not like to hear that. You may have your own ideas about things. But I've got a point of view, too. You're not so smart that your life's like it is. You're alone and people don't like you. When a man comes to you because he does like you, you treat him like a stupid bum.

Janice: We have nothing to talk about.

Huey: I reject that! We do too have things to talk about Miss High and Mighty. You shot my dog!

Janice: I'm not sorry.

Huey: It was a rotten thing to do.

Janice: It was a warning.

Huey: You killed a stupid loveable animal. All he wanted was love. To be patted on the head. Taken for a walk. Sit next to you and do nothing. What did he know? When he looked up at you with those eyes, how, how could you hurt him?

Janice: I tried to kill you. Why ain't you mad about that?

Huey: That's a good question. I don't know. Cause I was flattered.

Janice: You took it as a compliment?

Huey: At least you made a fuss over me. I was pretty starved for anything by that time.

Janice: That's pathetic.

Huey: Yeah, it is. It was. It was pathetic. I was pathetic. But what you need to hear, baby, is that you were pathetic, too.

Janice: I know about me.

Huey: You don't know the first thing about it. Every time I've ever tried to tell you somethin about yourself, you snap shut like a clam. You are beautiful! Do you hear me? You are intelligent. Capisce? You are a classy sensitive sexy woman, and I loved you and I married you cause I was smart. NOT CAUSE I WAS STUPID! Get it?

Janice: No.

Huey: I did not marry a nasty bitch who hated me.

Janice: Oh yes you did!

Huey: Oh no I didn't. Come down here.

Janice: No.

Huey: Whatever things mighta become, however things mighta gone wrong or not worked out, please don't take away from me that I loved you, that I married you, that to look at you and to be with you was the pleasure of my life. If I have to go back to the beginning, right or wrong, and win you again, an marry you again, and love you deeply, deeply, all over again, to dig up what is stolen an mine and true, I am willing. I'm telling you to come down here.

Janice: If I come down there, you'll kiss me.

Huey: Maybe.

Janice: I don't want you to.

Huey: If you don't come down, I'll stand here forever. Till I'm dead. You come down here. Leave your knives and guns up there, and come down here to me.

Janice leaves the balcony, and disappears within. The climactic music from "Turandot" begins to play. Huey is planted into the ground, the axis on which the world turns. Janice enters the garden through the garden gate.

Janice: Huey. Why did you come here?

Huey: I don't know everything.

He kisses her. The music swells. They break apart and look at each other. He picks her up. The music! The music! The music! Blackout. The music continues and resolves.

SCENE 2

Pop's Soup House. Daytime. May, dressed in a fresh apron, is behind the counter reading National Geographic. Something like Frank Sinatra singing "The Summer Wind" opens the scene. May puts a tablecloth on the table. Enter Aldo in a white dress shirt open at the collar, blue jeans with a red web belt, white socks and black shoes. Over his shoulder he carries a sports jacket.

Aldo: Hi.

May: Hi.

Aldo: Where's Teresa?

May: Gone.

Aldo: Gone? Where's she gone?

May: Canada.

Aldo: What are you talkin about?

May: She had a bad night and she got up and went to Canada.

Aldo: She promised me she'd keep an open mind.

May: She has an open mind, and she took her open mind to Canada. She's got a cousin there she's gonna stay with.

Aldo: How long?

May: She didn't say.

Aldo: Did she leave any word?

May: You mean like a note or somethin?

Aldo: Yeah.

May: No.

Aldo: Astonishing. I feel like I jump through hoops a fire and for what? Nobody has any sense a place but me.

May: You think Teresa shoulda done somethin different?

Aldo: Yeah, I think she shoulda done somethin different! Don't she have any sense of timing? Don't she have any hunger of curiosity about how last night went?

May: How did it go?

Aldo: I don't know. That is, I know my part of it, but I had to leave before the end. Then what you're tellin me is Teresa left Huey.

May: Teresa didn't leave Huey. Huey left Teresa.

Aldo: That's it! Stick together! You women always stick together. There was a time in our society when the woman stuck by the man till the ship went down and there was no more bubbles.

May: But this man wouldn't let her stick.

Aldo: She should've ignored him.

May: He made her listen. She begged him not to go. But he went.

Aldo: And he explained to her that he was in mental trouble and had to go, and that was her signal to hold tight.

May: Hold tight for what? Huey? He left.

Aldo: For today! For the clear light a day. For the conclusion to a drama that Huey needed to act out for his sanity. She shoulda held out for the punchline, and then made her move, good or bad.

May: You make Janice yours last night?

Aldo: No. Things went another way.

May: Uh-huh.

Aldo: Janice is this certain kinda woman who is very difficult to predict in advance.

May: But Teresa you knew, huh?

Aldo: I thought she was more reliable. Canada. Why you wearin the apron?

May: I'm fillin in. Not the worst job I've ever had. All the mine-strone I can eat.

Aldo: I should eat minestrone.

May: You wanna bowl?

Aldo: No. I should eat minestrone and work in a garden. I should wear a straw hat, like my grandfather, and never speak another English word again.

May: What are you talkin about?

Aldo: I am sick from being a man.

May: You seem upset.

Aldo: I seem upset? I am upset. I talked to this woman last night. What a case! Could I help her? Maybe. I couldn't tell. I don't think so. I tried to strike up a little romance with her, and her reaction was she tried to kill me.

May: She did not.

Aldo: You see, this is what you do not realize, May. *(During next, Aldo vaguely indicates the audience.)* There are women out there, wild troubled women, and they are trying to kill or dam-age the shit out of men. Men, me, men. And then when someone like you talks with the men, you think these men are overreacting because they are immature an can't handle love problems! I'm tellin you it's the Wild West out there!

May: I know.

Aldo: You gotta be freakin Wild Bill Hickok to function out there!

May: I know.

Aldo: I know. You know everything and I'm talkin to myself.

May: I didn't say that.

Aldo: Jesus. You know, I really am havin a nervous attack.

May: What's the matter?

Aldo: I wonder if I'm ever gonna get married?

May: Aw, sure you are.

Aldo: I don't know. The state of the women in this country! They're like bombs.

May: The men are like bombs, too.

Aldo: You're right. The men are like bombs and the women are like bombs and everybody's negotiating like it was the atomic talks. Little kids look like lawyers to me. I feel like we're all doin some kinda politics here, an love ain't politics an shouldn't be. Politics is make-believe an lies and love shouldn't be. I'm traumatized! These women have got me traumatized! There's no honor between the men an women anymore, no trust of the words they say, no courage and strength of vows. The vows! You make a pact with a woman these days, you're promising yourself into a country without a constitution!

May: Aldo, you are talkin too much.

Aldo: Maybe you're right.

May: You're shook up by gettin involved of this problem with Huey.

Aldo: That's true.

May: This whole thing has reminded you that you wanna get married and that you're afraid to get married.

Aldo: How did you know that?

May: I'm a witch.

Aldo: I am afraid. Can you blame me?

May: No.

Aldo: These women are crazy. They've gone crazy.

May: Well, the men have gone crazy, too.

Aldo: I ain't gone crazy. I'm nervous, but I haven't gone crazy.

May: Sit down a minute, let me talk with you. It's time to talk.

Aldo: My hands are sweating.

May: You poor thing. You mean well.

Aldo: I do.

May: Listen. Women ain't tryin to kill you.

Aldo: Janice took a gun an pointed at me and pulled the trigger. It's only stupid luck I wasn't killed.

May: Then Janice tried to kill you. It wasn't the race of women that tried to kill you.

Aldo: That's what it felt like.

May: I'm not tryin to kill you.

Aldo: No.

May: Does your mother wanna kill you?

Aldo: No. My mother loves me. My mother happens to be the greatest woman in the world. *(To the audience.)* And I'm not just sayin that cause you're here.

May: So I don't wanna kill you and your mamma don't wanna kill you, and Teresa didn't wanna kill you, either.

Aldo: No.

May: It was Janice who wanted to kill you. Do you wanna marry Janice?

Aldo: WHAT?

May: I'm just askin.

Aldo: No!

May: Then you don't have to be afraid that that woman who hates you and wants to kill you will be your wife.

Aldo: It could happen. It could be somebody like her I don't recognize. Huey made the mistake. I could too.

May: But Huey got married. You held out. There ain't no reason under the sun why you should marry such a woman.

Aldo: Oedipus didn't mean to marry his mother, but he did.

May: That's true. But Oedipus really did have exceptionally bad luck.

Aldo: What's all this trouble, trouble, trouble.

May: What d'you mean?

Aldo: Life. Don't it seem just unnecessarily dangerous? Why can't I just like get married, play with the kids, suck on my teeth and look out the window?

May: Because marriage is trouble. But trouble ain't the worst thing. I married the man I loved and went through hell for it. And when things got better, he almost immediately died. Now I'm alone. What d'you make a that? A mistake, a tragedy? No! It was the most excitement! I can feel my heart right behind my eyes when I say it! For the best in this life you've gotta pay Big Dollars! What are you afraid of anyway, Aldo? You're gonna get old and things are gonna go wrong and right and wrong, and then you're gonna keel over and die. Anybody you really want in the meanwhile is gonna be expensive in some way. There ain't no bargains in people. You get what you pay for and the currency is Trouble. You ain't no bargain. Any woman ends up with you's gotta man who's gonna compare her to his mother. And that's always a bitch.

Aldo: But don't you believe people just are a certain way?

May: Yes, and you do your best to choose somebody who ain't gonna bring you to a dead end. But what I'm sayin is wrong and not my advice. My advice is give up your fear of women as a race. If some women has done bad to you, see it is them that did it. Write their names down in a book if you want. Glue their pictures next to their names, and cross X's on their faces, and don't mistake them for all the other girls. But even then I don't think that's my advice. I think you're gonna have to forgive those specific women and throw away your book of fear. You're gonna haveta open your heart an leave it open. Like it's your apartment and you just don't lock the door no matter how many times you get robbed. You're gonna haveta open your heart and forget your fear, and then what will happen is you'll fall in love. And marry. And your mama will become your second best girl. And it will become whatever it will become because of the trouble you take between you. But this minute, you are upset because you are in a situation. You wanna get married, but you are not ready to get married.

Aldo: I can't find the right girl.

May: The right girl? There ain't no right girl! Or every fifth girl is the right girl. That ain't the issue. It's you. You ain't ready to get married cause you ain't ready to fall in love.

Aldo: So what do I do?

May: You don't haveta do nothing. The clock'ill take care of it. Time. But stop this scaredness of women. It's silly. You can hold your own.

Aldo: I'll try.

> *Huey enters in an old blue buttondown dress shirt and black jeans. He looks more relaxed.*

May: There he is.

Aldo: Huey, how you doin?

Huey: Pretty good. Can I get a glass of water?

May: Sure. *(She gives him the water. He drops two Alka-Seltzers in it.)* Stomach botherin you?

Huey: No. *(Offers glass to Aldo.)* Here, drink this. You look terrible.

Aldo: Thanks. *(Drinks.)* So, what happened? Did you reconcile with Janice?

Huey: Yeah.

Aldo: You did?

Huey: Yeah.

May: You an Janice gettin remarried?

Huey: No, no. We just, you know, made peace.

Aldo: I thought you wanted her back?

Huey: I got her back. Kind of. Somethin of her. An me.

May: What'd you get?

Huey: I guess it was … this idea … of what was. Last night, she gave me back … what was. I feel strong again.

May: Good.

Huey: Thanks for helping me out, Aldo.

Aldo: That's okay. It was very interesting.

Huey: I do love you, you know.

Aldo: Don't lie to me.

Huey: I'm not lying. Where's Teresa?

May: She's gone.

Huey: Where'd she go?

May: Canada.

Huey: How long?

May: Indefinitely.

Huey: She wouldn't wait, huh?

May: Nope.

Aldo: I think she shoulda waited.

Huey: I don't know. She took a lotta shit from me. Well, I'm gonna go home.

Aldo: Ain't you upset Teresa's gone?

Huey: She's not gone. She just went somewhere.

Aldo: But ain't you upset?

Huey: No. I guess it ain't hit me yet.

May: It will.

Aldo: I meant, I mean, I thought, since Janice is out, it might be Teresa.

Huey: It is Teresa. And I'll get her, wherever she is, whatever she's doin. I'll get her and I'll make her mine.

May: Maybe you will.

Huey: I will. You see, I got back my strength as a man to take. See you later.

Aldo: You goin to Canada?

Huey: Not yet. I'm gonna go home an be quiet for a few days. I've been in a nervous state for a long time. I deserve a rest.

Exit Huey. The concertina music begins to play.

Aldo: Well, what do you make a that? He seemed so relaxed.

May: Yeah.

Aldo: Do you think he's right? Do you think he'll get Teresa back?

May: I don't know.

Aldo: Maybe he's still crazy and he's gonna change his mind again?

May: I don't know.

Aldo: He seemed better.

May: Yes, he did. He seemed like a man who'd gotten his life back in the proper order.

The lights fade on May. The music ends. Aldo comes down to talk to the audience. He puts on his jacket.

Aldo: So Huey went home. Come on out, Huey. (*Huey enters from the wings. He has the music box. He sits at the table.*) He's sitting there now. I guess like collecting himself. When he's through collecting himself, he's gonna go and claim Teresa. Now whether or not Teresa is gonna go along with being claimed like a package from the post office, I don't know. Stranger things have happened, but... That'll probably be another whole big thing, and not the story I set out to tell. The story I set out to tell was about Huey Maximilian Bonfigliano an me, and what happened to him. And I've told it. And I'll probably tell it again and again, other nights, other places. Till it's done with being told. Till I'm done with tellin it. Which may never be. But I also said I told it to you with the purpose of teaching you something, so here's the lesson. In the end, you are dead. In the middle, you can love. In the beginning you are taken care of. When a man goes to reconcile with his ex-wife, he goes to die because he is failing to live. He goes to love because she is where he left the ability. He goes to be taken care of because he is sick from being, a little too soon, a man. If he succeeds in his quest, he comes away able to love again. And this is the lesson I have to teach: The greatest, the only success, is to be able to love. So there he is. Sitting at the same table he was at the start of the story. Only now, at least I would like to believe, no, I need to believe, he is reconciled with himself. So. I got this girl waitin for me at P.J. Clarkes. She and I have a certain history. Very stupid, fulla trouble. I'm gonna try not to worry that she might kill me, but we'll see. We will see. Always the Prince, never the King. Right, Ma? So far. *(Pulls a carnation out of his pocket and sticks it in his buttonhole. He whispers to an audience member.)* Wish me luck.

> *Then he turns and casts a spell on Huey. Huey's light comes up brighter. Huey opens the music box. Aldo slips away.*

Huey: Janice Janice Janice.

> *Janice comes D. into her own circle of light. She has gentle mischief in her eye, and a smile.*

Janice: Huey.

> *Huey closes the box. Janice turns away as her light fades.*

Huey: God, I'm going to miss you.

> *He makes the slightest gesture of farewell. The opening of "Come Back To Sorrento" * plays. Huey buries his face in his hands. The lights go down and the music goes out.*

THE END

*See Special Note on copyright page

The
Big
Funk

A Casual Play

This play is dedicated to
The Fool

THE BIG FUNK received its original New York production by New York Shakespeare Festival, Joseph Papp, Producer. It was directed by John Patrick Shanley; the set desiger was Nancy Winters; the costume designer was Lindsay W. Davis; the lighting designer was Arden Fingerhut; the sound designer was John Gromada; the production stage manager was Pamela Singer.

The cast, in order of appearance, was as follows:

Jill	Jeanne Tripplehorn
Fifi	Jayne Haynes
Omar	Graham Beckel
Austin	Jake Weber
Gregory	Skipp Sudduth

Author's Note

A man in our society is not left alone. Not in the cities. Not in the woods. We must have commerce with our fellows, and that commerce is difficult and uneasy. I do not understand how to live in this society. I don't get it. Each person has an enormous effect. Call it environmental impact if you like. Where my foot falls, I leave a mark, whether I want to or not. We are linked together, each to each. You can't breathe without taking a breath from somebody else. You can't smile without changing the landscape. And so I ask the question: Why is theatre so ineffectual, unnew, not exciting, fussy, not connected to the thrilling recognition possible in dreams?

It's a question of spirit. My ungainly spirit thrashes around inside me, making me feel lumpy and sick. My spirit is this moment dissatisfied with the outward life I inhabit. Why does my outward life not reflect the enormity of the miracle of existence? Why are my eyes blinded with always *new* scales, my ears stopped with thick chunks of *fresh* wax, why are my fingers calloused *again*? I don't ask these questions lightly. I beat on the stone door of my tomb. I want out! Some days I wake up in a tomb, some days on a grassy mound by a river. Today I woke up in a tomb. Why does my spirit sometimes retreat into a deathly closet? Perhaps it is not my spirit leading the way at such times, but my body, longing to lie down in marble gloom and rot away.

Theatre is a safe place to do the unsafe things that need to be done. When it's not a safe place, it's abusive to actors and audiences alike. When its safety is used to protect cowards masquerading as heroes, it's a boring travesty. An actor who is truly heroic reveals the divine that passes through him, that aspect of himself that he does not own and cannot control. The control and the artistry of the heroic actor is *in service* to his soul.

We live in an era of enormous cynicism. Do not be fooled.

Don't act for money. You'll start to feel dead and bitter.

Don't act for glory. You'll start to feel dead, fat and fearful.

We live in an era of enormous cynicism. Do not be fooled.

You can't avoid all the pitfalls. There are lies you must tell. But experience the lie. See it as something dead and unconnected you clutch. And let it go.

Act from the depth of your feeling imagination. Act for celebration, for search, for grieving, for worship, to express that desolate sensation of wandering through the howling wilderness. Don't worry about Art. Do these things and it will be Art.

ACT I

There's a lightweight blue curtain going across the Upstage area. Perhaps there are a couple of white Ionic columns around, a few marble steps.

As the house lights go out, some bright and hopeful song begins to play, something like Walk Right In* *or* You Were On My Mind*.

Darkness. Jill comes in in the dark holding a candle. Or the lights come up full and Jill enters and signals for the music to stop.

Jill 's dressed like a goddess. She's a very attractive woman.

Jill: Hello. My name is Jill. I am speaking to you directly from my subconscious mind. I do this to save time. I am a destructive person. I am not the hero of this play. I am not the hero of any play I could be in. Except a play I wrote. And even in my own play I wouldn't be the hero. It would be a tragedy of course. But it wouldn't be my tragedy. It would be the tragedy of existence. And it would be a bad play. Because it would be senseless. Because whatever had gone wrong with the world would've gone wrong long before the play even started. It would just be a whole bunch of victims. And I would just be one of them. It would just be a mess of senseless pain. I wouldn't want to see this play, much less be in it. In fact, if I wrote this play I'm describing, and it was performed, and afterwards someone asked: Who wrote this play? I would just look around to see who raised her hand. This is because I am a coward. Which is the root of my problem. So I am not in a play of my own. And I am not the hero. And this is not a tragedy. And this is where I would rather be. In a play where I will fail to prevail. I want to be stopped. I cannot stop myself. I am not easy to stop. And I can do a lot of harm before I'm knocked down. I do have a noose around my own neck. But if I pull up on the rope, I will not die. I am condemned. I carry around my means of execution. But it's not for me to do the job. This is what makes people like me a real bummer. Some-

*See Special Note on copyright page

body, for the sake of everybody, has to squash me and blot up my remains. God put me on earth. I am a villain. I have a job to do. I am going to do it.

Jill exits. We hear a single sweep of harp strings as Fifi enters, hiding behind a small umbrella. She reveals herself. She's dressed in the costume of a circus performer.

Fifi: My name is Fifi. My mother named me this because she was hostile to me. She felt I was a rival for my father's affections and so she tried to label me as someone not to be taken seriously by naming me Fifi. I like the name. My father was weak but crafty. He pitted my mother and me against one another so we wouldn't join forces and destroy him. His plan worked. My mother and I went to war, and my father worked in the garden. But the great pity is that his calculations did not include the possibility of love. As a result, my father has withered away. My mother continued to attempt to war with me until I threw her out of my life. This war was all she had left. She drinks now. My father is with her.

These things I am telling you. When I faced them, my world fell apart. I went into the desert tearing my hair and hurting myself with stones. A cry came out of me. And as it came out, the sky cracked open, the earth burst into flames, and I saw beauty. Again. When the spirit is roused, and you see it come out of you, that's a humbling thing. You realize that you've been arrogant and there is a God. Yes, folks, in case you were still wondering, There is a God. And your life is unknown country you go through. And everything has meaning. And every hair on your head *is* counted.

What I'm saying to you, in essence, by way of introduction, is that my name is Fifi. I am an adult. Which means my life is a war, a struggle, a journey towards beauty, toward a huge expanse in which community is possible. But there are bad people in the world. My parents were bad people. A child who does not grow into an adult does grow into something. A big ugly kid. There's a lotta big ugly kids in the world. These kids find you from time to time, and try to fuck up your life. Basically, they try to kill you. But they'd much rather die themselves. That's my opinion. But they won't kill themselves a lot of the time. They want you to do it. This makes me sick. I'm not going to kill these people just to give them pleasure. So a big part of the life of an adult, as I see it, is to keep these big ugly kids out of your life. Because if they get in, if they manage to wiggle their way into your house, you may just have to kill them. (*She thinks she's finished, but then remembers something.*) Oh, one other thing. Whatever house you were raised in, even if you successfully left it, leaves a certain smell on you. I have the smell of my rivalrous mom and my weak sneaky pop on me. People who were raised in a similar house, but stayed in that house if you know what I mean, they can smell this smell on me. These people are like ghosts and they try to grab you but their hands pass through you. Don't be afraid of these ghosts. They can't harm you. But never, never do what they want you to do.

I am not speaking from my subconscious. I know these things like I know hot from cold. Omar?

> *Omar enters through the audience. He's wearing a metal helmet which sports a few dents, a white circus performer blouse, a sash cinching his waist, and pantaloons of a dark color. He's carrying a well-seasoned briefcase. Fifi gives up her spot to Omar and retires up stage right. Omar addresses the audience.*

Omar: My name is Omar. I have been through more shit than I can possibly explain so lemme just say this. I have a family, a wife and two kids. I love my family. I am a man. I see the role of a family man to be a guard dog. I circle my family like a ring of fire. If anybody bothers my wife, I'll kill them. If anybody's mean to my kids, I'll kill them. The whole thing of having children brings every nut out of the woodwork. I bash these yahoos and throw them outside my family circle. Also, every person has a hell in them that contains demons. I have demons. My wife has demons. When you have kids, these demons jump outta your mouth and attack the kids. I have to beat the shit outta these demons, chuck them out into the sunlight where they shrink and scream into ugly little trinkets I call quirks. Quirks I can live with.

I am a real father. When I first saw my kids, I got terrified because the replacements had arrived for me and my wife. My wife is Fifi. The heroic thing that a father has to do is encourage his son to kill him and replace him. This is what Hamlet's really about in my opinion. It's a tragedy because the son fails to kill and replace the physical father. Which is what the spiritual side of the father, the ghost wants the son to do. All you can do is hope for anybody. Now when I was a kid, I had these parents and they were alright, except for one or two things. One of the things was they didn't praise me. So I got a hole there. As a result, I'm a sucker for praise.

Fifi pipes up from where she's lurking.

Fifi: You've got to watch that.

Omar: I know. But you can't watch it for me, Fifi. If you don't praise me because I'm a sucker for praise, then we're just recreating the bum deal I got as a boy in this regard. You've got to be free to praise me even though I'm a sucker for praise.

Fifi: If I feel like it.

Omar: If you feel like it. And if you're not just doing it to push my button which I've obviously got there to push.

Fifi: I wouldn't do that.

Omar: I know you wouldn't. Because you love me. *(Fifi, abashed, doesn't answer.)* You don't have to say it.

Fifi: It's hard for me.

Omar: That's 'cause your parents abused the word.

Fifi: That's right.

Omar: But that brings up the subject of love. A word so often abused or misunderstood that I feel I should right now define it for you. But I'm not going to. I mean I could go on and on, but love is simple. Love is profound. And talking about love is a lot of bullshit. *(Omar pushes up his sleeves and goes down into the audience.)* Now lemme tell you about me. If you think I am simple, I am not. If you think I'm complex, I am not. If you think I'm tough, you've got me wrong. If you think I'm soft, you're liable to make a big mistake. I confuse some people. But the only people I truly confuse are those who have a simplistic view of human beings. Each of us, at base, contains a mystery. I am mysterious. I look at myself and I am mystified. *(He sits down on the edge of the stage, next to his briefcase.)* Now I'm going to tell you a story. This story takes place in the Past. I should tell you what I do for a living. I throw knives at a one inch black dot thirty-five feet away. *(He opens the briefcase. It contains six gleaming throwing knives.)*

There are tens of thousands of people who make their living this way, but I've gained a reputation for doing it very well. That is, I hit the dot a lot. *(He takes out one of the knives.)* And when I don't hit the dot, I remain a gentleman. I don't point the finger at anyone else. I just missed the dot. It's going to happen. *(He stands up with knife in hand.)* One day, before Fifi and I had kids, I was in my loft, practicing. Hmmm. Yes. Yes. I see it. I see it. Yes.

Omar aims with eyes closed. He is about to throw the knife.

Austin: Wait a minute!

Omar abandons the throw.

Omar: Hiyaya!

Austin enters from the wing.

Austin: One minute, please!

Omar: Please don't ever do that again.

Austin: What?

Omar: Never mind.

Austin: Have you read the papers today?

Omar: I don't read the papers anymore.

Austin: A lot of interesting stuff!

Omar: I don't read the papers anymore.

Austin: *(Brandishing the paper like a sword.)* Here comes the millennium! Hi. My name's Austin. I believe in live and let live. I swear to God nobody believes in this but me. I'm in my house. I'm doing what I do when I'm not doing what I do. I'm an actor.

Fifi: A promising actor.

Austin: Thank you. And people come around, call, people try to get me to go here, do this, believe that, eat this, change my hair, change my clothes, my manners, my posture. I'll tell you this: It don't make me feel loved. And this is a battle. Cause people wanna tell you what to do. And they're looking for an angle, any angle, a way in. If they find out maybe you're a little shaky about your nose, then they'll talk about your nose all the time. How's your nose today? How do you feel about your nose? You must be upset about your nose. Until you tell 'em to get outta your business. Or you get a nose job. And if you do that, then they've got you. This one part a you's not you anymore. It's somebody else's idea of how you should be. You're on your way to becoming somebody you don't know. A doll in dress-up clothes.

Omar: I hate this fucking society.

Austin: I hate this fucking society! I wanna burn it down!

Fifi: Now, now, now.

Austin: But what? No, I don't. But sometimes I feel like it's me or them, me or society. I believe in live and let live. But society don't. You think we live in a time where everybody does what they want?

Omar: Yeah.

Austin: You're wrong!

Omar: You know what you are?

Austin: I am not an anarchist fuck you truly. I am a constructive person.

Omar: You are a young person.

Fifi: Hear him out.

Austin: I know. You can explain why I'm wrong. Why the streets have to be dirty and the politicians have to be corrupt and drugs and starvation, and why there's cruelty right there in your face and you can't do anything about it. But you're wrong!

Omar: You're wrong.

Fifi: Such contention.

Austin: Listen to me! I'm not wrong! We could make things better than they are. Living your life is supposed to make you weary. That's what death is for. Rest! You can't be lazy. You need to call up your guts. Cause it's just cowardice to say, Oh, that's the way things are. You can't do nothing about that. I'm telling you, Brothers and Sisters, we could be heroes!

Omar: Austin?

Austin: Yeah, Omar? *(To the audience.)* We're friends.

Omar: Come up here. *(Austin hops up on stage.)* I was just starting to tell a story and you made this whole big speech.

Austin: I'm sorry, Omar. But if I let you go ahead and start the story right there, the feeling would've been that you are the hero of this story. And I don't think you are.

Omar: Oh yeah? Well, who is the hero of this story?

Austin: I think I am.

Omar: You've got a lot to learn, Austin. But about storytelling you're pretty smart. You're right. If you hadn't interrupted right about when you did, you wouldn't have had a chance of being the hero of this play. And now you do. You have a shot.

Austin: Well, good. That's all I ask.

Omar: Now get back there and lemme tell this first bit.

Austin: Okay.

Omar: Anyway, I was in my loft …

Austin goes off into the wing from which he emerged, but then he immediately comes back.

Austin: Oh, just one other thing. When I was a kid, my mother cried a lot and had a lot of headaches, and I would try to cheer her up.

Omar: That's important?

Austin: I think so.

Austin leaves again. Omar resumes his storytelling. He produces his knife again.

Omar: Anyway, I was in my loft, with Fifi, before we had the kids, and I was practicing my knife throwing. Yes. Yes. I see it. I see it. (*He throws the knife, and then looks unhappy with the result.*) Yes! No. Hmmm.

Fifi: Not hitting the dot, Omar?

Omar: No.

Fifi: Well, you will.

Omar: No, once I start missing like this, I gotta stop.

Fifi: What's the matter?

Omar: I'm feeling a little jammed up. I think I'm gonna go out for a while. I think …

Enter Jill in a brightly colored vinyl dress. She is carrying 2 coffee mugs.

Jill: Wait a minute!

Omar: What do you want?

Jill: The next part really belongs to me, and if you tell it, I'm gonna look different than I should.

Fifi: She's right.

Omar: Well, at least let me say my exit line.

Jill: Sure.

Omar: (*To Fifi.*) I think I'll see if Austin wants to get a beer.

Omar and Fifi start to exit. Jill calls after them.

Jill: But bring me two chairs before you go.

Omar and Fifi reemerge with a chair each. They are surly.

Omar: We don't work for you, you know.

Jill: I know.

Fifi: I'm gonna need these chairs back.

Jill: You'll get them back. Thank you. *(Omar and Fifi exit.)* Married people. They gang up on you. That's like a definition. Anyway, I went to this party. I was seeing somebody but I went alone. I guess I was looking for a change. And I met this guy. I mean I saw him and I found out who he was, and I made it my business to stand in his face till he took the initiative. His name was Gregory. We talked. And we agreed to have coffee. This is Gregory. *(Enter Gregory, a seeming genial guy in a double-breasted suit. He's carrying a wrinkled, brown paper bag. He's English, very Public School. He's whistling a song like* It's A Long Way To Tipperary.**)* And this is coffee.

They sit. They sip the coffee.

Jill & Gregory: Ahhhh.

Gregory: So?

Jill: Good coffee.

Gregory: It's a little bitter.

Jill: I'd like to get to know you.

Gregory: I'd like to get to know you, too.

Jill: I have such a feeling about you.

Gregory: Do you?

Jill: I think you're really great.

Gregory: You think I'm great, huh?

Jill: Yeah, I really do.

Gregory: I hate myself. I'm worthless. My father was incredible. My father was this guy, unbelievably handsome, smart. He made a million dollars when he was twenty-two years old. You know how old I am?

Jill: How old?

Gregory: *(He's going to tell her, but decides against it.)* My mother

---

*See Special Note on copyright page

hounded my father to death. She was always on him for money.

Jill: But I thought he had a lot of money?

Gregory: He lost it! He lost it all. And then he started drinking. And looking at me. He looked at me like this. (*Makes a horrible face and a weird noise.*) She was behind it. If it wasn't for her, me and Daddy would've had love.

Jill: Your mother?

Gregory: She couldn't give him enough room! He was fighting for his life and she would be droning on about the BATHROOM or the SITTING ROOM or the KITCHEN!

Jill: What about them? (*He thinks about telling her, but decides she's out to get him, which makes him look at her with that horrible face.*) Greg?

Gregory: I would prefer to be called Gregory.

Jill: Alright. Gregory.

Gregory: Same as my father.

Jill: Oh. Uh-huh.

Gregory: My mother used to call me Greg, too.

Jill: Well, I guess having two in the house named Gregory was confusing.

Gregory: (*Laughs bitterly.*) Oh, it was confusing alright! It was very confusing. IT WAS A FUCKING NIGHTMARE! It was a nightmare, I was an ostrich, my mother wished a wish too fat to fit. There was a Grunt. Grunting. My father screamed and died. Then there was only one Gregory. The little he with his head pulled up like a potato to see with his potato eyes: my father dead, my mother big as a Clydesdale. You know the two halves of the brain are connected by something it's just like a rubber band. Snap that and you know what happens?

Jill: No. And I don't think I wanna know.

Gregory: That's probably very healthy of you, Jill. You know, your eyes really have a sparkle.

Jill: I don't know what it is. You have an effect on me that's really unusual.

Gregory: What is it?

Jill: Well, this is going to sound ... I feel like I've known you all my life.

Gregory: You do?

Jill: Yes.

Gregory: I've had that feeling sometimes. About people.

Jill: You have?

Gregory: Yes.

Jill: Like you've known them all your life?

Gregory: Yes. I don't have it now, but I know what you're talking about.

Jill: *(Disappointed.)* Oh.

Gregory: Oh. Hey. I was only joking with you.

Jill: What do you mean?

Gregory: I *am* having that feeling now.

Jill: You are?

Gregory: Yes.

Jill: Like you've known me all your life?

Gregory: Yes.

Jill: Alright then, who am I?

Gregory: You sure you want to know?

Jill: Yeah.

> *He concentrates on her, looking into her soul. He has a certain Rasputin quality.*

Gregory: You've always been apart. Lonely. In pain. You've tried very hard to be good. To do the right thing. To please everybody. But you've always failed. You've always done the wrong thing. You've been bad no matter how you struggled against it. So then finally, a lot of the time, you've given up and just said the hell with it, I'm going to be bad. A Two Face. A Liar. A Whore. In short, what your mother always predicted you would become. And here's the weird touch. Being really bad made you feel skinny! When you were trying to be good, you felt fat and puffy. But when you were bad, you felt skinny like you could wear the shortest skirt and get away with it. You cry all the time. All night sometimes. You cry with men but you really hold back. But with women! With women you cry fat fat tears. You're angry with women. The sight of them causes you anguish. But you're angry with men, too. Your life is a power struggle and you're losing. You feel a panic lately creeping up on you. You look in the mirror and it frightens you. There's a crazy look in your eye. Like you might really be crazy. Not wired and nervous and bloodshot as usual, but a real screaming Mimi. You have a sister. You got all the looks. Or so you always thought. But lately you've started to wonder, Maybe nobody got the looks! You don't even want to talk about your father. You bring him up, but you've gotta drop it before the animal in your head starts to murder your civilized self. You're small time. You know it in your heart. Even if you found somebody great and they wanted you, you'd lose them somehow. You got your whole life laid out. You know the whole thing. If something good happens, you'll destroy it. There's a noose around your neck. I can see it.

Jill: SHUT UP. You're a real monster.

Gregory: Talking to yourself again, Jill ? (*He begins whistling his tune. He takes out a quart jar of something from the bag, and puts it on the table.*) Do you know what this is?

Jill: No.

Gregory: Yes, you do.

Jill: No, I don't.

Gregory: I think you do. It's a family size jar of Vaseline petroleum jelly.

   Pause.

Jill: What do you mean?

Gregory: What do you mean what do I mean? I simply said it's a family size jar of Vaseline petroleum jelly.

Jill: Why did you put it on the table?

Gregory: I think we understand each other.

Jill: I don't know what you're talking about.

Gregory: I think we understand each other, Jill. (Pause.) I think you look a little … dull.

Jill: You're calling me dull?

Gregory: Yes. (*He starts to unscrew the jar.*) I think you want to get a little shiny.

Jill: No.

Gregory: I think you want to get a little greasy.

   He unscrews the jar. He sticks two fingers in it. He looks at her intently all the while. He sinks his whole hand into the jar. The jelly oozes up over the top.

Jill: No.

   He pulls his hand out of the jar. It's covered with jelly. Slowly, he reaches out and touches her face. He takes his hand away and inspects the result.

Gregory: See?

Jill: Don't.

Gregory: Stop me. *(She does nothing. Now he strokes her hair, greasing it with jelly. He gets more out of the jar.)* Stop me.

Jill: It's sick. *(Gregory whistles a little more of his tune as he covers her face and hair with grease.)* Why don't you just talk to me?

Gregory: No. This is what you want.

Enter Omar, disgusted.

Omar: Oh my God, what are you doing out here?

Jill: This is my scene!

Omar: It's giving me the creeps!

Jill: This is my life! You can't understand my story unless you feel my experience!

Omar: I think you've done enough. I think we've gotten the idea and you can stop now.

Gregory: We're not finished.

Omar: Well, can you finish offstage?

Jill and Gregory exchange a look of inquiry and assent. They gather up their stuff.

Jill: Alright.

The table and chairs remain.

Omar: So anyway, I was feeling a little jammed up, so I phoned Austin, and we met for a beer. *(Austin comes out with two mugs of beer. He and Omar sing a bit of something like* Walk Right In* *or* You Were On My Mind*, *and then drift into the scene.)* Fuck you.

Austin: Couldn't put it better myself.

Omar: What's new with you, citizen?

Austin: Out of work. What's new with you?

Omar: Missing the dot. This is a dangerous moment in a man's life.

Austin: How so?

Omar: These moments where there's no work. There's a slight feeling of dissatisfaction. This is the time when men look for trouble.

*See Special Note on copyright page

Austin: I'm not looking for trouble. I just want a job.

Omar: There are these dull spots along the road. No obvious karma. No obvious power sources. You're becalmed.

Austin: You're becalmed. I'm just unemployed.

Omar: Alright then, I'm becalmed.

Austin: So why don't you do something?

Omar: The point isn't to do something. The point always is that you are doing something and you've gotta notice what it is. Austin!

Austin: What?

Omar: I just realized why I asked you to have a beer with me!

Austin: Why?

Omar: I'm worried about you!

Austin: When did this happen?

Omar: I'm sitting here. I'm noticing how I'm feeling!

Austin: Good for you! Would you like to be alone?

Omar: You're about to go through a big one. A life crisis.

Austin: I think you're goin through one right now.

Omar: You know why we're friends?

Austin: Because we like each other?

Omar: Fuck you, I don't know what that means. We're friends cause we're similar except I've been through shit you're about to go through.

Austin: You mean you think you know something about my life?

Omar: That's why I can't hit the dot!

Austin: Are you bein obscure or am I dim?

Omar: I'm supposed to check in with you! I'm supposed to say: Watch out!

Austin: Watch out for what?

Omar: I don't know.

Austin: Even Agamemnon gotta more detailed warning than this. Watch out for what?

Omar: I don't know. I may never know. Austin, I'm hooked into you!

Austin: I think you're fucking crazy.

Omar: Go ahead and be glib, you pinhead fuck! I hope you choke!

Austin: What do you want me to say!

Omar: You're right! What could you say? We got no language to talk about this shit in our society!

Austin: I'm with you there. I hate this fuckin society!

Omar: I do too! I do too! I despise this fucking society! What do you hate about it?

Austin: Everything!

Omar: Comon, focus! What do you hate about this society?

Austin: It's unmasculine *and* unfeminine.

Omar: Yes! And that's why we're godless right now!

Austin: Yes! Exactly! How'd you get to that?

Omar: God's gotta have a big dick *or* big tits, right? Something!

Austin: That's true.

Omar: You know what I hate about this society?

Austin: What?

Omar: It's just so square!

Austin: You think so?

Omar: It's unbelievably square!

Austin: I guess that's true.

Omar: We haven't got the belief, the chops to talk about nothin. This psychobabble of the psychorabble. Parenting and bonding and safe sex? This is the squarest time in history.

Austin: You're right.

Omar: I listen to these morons talk about death, love, birth, it's a fucking T.V. show! I don't wanna see anything through the eyes of this stinking society! I feel like I could just walk down the street with a big mirror showing this city to itself and everybody would go insane, light their torches, march in the revolt!

Austin: You're right.

Omar: Like when I was just talking to you now, at least I'm trying to like break into a new way of speaking that'll rip the television set outta my head. Austin, we're in big trouble.

Austin: You're right.

Omar: This society's in big trouble.

Austin: I know!

Omar: I'm not talkin about money! I'm not talkin about disease, the global shithouse, the A bomb. The A bomb! At this point the A bomb is looking good to me! What I am talkin about is Everybody's just so frustrated with this gigantic rut, this bottomless fuckin rut, this same old shit with the politicians and the newspapers and the cars goin beep beep beep. The Ugliness! I've said it! I've said the words! The Ugliness has come to roost!

Austin: It has! It has!

Omar: There's nothing new it feels like for the last twenty something years. There's no like new beatniks. There's no new nothin. It's all RUST. We're rusted shut. The youth is despondent!

Austin: We're disorganized!

Omar: That's right! We're fucking disorganized!

Austin: We gotta do something about this society!

Omar: I know! You're right, we do! And we gotta do it while we still got the juice.

Austin: That's right!

Omar: But you're not ready.

Austin: Whadaya mean?

Omar: You're not ready. I wish you were.

Austin: What are you talking about? I am too ready.

Omar: No, I gotta wait for you.

Austin: What am I doing that you gotta wait?

Omar: I'm standing here and I can see in your eyes that you got this compulsion to dramatize a major feeling of waste. This is very common. You're going to do this or bust. I gotta wait for you to come out the other side of that.

Austin: I don't know what I'm supposed to say.

Omar: What is there to say? It's a waiting game now. Maybe I shouldn't a said nothing.

Austin: Fuck you making out like you're a prophet. You're the deadbeat. It's you that's holding us back from …

Goes mute.

Omar: Changing the world?

Austin: That's right.

Omar: But see, you didn't have the guts to say it. That's cause you're holding on to something wasteful that you're gonna have to dramatize. *(Stands abruptly.)* Come by for dinner tonight. Fifi's making steaks.

Omar exits.

Austin: So Omar left. I stood there and thought he was an arrogant asshole for presuming to know something about me. Then I felt lonely. I had another beer. And another beer. And then I saw this woman at the bar. *(Jill enters. Covered with grease. She looks a sight. She is humming "Gregory's tune.")* She was very … greasy. *(Calls to her.)* Excuse me? Join me for a beer?

> *Jill cautiously approaches. She's traumatized.*

Jill: Why not?

Austin: Sit down. *(She sits.)* How you doin?

Jill: I'm doing fine.

Austin: You coulda fooled me.

Jill: What's that supposed to mean?

Austin: I'm no fortune cookie. Figure it out. Listen. Are you alright?

Jill: I don't know.

Austin: A man do this to you?

Jill: Yes.

Austin: What's your name?

Jill: Jill.

Austin: Austin. *(Sticks out his hand.)* Nice to meet you.

> *She shakes his hand briefly.*

Jill: Austin?

Austin: That's right.

> *He surreptitiously wipes his hand with a handkerchief.*

Jill: Sure. Wipe it off.

Austin: Jill. That's a nice name.

Jill: Get your own. It's mine!

Austin: I know, I mean, yeah, okay. *(Pause.)* Can I be honest with you?

Jill: Why?

Austin: What?

Jill: Why do you want to be honest with me? Somebody was recently honest with me and I didn't like it.

Austin: Don't you think it's always better to be honest?

Jill: No.

Austin: But if you don't want to lie, what else is there to say?

Jill: Small talk. I like it!

Austin: But life is so short.

Jill: I haven't noticed that.

Austin: You've got an answer for everything.

Jill: You've got to be kidding.

Austin: I'm not attacking you.

Jill: I don't know you.

Austin: But you shouldn't assume attack.

Jill: Yes, I should.

Austin: Let's try to get into like a casual track.

Jill: I wish I had a gun.

Austin: What for? *(Jill throws mug of beer in Austin's face.)* Hey, look! Chill out! You're acting like I ate your kids or something. All I did was buy you a beer.

Jill: That was your first mistake.

Austin: What's wrong with you?

Jill: What do you care?

Austin: Just relax, sugar.

Jill: What are you calling me sugar?

Austin: Oh, so what?

Jill: I'm no sugar.

Austin: Yes, you are. Listen, I know what's the matter with you.

Jill: You do?

Austin: Yeah.

Jill: *(Struck by paranoia.)* Don't try to psyche me out!

Austin: I'm not trying to psyche you out.

Jill: These guys. I keep running into these guys who're game players. They're playing with my head like it was a football. My brain's cooked. I feel like I've been bit by a snake. I can't take anymore games!

Austin: What kind of games?

Jill: Any kinda games, all kinda games. I feel like I've been through the scumbag olympics. *(Calms down.)* Alright. Alright, lemme assume you're a nice guy.

Austin: That might be a good idea.

Jill: If you're a nice guy, what are you doing talking to me?

Austin: Why shouldn't I talk to you?

Jill: Because I'm a Two Face, a Liar, a Whore, my mother was totally right about me, AND I'M ALL GREASY.

Austin: I was gonna ask you about that.

Jill: I'm greasy. I'm greasy.

Austin: How'd you get so greasy?

Jill: I'm greasy.

Austin: Because?

Jill: Because I listened to some guy, some snakecharmer named Gregory. And the next thing I know he takes out this big jar.

Austin: What kind of jar?

Jill: *(Paranoid seizure.)* You don't have a jar, do you?

Austin: No.

Jill: If I even see a jar, I'm screamin.

Austin: I don't have a jar! No jar.

She subsides.

Jill: Alright.

Austin: Listen, Jill. I can help you.

Jill: Why would you?

Austin: Cause I'm in good shape myself, and I'm a little idle at the moment. And because I like to be constructive.

Jill: What did you have in mind?

Austin: My apartment's not far from here.

Jill: What are you saying?

Austin: I want you to go there with me.

Jill: I'm listening.

Austin: I want to give you a bath.

Jill: What's in it for you?

Austin: I'd like to get something done today. I have no work right now. There's a lot of things wrong with the world. It's wrong that you're greasy. I'd like to help you fix that. Then when I went to sleep tonight, I'd know I at least tried to correct a problem today. And listen, if everybody did that, attempted to accomplish something every day, fix something they saw was a problem every day, I think we could really turn the world around.

Jill: You do?

Austin: Yeah.

Jill: I don't.

Austin: Fair enough. But you see where your beliefs have gotten you, Jill. Maybe it's time you allowed yourself to be taken in hand by somebody who doesn't share your view of the world.

You've got nothing to lose. Except your grease. Now I don't wanna tell you what to do. I believe in live and let live. I'm just speaking to you as one citizen to another. But listen. Come on. Take a little walk with me and see where it leads. I'm not taking you to a church or a cult or a political meeting. I'm taking you to a bathtub. I've never done this before either. But that's what'll make it a day that was worth living.

Jill: Things couldn't be any worse. Alright. Take me. Take me to the tub.

They exit. Omar enters singing something noble and uplifting like Some Enchanted Evening* *or* Born Free*, *then breaks off and addresses the audience.*

Omar: Meanwhile, I had gone home to be given news by Fifi.

Enter Fifi, on the opposite side of the playing area from him.

Fifi: Omar, I'm pregnant.

Omar: What?

Fifi: I'm pregnant.

Omar: Fifi!

Fifi: Are you happy about it? I hope you're happy about it.

Omar: I am happy about it. It's just, you know, a revelation.

Fifi: Omar?

Omar: Yeah?

Fifi: It's twins.

Omar: What do you mean?

Fifi: Two.

Omar: Twins?

Fifi: Yeah. I was scared you might be freaked.

Omar: I'm not freaked. I'm not freaked. Well, this is just, NEWS.

Fifi: Are you alright?

Omar: No. Yeah! No, I'm just so happy! When are you, I mean, do you know when you're due?

Fifi: Tomorrow.

Omar: What?

Fifi: Tomorrow afternoon.

*See Special Note on copyright page

He freaks.

Omar: You're having twins tomorrow afternoon?!

Fifi: Yeah.

Omar: Yeah? How can you just say yeah?

Fifi: What am I gonna say?

Omar: I don't know.

Fifi: I know it seems soon, Omar. But if we plan it out, it'll be okay. We'll have all morning.

Omar: I'm gonna have a whole family tomorrow afternoon? I'm gonna have a whole family tomorrow afternoon! I'm gonna have a whole family tomorrow afternoon!

Omar breaks down completely.

Fifi: That's how life is sometimes, you know? *(She strikes the old circus pose, one arm lifted in a theatrical gesture.)* Omar!

An orchestral arrangement of the song Omar opened the scene with begins to play. Omar pulls himself together, clambers to his feet, strikes the answering pose, and cries out ...

Omar: Fifi! *(And now, still in the pose, they walk formally towards each other. Omar's a bit shaky but finding his courage. Fifi is calm and centered. They reach each other. Omar calls out again ...)* Fifi! *(And picks her up in his arms.)* I am with you!

He carries her off. The upstage blue curtain parts to reveal Austin's bathroom. Jill is in a big bathtub full of suds. The tub extends at right angles from the rear wall. To the left and right of the tub is window-seat style shelving. There's a pull-up shower nozzle on a long hose, as well as shampoo, a bar of white soap, two yellow rubber ducks of different sizes, a big sea sponge, a very large powder puff, and a portable tape player. On the wall, right, is a coat hook from which hangs an orange terrycloth robe. Left is an equal and opposite hook which is currently bare. And then there's Austin. He's dressed in a bright blue suit, white short-sleeve shirt, skinny black tie, and shiny black shoes. His hair is tonicked and combed. Establishing the downstage invisible walls of the bathroom are towel rings, one on either side, suspended in the air. From these rings are hung big fat white towels.

Jill: I feel naked. Very naked.

Austin: You are naked. Neither of us know how to do this and that's okay. I'm excited. I feel like a kid.

Jill: Can I ask you something?

Austin: Sure.

Jill: Why are you wearing a suit?

Austin: Well, I've never washed a woman before. Like this. I guess I didn't want to be misunderstood. I thought it was better to be kind of formal.

Jill: That doesn't make a lotta sense.

Austin: Yeah, it does. Clothes make the man. It's hard to prepare for anything really new. I'm going on intuition. Maybe you just wanna wash yourself?

Jill: No. I don't know. I don't feel like I know anything.

Austin: It was a guy who did this to you. I think a guy should undo it.

Jill: I do know I need a new twist. Maybe this is it.

Austin: That's right.

Jill: I've washed myself and that didn't do shit.

Austin: You've got to violate your style.

Jill: Your intuition told you to wear a suit?

Austin: Yeah.

Jill: A blue suit?

Austin: A suit. It happens to be blue. It's drip dry. Is the water too hot?

Austin takes off his suitjacket and hangs it on the free hook.

Jill: No, it's good. What's the smell?

Austin: Eucalyptus.

Jill: Very aromatic.

Austin: It's supposed to relax you.

Jill: I hate baths.

Austin darts over, picks up the sea sponge, dunks it in the bathwater, and squeezes it over her head. Then he puts the sponge back.

Austin: This is so pleasant!

Jill: I'm still thinking about it.

Austin: This is so much better than fighting with people in the street, in their houses, in the marketplaces, anything like that! A little harmless fun. Everything is such a struggle. Everybody's always pushing and pulling. I remember when I was a kid there were these moments, you would just blow a feather or something and laugh. I miss that. When I was a kid, my mother would wash me in the tub. I can't remember ... I do remember that she was rough with me. She'd jam this soapy washrag in my ear. I don't know what she thought she was doing. I doubt she jammed washrags in her ears. Soap in my eyes. I was very sensitive. She didn't know that. She was a tough old broad. An adult. She was an adult. We adults are used to having things rough. But then, see, I was an innocent child. And I wasn't used to that kinda treatment. That's how I wanna wash you. Like you were an innocent child.

Jill: Okay.

Austin: I got some music here I chose. I'm gonna turn it on and I'm gonna wash your hair.

Jill: Okay.

> *Austin taps the button on the tape player. Something like* The Girl From Ipanema *performed by Getz & Gilberto* comes on. Austin listens to the music and does a little bossa nova. He pulls up the rubber shower nozzle, turns on and tests the water, and wets down Jill's head. He puts down the nozzle, bossa novas around to the other side of the tub, sits down and begins to shampoo Jill's hair. She turns into a little girl in her own little world. She sings little bits of the song to herself. Austin throws the ducks in the water. She begins to play with them. Austin briefly rinses her hair, and then shampoos it a second time. He gets up, bossa novas around to the other side of the tub again, and gives her hair a final rinse. He gets a towel and wraps her hair in a turban. He gets one of the big bath towels and holds it up for her. She stands up, does a little dancing of her own as she gets into the towel, and tucks in the final fold. Austin puts down a towel where she will step out, then takes her hand. She steps up on the tub's edge, bossa novas there briefly, and then steps down on to the towel. For a moment, they dance together, a quiet little turning. Then Austin steps away, removes her towel, produces the enormous powder puff, and powders her all over quickly. He takes the beautiful orange robe off its hooks as the music ends,*

*See Special Note on copyright page

296

and helps her into it. He stands back from her again.

Austin: Good as new.

Jill: This is like another world.

Austin: There are some friends of mine I want you to meet.
Omar and Fifi. Are you free for dinner?

> *She nods gently as the lights fade, leaving them in silhouette.*
> *They both laugh a gentle laugh. Fade to black. Some great coffee*
> *house jazz begins to play. Maybe Sonny Rollins'* **Sunny Moon**
> **For Two***. Whatever the selection of music, it should play a few*
> *minutes into intermission and end a few minutes before the com-*
> *mencement of Act II.)*

END OF ACT I

ACT II

A half-moon shaped dining table set for four. It's a big table.
There are a few feet of space between each of the diners. The table
settings are thorough, but of restaurant quality. Except for the
steak knives; these are actually Omar's old throwing knives. They
are chipped, nicked. One is missing a point.

All of the diners are seated at the Upstage side of the table. Omar
is the furthest right, next is Fifi, then Austin, and finally, Jill .

On the table, at the meal's outset, is a magnum of red wine, an oil
and vinegar set-up, and a salt cellar. Downstage of the table is a
big bear rug growling at the audience.

As the lights rise on the scene, we see that Omar is wearing a
horned helmet, Fifi an apron over a dress, Austin a leather sports
jacket, and Jill is dressed to the nines. The ensemble sings this
song to the tune of God Rest You Merry, Gentlemen.

Ensemble: God rest you merry, gentlemen
Let nothing ye dismay
Remember that the Super Bowl
Is not the Passion Play

* See Special Note on copyright page

I drink some booze
I take a snooze
I eat a Milky Way
O tidings of comfort and joy

Men: Where are you now?
Ensemble: O tidings of comfort and joy!

I had a dog, his name was Spot,
I found him at the pound
I looked at him, he looked at me,
I loved that little hound!
He died in 1981,
I wish he were around!
O friends we are missing much this year

Ladies: Missing this year!
Ensemble: O friends we are missing much this year.

I count my money twice a day,
And look at all my clothes,
I've learned to speak without a squeak,
And whittled down my nose,
I hear quite clear as they draw near
The Wreckers' hammerblows!
O spirit of peace I once held dear
Dear to my heart!
O spirit of peace I once held dear

Now the song switches to the tune of Good King Wenceslas.

Austin: Bring in flowers!
Omar: Bring in wine!
Ensemble: Start a roaring fire!
Sing a ringing roundelay
Raise your glasses higher!
Though the night is everywhere
Though the stars are hiding
We have breath and life is sweet
That there's no denying.

The song ends, and now Omar announces …

Omar: Act Two!

As the lights change and the attitudes of the players adjust.

Austin: Omar. I haven't really introduced my friend. This is Jill.

Omar doesn't answer.

Fifi: I should warn you. Omar is in a bad mood.

Omar: I am not in a bad mood. I am in a practical mood. I'm not interested in the niceties. We are gathered here to eat dinner. Let's eat fucking dinner.

Fifi: Do you want to start with the steak or the salad?

Omar: Steak.

Jill: Oh, I don't eat steak.

Omar: What?

Jill: I don't eat steak.

Omar slams a fist down on the table. Silence.

Omar: Alright. Let's start with a glass of red wine.

Fifi: I can't drink wine. I'm pregnant. *(Omar slams a fist down on the table. Silence.)* But that doesn't mean the rest of you shouldn't have any.

She gets up and pours wine for the others.

Austin: You're pregnant?

Fifi: Yeah.

Austin: That's great! That's wonderful.

Jill: Congratulations.

Fifi: Thank you.

Omar is grim.

Omar: Aren't you going to congratulate me?

Jill: Of course. Congratulations.

Omar: Thank you.

Austin: I can't believe it.

Omar: Why don't you eat steak? You don't like steak?

Jill: I used to. But then I started thinking about the cows. I really like cows.

Omar: I like cows.

Austin: Fifi, when did you find out?

Fifi: Today.

Austin: God.

Fifi: It's twins. I'm gonna have twins. They told me. A boy and a girl.

Jill: Really? Wow. That's a lot to take in.

Austin: When are you due?

Fifi: How do you like your steak cooked?

Omar: TOMORROW! She's having fucking twins tomorrow! And there's gonna be doctors and birthdays and babysitters and college and maybe fucking cars! It's gonna cost millions of dollars and I'm never gonna get a good night's sleep again!

Fifi: You told me you were happy about it!

Fifi exits.

Omar: I am happy about it! I am. I am happy about it! But just fucking shoot me, okay? So I can die happy.

Jill: I don't blame you for being nervous. It's scary.

Omar: What do you know?

Austin: Hey, Omar, make an effort, huh? This is my date.

Omar: Sorry.

Austin: That's okay.

Omar: It's just when she.... What's your name?

Jill: Jill.

Omar: It's just when she tells me she's worried about some fucking cow's well-being while my life's falling apart ... I don't see how I'm ever gonna hit the dot again.

Jill: I just happen to like cows. What's the big deal? I'm not asking you not to eat meat.

Omar: That's very wise of you, Jill. Because if you were to suggest that I shouldn't eat meat, I'd throw you out the fuckin window.

Fifi returns with a pitcher of water.

Austin: No, you wouldn't.

Fifi: Boys, boys.

Omar: I'm not a boy.

Fifi: Then don't act like one.

Omar: I'm a man.

Fifi: Then act like one.

Omar: I can't act it. So where did you two meet?

Austin: After you and me had that beer today, I stuck around. Then Jill walked in and we got to talking.

Omar: So you're a pick-up.

Fifi: Omar!

Austin: That's it!

Jill: No, that's alright. Yes, I am a pick-up. I'm a pick-up.

Omar nods, satisfied.

Omar: Gimme some more wine. *(To Jill)* You're a stranger.

Fifi gets up and serves everybody but Omar more wine.

Fifi: I'm thinking about names.

Austin: How about Austin?

Omar: I like the name Austin.

Jill: I love thinking up names for kids.

Omar: Fifi, you have any names in mind for our children?

Fifi: Yeah, I had a couple of ideas.

Omar: Don't say them in front of this woman. And I don't want to hear your ideas.

Austin: How about Charles?

Omar: I like the name Charles.

Austin: I thought you didn't want to hear any suggestions?

Omar: Just from her.

Jill: What's wrong with me?

Omar: I don't know. I have an idea about dinner. Jill, me and Fifi and Austin will have steak, and you can have the salad. We'll just have steak. You'll just have salad. Is that alright with you?

Jill: Sure.

Omar: I want to apologize for my behavior so far this evening, Jill. I had a terrifying shock today. It's altered my behavior. I'm usually a very casual person. See, I was just pissing around. Then FATE came here. My fate. I forgot about that, you know? Austin, you hear what I'm saying?

Austin: You've been acting unbelievably awful.

Omar: I know. I apologize. I apologize.

Austin: Apology accepted.

Omar: Maybe that premonition I had about you was actually about me.

Austin: I wouldn't be surprised.

Omar: I would.

Fifi: I'm going to get the steaks on.

Fifi goes.

Omar: I asked Fifi to make steak for you, Austin, but now it's just what I want for myself.

Austin: Why steak for me?

Omar: I had that premonition you were approaching a high mountain, a deep ditch. I'm talking about karma, Jill.

Jill: I guessed that.

Omar: And I always think at such times a steak is good.

Jill: Why?

Omar: The blood. All that blood. It's like a hot shot. You remember shit you don't even know.

Jill: I don't think it's good to remember everything.

Omar: It's good to remember everything. Everything. And if you can't remember, make it up.

Austin: OMAR.

Omar: What?

Austin: I'm sitting here, I'm watching your act, what are you doing?

Omar: We're having a dinner conversation.

Austin: You acting like a.... You're acting like a medicine man.

Omar: Thank you.

Austin: Fuck you.

Omar: Why you say that?

Austin: You ain't a medicine man.

Omar: Now it used to be that there were medicine men, right?

Austin: A long time ago. Not now.

Omar: You say. What do you say, Jill?

Jill: If you're a medicine man ...

Omar: Or a holy man.

Jill: Or a holy man. You would be gentle.

Omar: How you figure that?

Jill: To be holy is to be gentle.

Omar: By holy you mean close to God?

Jill: Yeah. I mean, spiritual things. Maybe God.

Omar: God is not gentle.

Jill: Maybe not your God.

Omar: You got a God?

Jill: Sort of.

Omar: Are you embarrassed?

Austin: People who talk about God tend to be schmucks or insane.

Omar: True. Why is that?

Austin: Either because they're weak or because they're looking for a victim to bullshit to death.

Omar: I'm talking about God. Am I a schmuck?

Austin: Right now, absolutely.

Fifi enters with a big aluminum tray. She comes down and serves up the three steaks.

Fifi: Dinner's ready!

Omar: Hot Dog!

Fifi: Rare. Rare. And Rare.

Austin: Thanks, Fifi. It looks great.

Fifi: Good. Jill, I'm getting your salad.

Jill: Oh no. We should really be serving you.

Fifi: Why?

Jill: Because you're pregnant.

Fifi: Oh, I'm fine.

Jill: You shouldn't push it.

Fifi: Oh, please.

Fifi exits.

Jill: I hope she's alright.

Austin: What do you mean?

Jill: It's scary. A lot can go wrong.

Austin: Like what?

Jill: Toxoplasmosis.

Austin: What's that?

Jill: It's this horrible parasite. A pregnant woman can get it from a cat, and then the baby gets it. I know a woman it happened to. The baby was born blind. You don't have a cat, do you?

Omar: No.

A pause.

Jill: These are really unusual steak knives.

Omar: They're my old throwing knives. I can't bear to part with them. We use them as steak knives. I haven't thrown them away because of sentimentality. But I have to be very careful when I cut my meat. Otherwise, I'm in for a nasty gash. Sentimentality has a romantic attraction, but it's dangerous and impractical. These knives serve to remind me. You could lose your thumb. What do you do for a living?

Jill: I'm in politics.

Austin: You are?

Jill: Yeah.

Austin: What kind of politics?

Jill: I'm a campaign manager. I'm not doing anything now. I'm between campaigns. I mean, I'm doing volunteer work. I work with The Battered Women's Bowling League.

Fifi enters carrying an enormous plate of green salad. She puts it in front of Jill.

Fifi: Here's your salad.

Jill: It's so big.

Fifi: I know it seems big, but it's really just air and water and minerals.

Jill: It still seems awfully big.

Fifi: Well, it was supposed to be for the four of us. You know, that and the steak. But you didn't want steak, and Omar proposed this solution ...

Omar: So eat it. Fifi.

Fifi: Yeah?

Omar: How about some pepper?

Fifi: Sure.

Fifi exits.

Jill: You really keep her running.

Omar: So, as I was saying. Or thinking. You see a dog. The dog has a litter. The dog has tits. The pups fight to suck on the tits. The mother doesn't stick the tit in the pup's mouth. It's up to the pup.

Austin: What's your point, Omar?

Omar: Maybe that's what our relationship with God is. We can't just mope around and hope for sustenance. We gotta go to God. Otherwise you'll be the runt. You don't wanna be the runt. You gotta choose to suck.

Austin: I can't believe you're talking about God again. *(To Jill.)* I've never heard him talk about God till today.

Omar: It's in bad taste, isn't it? God's in bad taste.

Austin: Well, I don't know about that.

Omar: No, it's true. Right now. God's in bad taste.

> *Enter Fifi, with an enormous pepper mill. It's four feet long. She handles it ably, but it is heavy for her. She goes to Omar and grinds some pepper on to his steak. He holds up his hand when he's satisfied. Then Fifi goes to Austin.*

Fifi: Pepper?

Austin: Sure. *(She grinds some.)* That's good.

> *Fifi goes to Jill.*

Fifi: Pepper?

Jill: Put that down!

Fifi: Why?

Jill: You're a pregnant woman.

Fifi: *(Carefree.)* Oh, so what?

Jill: *(To Omar.)* You should be grinding the pepper for her!

Omar: That's not our arrangement.

Jill: Well, you should change your arrangement!

Fifi: Do you want pepper or not? This is heavy.

Jill: That's my point!

Omar: Look, Jill. I apologized to you for my rudeness. But there's something you have to understand.

Jill: I understand that you are abusing your wife!

Fifi: Forget it.

> *Fifi exits with the Pepper Mill.*

Austin: Jill, don't put your nose in anybody's marriage.

Jill: Oh, so you're with him now.

Austin: No. I'm with me. He's with him. You're with you. But do yourself a favor and don't put your nose in anybody's marriage but your own.

Jill: I'm not married.

Omar: No kidding.

Jill: What's that supposed to mean?

Omar: Austin, member how we were talking about society?

Austin: Yeah?

Omar: This is society. We sit at this table. I am married to Fifi, who's in the kitchen. You are an old friend. And Jill, you're new to the group. This is a classic social situation.

Austin: Omar …

Omar: So. If we are critics of society, and this is a unit, a molecule of society, then we've got to explode this, change it. Something. If we are to be effective.

Austin: So do we do that by being rude to each other? I mean, before Jill and I came here tonight, I gave her a bath. She was basically a stranger and I brought her home and I put her in the tub and I gave her a bath.

Omar: Why?

Fifi enters and goes to her place.

Austin: She was greasy. She was covered with grease. *(Jill lowers her head.)* Is it alright that I'm saying this? *(Jill nods her lowered head.)* Some guy had upset her and put grease on her. When I ran into her, she was in shock. I took her home. I gave her a bath. I saw something wrong, Omar, in the world, and I did something about it! I think if you're out to change the world then we should all be nicer to each other.

Fifi, eating her steak, giggles.

Omar: Fifi. Show a little sensitivity.

Fifi stops giggling and goes back to eating.

Austin: She wasn't laughing at me.

Omar: Yes, she was.

Austin: No, she wasn't.

Omar: Fifi.

Fifi: *(To Austin.)* I was laughing at you.

Fifi goes back to eating.

Jill: Austin, these are evil people.

Austin: Jill.

Omar: We're not evil people, Jill. Though I'll admit we bear some similarities to evil people I've run into. I've been rude to you. I've mentioned God a number of times. I'm eating a steak. Evil people sometimes eat steak. But it's not that we're evil.

Austin: They aren't evil.

Omar: But what's happened is, we've come up against the verities. Actually, Fifi had probably come against the verities before this, but now I've come up against the verities.

Jill: And what are the verities?

Omar: Okay. First, I must say, I don't know. Then I can go on and say some other things. My wife is having babies. This makes me aware that tremendous powers are at work. The whole thing's a miracle. Not just the babies. The whole thing. You. Me. Austin. The table. France. A cavalcade of miracles.

Austin: I think you're scared. I think you've got your wagons pulled in a circle, and I'm supposed to be the novice cause I'm not living my life that way.

Omar: Yet.

Austin: Yet. I'm not dead yet, either. And I'm not gonna do a vamp till I am.

Omar: You think that's what I'm doing?

Austin: I don't know what you're doing.

Omar: I'm a family man.

Austin: Well, a family can't float in outer space, Omar! There's people outside the door you gotta deal with!

Omar: I deal with you.

Austin: What about the neurotics?

Omar: You mean her?

Indicates Jill.

Austin: I'm not naming names here, but what about the freakin neurotics?

Omar: They're not my problem and I'm not gonna make 'em my problem.

Austin: Whose problem are they?

Omar: I don't know.

Austin: You're a fucking hypocrite with your change-the-world shit then!

Omar: How so?

Austin: If you're in your house worshipping the fucking fireplace or something, and then outside the door it's all Charles Darwin to you, what do you think's gonna happen?

Omar: I don't know.

Austin: Well, it's easy to find out cause it's right out the window and in the paper! We're disorganized cause we're in the house, and the neurotics, the people who can't get their houses straight, they own the street. They're running the country. They're burning down the world. And lemme tell you something, they're right to burn it down! They're pissed and they're right to be pissed. We're supposed to be taking care of them!

Jill: Are you calling me a neurotic?

Austin: No. *(To Omar.)* The neurotics are the shock troops of the damaged people. They're in the best shape so they lead the charge. They're the ones we have to deal with. They want to be stopped. They want us to say no. Don't do that. But we've gone home, Omar. Do you hear what I'm saying? *(He addresses the audience.)* The men of the city have hung up their togas. And gone home.

Omar: *(Examines audience.)* That's true.

Austin: *(To audience.)* We can't keep doin that.

Omar: *(Thinking about the audience.)* No.

Now they drop this attitude and resume normal conversation.

Fifi: Jill, why would a guy put grease on you?

Jill: I have no idea. You can't imagine what it's like to be a single woman now.

Fifi: You're not eating your salad.

Jill: It's so big I'm afraid I'll choke on it.

Fifi: That's ridiculous. You just have to chew.

Jill eats a leaf.

Jill: It's delicious.

Fifi: Put some dressing on it.

Jill: Dressing?

Austin passes Jill the dressing.

Omar: Are things miraculous to you, Austin?

Austin: I go in and out.

Omar: I did, too. But now a miracle's happened that gives me a job. A miracle that gives you a job is called Fate.

Austin: You mean you've got to take care of a family now.

Omar: Exactly! I am the guard dog. She's the cradle of conception and I'm the guard dog appointed to protect her. *(To Jill.)* You think I'm treating Fifi in a demeaning way. There may be some truth in that. I may be a little angry at my fate. Fifi has been designated by a great unseen power to be the cradle of conception. The same power has made it clear that I am not where it's happening. I walk the perimeter. I'm not in the Command Tent. Manhood is a humbling thing. I may not wander too far. I am needed.

Jill: I have to admire what you're saying.

Omar: Why?

Jill: It's just very masculine. I'm not masculine. Our disagreement's almost biological. *(Jill puts dressing on her salad and eats some.)* And I admire you, too, Fifi. Now that I think about it. The way you slave for him looks bad. But you don't care. You know who you are. What other people think is their business.

Fifi: I don't know.

Omar: I do. She's right.

Jill: You see, he's very masculine.

Austin: What about me?

Jill: That goes without saying.

Austin: It went without saying.

Fifi: Was the guy who put the grease on you masculine?

Jill: I don't know what he was. He was very fucked up. His identity was all over the place. I feel sorry for him. But fuck him. He treated me rotten. Why should I feel for him? This salad is just the thing for me.

She's eating away.

Omar: You make it look good.

She puts more dressing on it.

Jill: You're embarrassing me.

More dressing.

Fifi: Did I just see you flirt? Was that a flirting smile?

Omar: She's just enjoying her salad.

Fifi: Omar! Your parents didn't praise you. You have a hole there.

Omar: Yeah. Right.

Fifi: I think you're great.

Omar: Thanks.

Fifi: Do you want some more wine?

Omar: Yeah.

Fifi: Let me get it for you.

Fifi gets up, serves him wine, and sits again.

Austin: Well, I know what I think!

Omar: What?

Austin: *(Standing up.)* I have a good feeling. I feel dissatisfied.

Jill: *(Standing up.)* Me, too!

Omar: I wouldn't describe that as my feeling.

Fifi: *(Standing up.)* I'm happy.

Omar: *(Standing up.)* I'm awestruck. I'm awestruck and alienated from everyday life.

Austin: I'm alienated from you.

Omar: I'm alienated from the mundane by the miraculous.

Jill: I'm alienated because I've been abused.

Fifi: Who abused you?

Jill: Men.

Austin: I haven't abused you. *(She doesn't answer.)* I haven't abused you.

Jill: No.

They all sit.

Austin: *(Standing up again, throwing down his napkin.)* I don't feel helpless! Everything is always the same. Finally. But I don't feel helpless. You can't think in a straight line. You can't describe the phenomenon of being a man like this. *(Indicates a flat plane.)* Everything is wild and you have to make believe it isn't to keep from flipping out. My name is Austin. I'm in this body. We have dinner. I poured water on you. Why? There's an explanation for that. King Kong carries the woman, the woman doesn't carry King Kong. That makes sense, right? If the woman carried King Kong, the scientists could explain that, too. Icarus. If, in the myth, Icarus flew to the sun, and blew it out like a candle, then now we would say of course, and explain it. Hadda be that way. I'm Austin. It hadda be that way. I agree with you, Omar, it's all a miracle. But that's very frightening. Planes don't have to fly, you know. But it hadda be that way. Why! I can explain it! Fuck, I can explain anything! But hey, by the same token, I can refute anything! Jill, why are you so unhappy?

Jill: I'm not unhappy.

Austin: Okay. Omar, you got a job. It's going to spirit you away.

Omar: I know. I feel like I should wave. I don't wanna go but what are you gonna do?

Austin: You can't fight fate.

Omar: Nope.

Austin: And I know that! But still, I don't feel helpless.

Fifi: I feel happy.

Austin: I know you do.

Jill: You should be scared stiff.

Fifi: Why?

Jill: Cause horrible things can happen. Horrible things happen all the time.

Austin: Can't argue with that.

Fifi: Wonderful things happen all the time, too.

Austin: You can't argue with that, either. Both of these women are absolutely right.

Omar: I see now why philosophers are almost always single.

Austin: Why?

Omar: Cause I'm losing interest in philosophy. A miracle gave me a job, and the job ain't philosophy.

Jill has quietly taken the salad oil and put it on her face.

Austin: Now, when I was a kid, my mother cried all the time and I would try to comfort her. Does that ring a bell with you, Jill?

Jill: What?

Austin: You put the salad dressing on your face.

Jill: No, I didn't. I mean, a little might've splashed on me, but I didn't intentionally put it on my face.

Austin: When I met you today, you were devastated because some man put grease on you. Has that ever happened to you before?

Jill: What?

Austin: Did a man ever put grease on you before?

Jill: No! Never!

Austin: Think!

Jill: Well, maybe it happened once before.

Austin: Once?

Jill: A couple of times then!

Austin: I'd bet it's the story of your life. Just like the story of my life is comforting women who have this view of life that lets them cry. Let's go back to Chapter One of your story. Did your father every put grease on you?

Jill: Go screw yourself!

Austin: Did your father ever put grease on you?

Jill: My father loved me!

Austin: Come on! Answer the question!

Jill: A little butter.

Austin: Butter?

Jill: At dinner. He used to put butter on my nose. It was love!

Fifi: You should've been a lawyer, Austin.

Austin: I'm gonna tell you something about yourself, Jill.

Jill: You don't know me!

Austin: I'm gonna tell you something about the way things are. You're not a villain.

Jill: Who said I was?

Austin: You don't have a noose around your neck.

Jill: What are you talking about?

Austin: I know you. But you are a neurotic person.

Jill: You don't know me!

Austin: And you don't currently have the strength to face that. My mother died without changing. She went to her grave a victim. You're like her.

Jill: You're scaring me.

Austin: I'm sorry, but good. I've got something to tell you, Jill. Grease is not love. Some women think brutality is love. Some women think money is love. Some women think power is love. There are a lot of misconceptions. Some guys wanna kiss shoes. There's a naked girl there, and they wanna kiss the shoe. With you, it's grease. It's like you make a long distance call, and the switchboard makes a mistake. You were calling for love, but they connected you with grease. It's not your fault. You were in the hands of others, and they got you the wrong number. But it's time to break the connection and call again.

Jill: You don't know what you're talking about.

Austin: My mother died without facing herself.

Omar: Well, what's for dessert?

Fifi: An apple tart. A cookie. A dozen raspberries. A broken piece of white chocolate.

Austin: Excuse me, please.

Austin exits.

Fifi: *(To Jill.)* Do you want some coffee? Do you want some coffee, Jill?

Jill: You're happy?

Fifi: Yeah.

Jill: *(To Omar.)* You're happy?

Omar: No. Not at the moment. Happiness ain't the measure, you know. Happiness is a side issue. A necessary element. But not the *raison d'etre*. Life? Absolutely. Liberty? Yes. The Pursuit of Happiness? A big mistake. You don't pursue happiness. It comes to you while you do other things. Occasionally. Like grace. I'm not against you, Jill. You're alright. But children are coming here.

Jill: Yeah, I'll take coffee. *(Fifi exits.)* Do you think there's life after death?

Omar: Yes. Maybe not my life, but there's life.

Jill: I am a villain, you know.

Omar: No, you're not.

Jill: Don't you believe in villains?

Omar: There are villains. I think. You are not one.

Jill: How do you know?

Omar: You're just unhappy. You have an unhappy mark on you.

Jill: Austin cleaned me up this afternoon. And we danced. It was very calm.

Omar: Austin's a good person. He feels grief over the plight of his mother. If he can ghost her up in you for a few hours, and wash her troubled brow free of care, and dance with her a faded little dance. Why not? Why not?

Fifi enters with a tray on which sits a coffee pot, and cream and sugar. She serves it up.

Fifi: This is good coffee. It'll make you think.

Fifi sits and drinks a sip.

Omar: It is good.

Jill: *(Sips it.)* It is good.

Omar: Life is sweet.

Fifi: You're in a better mood?

Omar: Yeah.

Enter Austin, naked, carrying a mirror. Everyone looks at him. No one seems shook up.

Fifi: Austin, where are your clothes?

Austin: I took em off.

Omar: Why?

Austin: I don't know. It's not sex.

Omar: I can see that.

Austin: It's not anger, either.

Omar: I believe you.

Austin: I hope you're not offended, Fifi.

Fifi: Oh no. Why'd you take the mirror out of the bathroom?

Austin: The mirror's for Jill. To look in. *(Austin goes to Jill. Holds the mirror for her to look in.)* What do you see in the mirror, Jill?

Jill: I see myself.

Austin: Do you?

Jill: Yeah.

Austin: Do you see yourself?

Jill: Yeah.

Austin: Cause that's all I'm asking.

She starts to cry a little.

Jill: Okay.

Austin: Why is it such a big thing to be naked? And it's supposed to be like a bigger thing for men than women, don't you think? Men ain't supposed to look as good naked as women. They say women show their feelings more than men. Maybe that's why it's supposed to be more right for them to be naked than men. They can show more easily. Not that I'm not sure it's not all total bullshit. But it's good to talk about possible things.

Fifi: You want some coffee, Austin?

Austin: Yeah, I'll have some coffee with you. In a minute. As a reward. That's what I like. The casual. I was wrestling with the world of people for a long time. I'd be pushing and pulling them around like they were toys. What nonsense. If you're casual, things unfold, and it's all a surprise. Human beings are the absolute home of the unexpected. But only if you're casual. The best you can hope to do, to speed along the possibilities of life, is approach another human being, be naked, and hold up a good mirror. Omar, am I the hero of this play or what?

Omar: Yeah, you're the hero.

Austin: And Jill, you're not the villain.

Jill goes to Austin and kisses him chastely.

Jill: No.

She exits.

Austin: And Fifi, you're happy?

Fifi: Yeah.

Fifi exits.

Austin: And tomorrow, when Fifi goes into the hospital and you've got a wife and kids, then you can start providing. And then you'll be the hero of the house.

Omar: I'll do my best.

Omar exits. Austin steps off the stage and addresses the audience.

Austin: You can't describe the phenomenon of being a man. Everything is wild and you have to make believe it isn't to keep from flipping out. Society is make-believe. You think this play is make-believe? Society is make-believe. I hate this fuckin society. *(Austin walks further down, a little closer to the audience.)* There's a naked man among you. With a mirror. And it isn't about sex. And it isn't about anger. Now relax. Be casual. How delicate life is. You're the same as me. *(Austin thinks, takes on a more formal attitude, and calls out.)* I wish to put on my robes, please. Citizens, I wish to put on my robes! *(Omar enters, carrying a big white Turkishrobe with a hood. Fifi follows, carrying a cup of coffee. Fifi takes the mirror from Austin and lays it down on the stage. Meanwhile, Omar helps Austin into the robe. Austin thanks Omar, Thank You, and Omar exits. Fifi hands Austin the coffee, and he thanks her. She kisses him on the cheek and goes. Austin takes in the audience and then speaks.)* Now one social speech and it's the end. This is the big funk. The big fear. The big before. There are flashes of light in the sky. But everything is still. We were doing stuff, but then the funk got really big and we stopped. All we're doing now is sweating. We can hear our breathing. Everything is halted. We're waiting for the Big Storm. It's coming. The storm is coming. All we are now is in our death which is premature. It's not time for death. Death will take care of itself. We're frightened anyway. We can feel every vein in our bodies, our hearts ticking like bombs, our breaths like respirators waiting to be disconnected. But it's all premature. I hadda dream I was in Saigon, sleeping on a balcony.

The army was gone. The city was protected by boobytraps and bombs and mechanical soldiers, and something set the whole system off. A bird had tripped a wire. And this huge network of defense started to fight a fierce war with an enemy that hadn't come. I was lying in my bed on the balcony. Bullets going off all around me. I didn't bother to get up. I knew it was a huge defense against nothing. I woke up and I knew I was in the big funk. That the storm was coming. I'm lying here, in my life, waiting for the storm. I'm not alone. I wish it would break. I wish it would rain. Nothing's gonna happen till it rains. And it is going to rain. That is known to me. It's not just hope. A hope. That discredited virtue. It's not in politics that the funk is going to end. It's not in the religions of men. The rumble of thunder is in our human soul. Our spirits have lain down in terror before an eyeless skull. When I'm afraid I'm gonna die from a heart attack and I won't go to the doctor because I don't want him to see my death in me, you know what I do? I eat steak, I drink liquor. I butter my bread. I eat eggs. And I say, See? Wouldn't this give me a heart attack if I was going to have one? But then I feel these twinges in my chest and I get scared and I have to eat more steak and butter to prove what all over again? We're frightened that it's already over and we're whistling in the dark till the madman comes with the knife. (Holds up the mirror.) Here he comes. (Puts down the mirror.) Our fear is heavy. Our fear is thick. It's casting a shadow like a thunderhead. It's growling. It's flashing. It's been growing for a long time. We have lain down on the hillsides to watch it now. Occasionally, lightning forks down and takes one of us. But where's the storm? When the storm? It's coming. It is coming. Is there anything to do in the meanwhile? Yes. Look at your fear. See the funk. See the funk we're in. Look at nothing else. It's our fear that's created the thunderhead. And we can make it rain. The end.

> *Austin puts out his hand and blows on the palm. The lights go out like a candle. Whatever song opened the show comes up again. It plays through the happy curtain call.*

THE END

Beggars in the House of Plenty

BEGGARS IN THE HOUSE OF PLENTY was originally produced by the Manhattan Theatre Club on October 3, 1991. It was directed by John Patrick Shanley; the scenery was designed by Santo Loquasto; the lighting was designed by Natasha Katz; the costumes were designed by Lindsay W. Davis; and the production stage manager was Renee Lutz.

The cast was as follows:

Johnny	Loren Dean
Ma (Noreen)	Dana Ivey
Pop	Daniel von Bargen
Sheila	Laura Linney
Joey	Jon Tenney
Sister Mary Kate	Jayne Haynes

CHARACTERS

Johnny: Irish American, in his 20's. Bronx accent.

Ma: Irish American, somewhere between 45 and 60. She was raised in Brooklyn.

Pop: Came to America from Ireland, when he was 20. Now he's 45 to 60.

Sheila: Pretty Irish-American girl in her early 20's. Bronx accent.

Joey: Handsome, charismatic, charming, in his late 20's.

ACT I

The Old House, all of it jumbled together, as such things are in memory. No ceiling. Walls only as needed. Up Right there's a staircase going up to a small landing. Up Left a door and a doorless doorway form the corner. The doorway, which faces us, leads to the basement. The door, which faces Right, has a pane of frosted glass; it leads to the front entrance of the house.

On Stage, to the Right, is a small kitchen table, on which sits a cleaver.

The back wall is a painted drop depicting a decorated Christmas tree.

House goes to dark. A sentimental American version of DANNY BOY plays.

Lights up, Johnny enters in fanciful pajamas that are too big for him, and a coonskin hat. He's a young man of about 20, and at the same time he's a child. He's holding a box of kitchen matches from which he's drawing one.

He speaks to the audience. He's telling a story.

Johnny: When I was one, two, three, four, five freakin years of my life…

Ma: *(Shouting from Off.)* Johnny!

Johnny: In the old house.

Ma: *(From Off.)* Johnny!

Johnny: *(Striking a match, smiling.)* I discovered fire!

Ma enters from the basement holding a basket of laundry.

Ma: What's that smell?

Johnny: *(Holding the match behind his back.)* I don't know.

She sniffs but doesn't see.

Ma: Smoke.

Johnny: Maybe.

Ma: Something's burning.

Johnny: Maybe.

Ma: False alarm I guess. *(She crosses, heading for the staircase. Johnny blows out the match.)* I don't know who dirties all these clothes, I always wear the same thing. *(She stows the basket of laundry under the staircase, trading it for a broom. She begins to sweep. Johnny's hiding his box of matches.)* Hey, I can eat a whole pizza pie by myself.

Johnny: Yippee, what an achievement. Where's Aunt Annie?

Ma's suddenly on guard.

Ma: She'll be back. You're like a little animal. I've gotta keep my eyes on you.

Johnny: Whaddaya mean?

Ma produces a sewing hoop with a piece of cloth on it. She throws it to Johnny.

Ma: Take this sewing hoop. Sew your name in it. That should keep you.

Johnny takes it and starts sewing his name. He sits on the foot of the stairs.

Johnny: *(Sings.)* Davy, Davy Crockett... Davy, Davy Crockett...

Ma stops sweeping and looks at him.

Ma: Today's the day your brother Joey's coming home from the Navy.

Johnny: I saw a bird in the house yesterday.

Ma: That's bad luck.

Johnny: In the hall at the top of the staircase. He was so scared, trying to get out.

Ma: A bird in the house is very bad luck.

Johnny: What about a bird outside?

Ma: A bird outside is a bird.

There is a great coughing and slamming and muttering outside the entrance door. An approaching menace. Ma and Johnny look to the door, still and fearful.

Ma: It's your father.

Something is slammed, as in anger, outside the entrance door.

Johnny: I'm scared.

Ma: Shut up. We've gotta be very quiet. He works so hard. In the slaughterhouse. *(To Johnny, with sudden accusing violence.)* All he wants is peace!

Johnny: And the Daily News.

Ma: Yeah, that's right. Peace and the Daily News.

Enter Pop, an intense silent angry man with a great shock of salt and pepper hair standing up on his head. His coat is blood-spattered, his boots caked. There's a smudge of blood on his face. He takes off his coat, hangs it from a hook, takes off his boots. He's wearing a blood-spattered apron underneath, and his socks are spotted with red. He speaks to himself the while in a low clenched voice of barely contained rage. He has a package wrapped in bloody paper.

Pop: I went to the dentist. He told me I had cavities. I told him, listen here. I don't need these god damn teeth if they're gonna give me trouble. Rip 'em out and gimme a plate. Let's be done with it. *(He dumps the contents of his package on the table: a bloody chunk of meat. He starts chopping the meat.)* I got a hemorrhoid. I went to the doctor. I told him, listen here. Cut that son-of-a-bitch out, rip it the hell out before it multiplies. And I haven't had a god damn hemorrhoid since. *(Explodes, waving the cleaver toward the door.)* I BUILT THAT BENCH OUT FRONT!

Ma: It's a beautiful bench. The Adirondack style.

She gives Johnny a prompting look.

Johnny: I like the bench.

Pop: I PAINTED IT!

Ma: It's a lovely color.

Johnny: Yeah. Green.

Pop: *(His fit abating.)* You're darn right. It'll last for years. Years and years. It's all-weather.

He stops chopping, produces a copy of the Daily News *with a headline from the early 1950's, starts to read, immediately falls asleep standing up, and snores.*

Ma: He's asleep. I hope to God he doesn't die on me.

Johnny: Why does he work in the slaughterhouse?

Ma: He likes it.

Laughter tinkles from out of view; it comes from the top of the stairs.

Johnny: Who's that laughing?

Ma: I can eat two big rolls every morning. With lots of yellow-butter.

Johnny: Hooray. I hear laughing.

Ma: That's your sister Sheila. Today's her wedding day.

Johnny: Can I go to the wedding?

Ma: No. You have double-pneumonia.

Enter Sheila, on to the landing. She's in her wedding dress, incredibly happy. She carries a little overnight suitcase.

Sheila: Mommy!

Ma: You look beautiful, baby.

Sheila: I'm so happy. I keep crying. Ray told me he bought blue silk p.j.'s for the honeymoon.

Johnny: Silk p.j.'s?

Ma: That Ray's a strange one. He's quite a character.

Sheila: It's his way. He's shy.

Johnny: Silk p.j.'s! Can I have a pair?

Ma: It's what a Chinaman would wear. It took forever just to get a look at him. He acts like a fugitive from justice.

Sheila: He's shy.

Pop: *(Waking up suddenly.)* He's furtive and stealthy. I never acted like that Polack. What's he got to hide?

Sheila: There's nothing wrong with him.

Pop: Two weeks. That's all I give it. Two weeks, you'll be home again. And you'll have squandered your precious innocence.

Pop sneakily lifts a wedding bouquet up, sniffs it.

Ma: I've got to go back down to the cellar.

Sheila: On my wedding day?

Ma: There's laundry I gotta do today just like any. Always more laundry. And there's a bum down there I smell. He must've crawled in during the night. One of the last bums from the Great Depression, I guess. I gotta do laundry and throw out the bum. Watch your brother! He runs out the back door and off down the block every time my back is turned. I have to run after him in my nightgown. Everyone on Benedict Avenue has seen my nightgown. He's a devil. He won't eat all his mashed potatoes.

Exit Ma. Pop, bouquet in hand, calls out craftily.

Pop: Hi ho!

And darts down the stairs after her.

Johnny: She mashes the carrots into the potatoes so they ain't really mashed potatoes. I don't know what they are! They have dots.

Sheila: Watch this. *(Humming the* Wedding March *under her breath, she comes down the stairs to take position. Along the way, she thanks an imaginary well-wisher for a compliment.)* Thank you! *(Having gotten to an open space, she advises Johnny.)* Get ready!

She hums romantic music and does an awkward pirouette.

Johnny: What's that?

Sheila: It's a pirouette. Wanna see another?

Johnny: *(Laughing.)* No.

She ignores him, hums again, and does another one, enjoying her dress.

Sheila: It's ballet! *(She picks up her suitcase from where she rested it.)* Let me put makeup on you.

Johnny: Okay.

Sheila: Well, come on!

Johnny runs Down and sits dutifully on a box.

Johnny: I'm only doing this because you want me to.

She takes out a lipstick and draws a big smile on Johnny's face. She sings Hark, The Herald Angels Sing *as she does so.*

Johnny: You're beautiful. I saw a girl on the street and I thought she was you and I said hello and she didn't know who I was.

Sheila: Ain't this fun?

Johnny: Not exactly.

Sheila: Yes, it is.

Johnny: Okay.

Sheila: There. It's a smile. Now you'll always have a smile on your face.

Offstage lascivious laughter is heard. It's Ma and Pop. Johnny takes it in and it alarms him.

Johnny: Don't get married, Sheila!

Sheila: I've got to. I've got to get out of this house.

Johnny: Why?

Sheila: Because this is my chance.

Johnny: I want you to love me.

Sheila: I can't. Not past today. You won't be in my life after today.

Johnny: Why not?

Sheila: I'll have my husband Ray, and my own children. And when you come and see us, I won't care about you very much.

Pop reenters without bouquet.

Pop: She was my jewel. When she was a little girl, I'd take her to Kelly's and let her walk up and down on the bar like the Queen on her ramp. She was a doll. If a man smiled at her in those days, I DON'T CARE EVEN IF HE WAS BLACK, he was alright in my book.

Johnny: Pop? Pop? (*Pop goes back to sleep with his paper. Johnny gives up and asks Sheila.*) What's wrong with that guy?

Sheila: Be quiet. Don't say anything to upset him. He works so hard.

Johnny: Where's your bouquet?

Sheila: In the fridge.

Johnny: You're gonna be sorry.

Sheila: Who's gonna make me sorry?

Johnny: Don't be stupid. Take this stuff off my face. I'm not a clown, you know.

She takes out cold cream and wipes his face tenderly.

Sheila: I know.

Johnny: I gonna get a scissors and cut off all my hair.

Sheila: Don't you dare. You wanna get me in hot water?

Johnny: What are you doing to me?

Sheila: Cold cream.

Johnny: Where's Aunt Annie? She's supposed to look after me.

Sheila: She'll be back.

Johnny: There's something fake about all this.

Sheila: I know. Ain't it something, Johnny? Things have gotten more like a magic story every day. I'm outta high school! Think a that. And now there's Ray. And the weddin. And it's Christmas!

A thunderous knocking on the door.

Johnny: Who's that?

Sheila: This is so exciting! Everything is so exciting! I'm the center of everything!

Enter Ma, excited, with the bouquet and another basket of laun-

dry. She crosses hurriedly to deposit it with the first, under the staircase. As she goes, she tosses Sheila the bouquet.

Ma: Jesus, Mary and Joseph! It's him! It's Joey! Home after a year! He's been voyaging all over the world. Spain and Ethiopia! I told him. Don't come home with nothin! I told him, if you come home with nothing, I'll slam the door in your face!

The door opens. Enter Joey, all in the white sailor suit and black tie. He's got a white seabag slung over his shoulder. He's young, handsome, healthy as a dog. He knows everyone loves him.

Sheila: Joey! It's Joey!

Joey salutes, beaming, and yells.

Joey: I'M BACK!

Johnny: Who is he?

Ma: It's your brother! And he didn't come home empty-handed!

Joey swings his bag, crying.

Joey: Yo Ho! Yo Ho! *(He throws open his arms. His mother runs into them. He twirls her. She shrieks, happy.)* Hi, Ma! How's my girl! Hello, Sheila!

He twirls Sheila. She shrieks with pleasure in turn.

Sheila: You look so handsome!

Ma: Hello, Joey me boy. Don't you look great!

Joey: Thanks, Ma.

Ma: I see you listen to your mother. You'll never go wrong as long as you do that, kid. Now what did you bring home?

Joey: Don't you wanna hear about all the places I've been?

Ma: No. I want to see what's in the bag.

Joey: That's my Ma! I could never put anything over on you.

Ma: And don't you ever try! *(To Johnny.)* I can see through doors!

Sheila: Joey, it's my wedding day!

Joey: I know. I didn't break any rules so I could stay out of the brig and be here. You look so beautiful! This guy's not good enough for you!

He cries a little, pulling out a big red handkerchief to dab his eyes.

Sheila: Don't cry, Joey. Aw, you're so sentimental.

Joey: I am. I know it.

Ma: He'd cry over spilt milk.

Joey: I would! And movies. And things drunks say to me when I'm drunk. But this is different. This is my sister getting married. You know how I feel about you.

Sheila: I know. And don't you know I feel that way about you, too?

Johnny: I can't go to the wedding because I've got double-pneumonia.

Joey: Hi, Johnny.

Johnny: Howdy Doody. You look like a god.

Joey: *(Smiling broadly.)* If you're ever disrespectful to Mommy or Daddy, I'll kill you, understand?

Johnny: But you lied and cheated and stole and everything!

Joey: Yeah, well so what? I should lie. I should steal. I should cheat.

Johnny: Why?

Joey: Women love a bad boy.

Johnny: What about a bad man?

Joey: I am who I am! I'm myself! And I'll rip you ta pieces if you ever cross me!

Johnny: Fuck you!

> *They both recoil at the language.*

Joey: I said that in front of Pop once, at the zoo. He punched me right in the face.

Johnny: You're not Pop and I'm not you!

Joey: I'm more Pop than you are!

Johnny: You're not Pop!

Joey: You wanna showdown?

Johnny: I'm five years old, you gorilla, and you're asking me if I want a showdown?

Joey: I was five at the zoo.

Johnny: That was you.

Joey: Later then.

Johnny: That's right. Later.

Ma: Alright already, open the bag! My feet are killing me.

Joey: Okay.

Ma: If I'm runnin around, they're not too bad, but if I stand still, they throb. It's the Fitzgerald Curse.

Joey, Sheila: *(Simultaneous with above.)* It's the Fitzgerald Curse!
He sets the bag down and opens it. He takes out a box and lifts the lid: crystal glasses. Another box: a dancer pops up, music plays. He takes out a small, wind-up car, and lets it go toward Johnny, who picks it up and is happy. Then hardwood jars. A box inlaid with mother-of-pearl. A pith helmet. And lastly, an Ethiopian flag.

Joey: This is it. OK... Spanish crystal.

Ma: Oh God, beautiful.

Joey: A music box. Sheila?

Sheila: For me?

Ma: Lucky girl.

Sheila: This goes on my night table.

Joey: A mechanical car from Germany. Don't break it.

Johnny: I won't.

Ma: He will.

Joey: Fruitwood jars from Africa for holding stuff.

Ma: That's a little weird.

Joey: You gotta smell 'em. A jewelry box inlaid with mother-of-pearl.

Ma: Now all's I need's some jewelry.

Joey: Next year. Now get ready. The sun hat of the emperor of Ethiopia.

Ma: Oh my God.

Joey: And the flag from his yacht.

Sheila: Oo! How'd you get it from his yacht?

Pop: *(Snapping awake, cleaver in hand.)* How else do you think? He stole it! The old story! He's a thief! He's got dirty habits! Women. Drink. Maybe even drugs, who knows?

Joey: Oh Pop.

Pop: Why wouldn't you finish high school? Broke my heart. You know it. It'll haunt you the rest of your life. After I'm dead and you realize how good I was. I'm a quiet man. I don't talk much, but how could you, son? What was I asking? Three months? Four? But you, you had to go in the Navy. Couldn't wait another day. How could you?

Joey: I worship the ground you walk on.

Pop: I know.

Joey: And I can tell a joke. I can tell a dirty joke so that good people laugh.

Pop: You've got the gift of gab, alright. And you're handsome as a hound.

Joey: So love me!

Pop: No.

Joey: Don't do this to me!

Pop: It'll haunt you all your life, this thing between us. I'll hold something back from you and you'll try to get it.

Sheila: But not me, Daddy.

Pop: No, not you. You were my darlin. You were my jewel.

Sheila: That's why I'll be the only one who isn't crazy.

Johnny: Your day's gonna come. Everybody's day's gonna come with this guy.

Sheila: Who says?

Ma: You'll hyperventilate.

Sheila: I will not.

Ma: You'll see spots.

Sheila: Spots?

Ma: You'll give up your gall bladder.

Sheila: Never!

Ma: You'll have thirty years of serious constipation.

Sheila: I don't care!

Ma: Your children will be crazy. Your husband Ray 'ill do it to 'em. He's crazy and he'll make them crazy, too.

Pop: I don't like that Ray. I don't care if he was in Korea. I don't care if he did win the Purple Heart. He's not good enough for my darlin Sheila.

Ma: He has a homicidal temper.

Sheila: He has a bad back.

Ma: I can eat two big lollipops, grape and cherry, suck 'em ta the bone!

Johnny: Oh, would you shut up with that weird bragging! And tell me. Do you love me?

Ma: Shut up yourself!

Johnny: And where's Aunt Annie?

Ma: She was hit by a car yesterday afternoon. Hit and run. Your Aunt Annie is dead.

Johnny: But she was the one who took care of me.

Ma: She's dead. Goodbye. End of story.

Johnny: Why didn't you tell me?

Ma: We didn't want to spoil Christmas! Why do you think we ain't opened these presents? They're from Annie.

Everyone looks at the base of the Christmas tree and shudders.

All: Ugh.

There's a violent knocking at the door. They all clutch their hearts. Then Joey smiles.

Joey: People! More people! Good! I love a crowd. I'll be in charge of the laughs.

Sheila: Everybody's coming for my wedding! They honor me!

Violent knocking again, and then the door swings open.

Ma: Oh my God! It's your wonderful cousin, children! Oh, what a wonderful day! It's your cousin Sister Mary Kate!

Enter Sister Mary Kate, a nun, all splendid in black and white. In her hands she holds several strings of white plastic rosary beads. Johnny hides. She has an Irish brogue.

Mary Kate: Bless you! Bless you all! Merry Christmas!

All: Merry Christmas, Sister Mary Kate!

Mary Kate: I've been on a Greyhound bus for four days, I smell like a ditchdigger! I've brought you all rosary beads that glow in the dark! You all look beautiful. At the hospital where I work in Texas, everyone is sick, everyone is in pain. I do hope you savor this time in your life which is so rich. What a beautiful tree!

Sheila: I picked it! I picked it!

Mary Kate: Self-praise stinks, dear. God bless them and keep them in this happy time.

Johnny: *(Sneezing.)* Ah-choo.

Mary Kate: And here's little Johnny!

Johnny: *(Discovered.)* Uh-oh.

Mary Kate spies him, pursues him, and catches him during next.

Mary Kate: Look how beautiful you are! I could eat you like an apple! I could eat you! I could eat you! You're like sugar to me! Come here now. Come here. *(She's got him now.)* Can you read yet?

Johnny: Yeah.

Mary Kate: Watch what you read! How's kindergarten?

Johnny: They threw me out.

Mary Kate: What! Thrown out of kindergarten! Whatever why?

Johnny: I don't remember.

Mary Kate: Now open your heart to me entirely and I will give you counsel.

Johnny: Okay. Listen, Sister, something's wrong! I started a fire in the bathroom that scared me, but it went out.

Mary Kate raps his hand.

Mary Kate: Don't start fires. That's the Devil's job.

Johnny: I feel like stealin something from Aunt Annie. Can ya steal from the dead?

She pokes him for emphasis.

Mary Kate: Yes! Steal stuff and you'll burn. That's basics. What else?

Johnny: I saw a cat kill a bird today. It was the most awful thing I've ever seen.

She thinks this over briefly, then snaps her fingers.

Mary Kate: Don't look at things like that!

Johnny: I don't know where to look!

Mary Kate: Take a rosary and pray when you're alone. It glows in the dark.

Johnny: Does it shine from holiness?

Mary Kate: Yes. And a chemical.

Joey's drinking a can of beer.

Joey: Hey, listen to this. Why did the moron get off the bus?

Pop: No dirty jokes now. With the clergy here. None of your Navy jokes.

Joey: No, no. This one is clean!

Pop: (*Terrorizing him with the cleaver.*) I will never approve of you! You dropped out of high school. And you'll get a bad discharge out of the Navy. You'll bum around with your bum friend Burke. And you'll get a job on Wall Street. The years will pass and you'll get to be a big muckity-muck on Wall Street. You'll have a wife named Betty and three children named Donna and Tommy and Joey, and you'll desert them! You'll look for love to stop the starving thing in you that I put there, but nothing will stop the starving thing. I'll never approve of you. Even after you're dead, there will be no rest. Your ashes will blow in the wind, and your soul will be in Hell!

Johnny: Leave him alone!

Pop, snapping around, looks at Johnny with pleasure.

Pop: Hey, look who's up on his hind legs!

Joey: Hey, are you going against Pop, you little crumb! I'll kill ya!

Johnny is dumbfounded.

Johnny: I... don't understand.

Pop laughs and goes back up to the dining table. Joey follows close behind Pop, aping his father's laugh and walk. Pop speaks to the chopped meat.

Pop: Meat and viscera. My old companions.

Joey: Pop. Did you see how I told him?

Pop: Sing "Danny Boy".

Joey: *(Sings.)* O Danny Boy... *(Stops, panicked.)* I don't know the rest!

Pop: God love ya, may ya not die till I kill ya.

Mary Kate: How are ya, Noreen?

Ma: My feet are killing me. All the Fitzgerald's got these feet, and I'm a Fitzgerald.

Mary Kate: Offer it up.

Ma: I do.

Mary Kate: If you saw the pain I see.

Ma: I see enough.

Sheila: Did you see Elvis on Ed Sullivan?

Ma: No!

Mary Kate: *(Simultaneously.)* Yes! *(Then defensively, to Ma.)* I saw it by chance!

Sheila: Everybody's special. Special.

Joey: I love beer. I love it.

Sheila: *(Taking Joey in.)* Yes.

Mary Kate: So you're getting married today.

Sheila: Yes, Sister Mary Kate!

Mary Kate: Is he a good Catholic?

Sheila: Oh yes. He's a Polish Catholic.

Mary Kate: You're not marrying an Irishman?

Sheila: No, is that wrong?

Mary Kate: No, it's not wrong. But it seems unnatural and no good will come of it. *(Switching to Ma.)* So poor dumb Annie stepped in front of a car and was obliterated!

Ma: I'll tell you one thing. I'm gettin the insurance. We're the ones who took Annie in, not my sisters. If she's been smashed with a car, the insurance money falls to us.

Mary Kate: That will be the cause of some bitterness.

Ma: Let there be a falling out then. They'll be wrong and I'll be hurt.

Mary Kate: Things will be awry ever after.

Ma: True perhaps, but I get the money!

Mary Kate: Head of the House, lead us in prayer!

Pop: Everybody kneel down! *(Everybody does.)* We're going to pray now. *(Everybody presses palms together. Pop continues to stand. He prays rapid-fire.)* Hail Mary, full of grace, the Lord sides with you. Blessed art thou amongst chicken houses fulla squallin women, and blessed is the lucky fine fat of yer womb, Jesus.

>   *They all bow their heads and say the name "Jesus." They say the next part with Pop.*

All: Holy Mary, Mother of Misery, Mother of this mindless muttering, Mistress of us grey galley slaves in this DEAD religion of the DEfunct Roman Empire, pray for us now, and at the hour of our death, now, and at the hour of our death. Amen!

>   *The prayer over, they all immediately rise to their feet.*

Pop: I get in and outta the meat locker thirty times per day. Cold, hot, cold, hot. The sweat freezes on my back but I never get sick. And that's why, no matter how long you live, you sons a bitches, no matter how goddamn long, I'll outlive ya!

Sheila: Look! It's snowing outside. Big big flakes. Like first communion dresses.

Johnny: Oh, look at it! Look at it!

Ma: It'll be a foot high on all the garbage can covers.

Mary Kate: It'll be in all the old photographs. Black and white. Like me.

Johnny: A white Christmas.

>   *Joey sings, very sentimentally and well, two lines of some Tin Pan Alley Christmas song.**

* See Special Note on copyright page

Pop: You're no Bing Crosby, are ya?

Joey falters, stops singing, but continues to hum the tune under Ma's speech. Perhaps Sheila hums with him.

Ma: I remember when your Aunt Della died. Mama was having a party out in Greenpoint. Della came. She looked especially beautiful. Everybody was telling her so. And then Mama came out and looked at her, she took one look at her, and she said, Get that girl to a hospital. She's got the T.B. Della was double-jointed in every part of her body. She could tie her arm in a knot. They took her to Lourdes, hoping for a miracle. She died on the boat, on the way back.

Pop: She was a whore!

Ma: SHUT UP!

A collective gasp comes from the others.

Others: *(Said short.)* Oh!

Pop: She was my sister.

Ma: *(Warning him.)* Don't step over the line, Pop.

It's a faceoff. The others look to see what Pop will do, saying the while.

Others: *(Said long.)* Oh!

Pop backs down, muttering to himself.

Pop: I had stomach trouble. I went to the doctor. I said, Listen here. I don't need this god damn stomach if it's gonna back up on me.

Pop's volume drops to an almost inaudible level after "I went to the doctor," and Joey overlaps the rest.

Joey: *(To Johnny, through clenched teeth.)* If you're ever disrespectful to Ma or Pop, I'll kill you. I swear to God I'll kill you, understand me? Pop, did you hear what I told him?

Johnny: *(To Joey.)* What's the matter with you?

Joey: There's nothing the matter with me. I feel like a million bucks.

Johnny: You drink too much beer.

Joey: I like a good time.

Ma: Lord have mercy on beautiful Della. May she rest in peace.

Joey: I'll drink to that.

Sheila: There's a shadow on my wedding day.

Ma: You had an uncle. The Blessed Virgin Mary appeared to him in the basement of an apartment building while he was shovelling coal.

Johnny: Ma? Whaddaya say? How 'bout we cut short the recollections? Whaddaya say? How 'bout some breast milk?

Ma: When I was having one of the babies, the woman in the next bed was dying. She called to me. She saw a white bird in the window. She wanted me to see. I looked, but there wasn't any white bird. But she saw it. She died soon after. Lord have mercy on that woman. May she rest in peace.

Mary Kate: *(Simultaneously.)* Lord have mercy on that woman. May she rest in peace.

Joey: I love beer. That's one thing I'll always have. I'll always love a cold beer.

Mary Kate: It's snowing. It's snowing. It's snowing.

Pop: It's bad weather.

Johnny: Can anybody hear me?

Sheila: Do you remember how we all used to play in the big lot out back?

Joey: With the dog?

Sheila: Big Red.

Joey: What a dog!

Ma: He died from eating five pounds of pure fat.

Johnny: Who gave it to him?

> *Pop brandishes a piece of meat in Johnny's face.*

Pop: Maybe it was me! *(Johnny runs away, hiding under the staircase. Pop calls after him.)* What would you think of that?

Ma: Mama was always so strict. Then one time she got real sick, and it looked like she was going to die. And she said to us, If I get well, I swear to God, I'm going to change. And, would you believe it? She did get well, and she did change. She was a better person. Lord have mercy on Mama.

Ma & Mary Kate: May she rest in peace.

Mary Kate: Oh Death, where is thy sting?

Ma: *(Pointing at her breast.)* Here.

Sheila: They've started building a police station out back, in the lot where we played with Big Red. One day it'll be the Forty-Third Precinct.

Pop: I told 'em to rip that stupid stomach outta me like an old blowed tire!

Mary Kate: I envy you your family.

Ma: I envy you your chastity.

Mary Kate: I'll never be back here again. I'll go back to the hospital in Texas, and I'll never see these people again. I'll correspond.

Sheila: And then one day later on yet, they'll shut that precinct down, and it'll just be a dead building and hurricane fence.

Johnny comes out from under the staircase. A little smoke starts to issue from under the stairs.

Johnny: And they'll have killed every living thing in the lot behind this house to do it! Listen! I'm five years old and everybody's like wrapping it up, saying goodnight. Now that ain't gonna fly, do you hear me?

Joey: I'll never be a sailor again. I'll never be this young again.

Sheila: I'll never be a bride anymore.

Pop: I'll sell this house and we'll move away to another neighborhood.

Johnny checks the progress of the fire under the stairs and makes a good point.

Johnny: If you wanna house to sell, you better start payin attention to me! *(To Ma.)* And I'm gonna get that nipple in my mouth, understand? If Aunt Annie is dead, somebody else is gonna have ta love me!

Joey: Jeez, I'm gettin sentimental. I'm getting all misty.

Sheila: *(Putting on her veil.)* It's time I put on my veil. I wanna see it all through a veil.

Johnny: Don't be stupid, Sheila! You've got to go on and on! It's a constant thing! A trance won't take you through it!

Sheila: God, what if this is the happiest day of my life?

Mary Kate: The past is such a beautiful thing. Somebody take a picture!

Pop: Hold it. How do you work this gizmo?

Pop produces a camera with a flash and fiddles with it as the group, excepting Johnny, gathers for the picture.

Johnny: When I was one, two, three, four, five freakin years of my life...

Ma: Johnny?

Johnny: In the old house.

Pop: What's the matter with that kid?

Johnny: *(Yelling at the group, pointing to all the smoke.)* What do you see? What do you see?

Group: FIRE! FIRE! FIRE!

Johnny: I discovered fire.

> *Pop's flash accidentally goes off as he stares, along with the others, at the fire under the stairs. Blackout.*

INTERMEZZO

> *In the darkness, a Lawrence Welk style orchestra concludes a Cha Cha number smartly to generous applause. We hear the Master of Ceremonies. He's an Irish charmer.*

M.C.: And haven't they been supplying us with a lovely bit a music? *(Applause.)* That's the band. None finer. *(More applause.)* Oh, you're a grand bunch. A real pleasure. Now about this bride. Isn't she beautiful? *(Applause.)* Would you step out here where we can see you? *(A spotlight appears in front of the stage. Or to the side. Sheila steps into it. She's glowing.)* Thank you. Marvelous. *(Applause and a few friendly hoots and exclamations.)* May I now ask the father of the bride to join his daughter on the dance floor. For one last dance with his little girl. And here he comes. *(Pop appears in a tuxedo and joins Sheila in the spotlight. Applause. Pop is formal, calm, emotional.)* And the number the bride has selected is… is… is…

> *The M.C.'s voice reverberates and dies away. A Sixties Heavy Metal Classic comes crashing on. Pop and Sheila come together and dance as if it were a waltz. The spot fades. Darkness. After a moment, the music chops off. And the lights bump up for Act II.*

ACT II

The New House. The back wall is a painted drop, peach in color, depicting a starburst clock from the Sixties. The scene is flooded with light.

There are two upholstered black chairs with flecks of gold running through the fabric; they stand on wooden legs. Downstage Center is the television. We can't see the screen, but it emits a pale blue light.

Johnny sits in the Right chair, watching television. On the floor before him are seven pairs of shoes, and an old shoeshine box of the homemade variety. Johnny's 18. He's absently touching up a pair of white, woman's shoes with white shoe dye. He's dressed in white jeans, ripped tennis sneakers and no socks, a white T-shirt with a homemade drawing of Snoopy on it. He has on pale blue rimless glasses.

Unbeknownst to Johnny, Joey is watching him from the landing. Joey's wearing white jeans, ripped sneakers just like Johnny's. He's sockless. He sports an incredibly yellow windbreaker. His jeans fit much, much more tightly than his brother's. It's sort've 1968.

Joey, arms folded, regards Johnny with a too big smile.

Joey: Hey, fucknuckle.

Johnny: What's that?

Joey: What's with all the shoes?

Johnny: This is my job. Pop gave me all these shoes to shine.

Joey: Whose shoes are they?

Johnny: Pop's. Yours. Mine. And then some of them, I don't know whose they are. They're just shoes.

Joey: Are you on acid?

Johnny: Am I what?

Joey: Are you on acid?

Johnny: No.

Joey: Mind doin me a favor?

Johnny: What?

Joey: Walk to me.

Johnny: Why?

Joey: Just walk to me.

Johnny walks to Joey. Joey looks into his face briefly, still smiling.

Johnny: Are you done?

Joey: You're not on acid.

Johnny: No?

Joey: No. *(Joey takes Johnny's chair.)* You know how I can tell?

Johnny: How?

Joey: Never mind. Why aren't you out getting girls?

Johnny: I'm going out later.

Joey: You're pretty lame, pardner.

Johnny: You're a faggot.

Joey gives a false hearty guffaw to this.

Joey: When I was in the Corps, if you said that to me, I woulda ripped your fuckin head off. But I've mellowed out some. Yessir. I just feel too good to let you bother me.

Johnny: You feel good?

Joey: I feel great.

Johnny: I thought you hadda bleedin ulcer?

Joey: I'm not talking about physically. Physically I've had a few problems.

Johnny: Then how is it you feel great? What is it you feel great about?

Joey: Life! Freedom! The Future.

Johnny tells his story to the audience.

Johnny: When I was sixteen, seventeen, eighteen fucking years of my life...

Joey: Johnny.

Johnny: In the new house...

Joey: Johnny.

Johnny: Another brother appeared, who I will also call Joey.

Joey: You want me to take it out?

Johnny: What?

Joey: My dick. You want me to take my dick out?

Johnny: No.

Joey: Are you sure?

Johnny: Yeah.

Joey: You shitass. I was just testing you. *(Noticing the t.v.)* Whats the show?

Johnny: It's called *Treasure*. It's about, you know, treasures. Where they are. How they got there. It sucks really.

Joey: I was just testing you.

Johnny: Who cares?

Joey: I feel like I don't know you anymore.

Johnny: When did you know me?

Joey: Still set fires?

Johnny: No.

Joey: When did you stop?

Johnny: Well, I didn't stop. It's just very rare that I start a fire now.

Joey: So what do you do now?

Johnny: Now I have language.

Joey: We all have language.

Johnny: Yeah. But I have language *at my disposal*.

Joey: What the fuck does that mean?

Johnny: I don't know.

   Joey speaks with sudden decision.

Joey: I'm gonna write a book.

Johnny: You?

Joey: Oh yeah.

Johnny: When did you decide that?

Joey: A long time ago. Are you as hated and despised in this neighborhood as much now as when I left?

Johnny: Nope. These days I'm verging on popular.

Joey: Is that right? That's some turnaround from the way it was.

Johnny: I was never hated and despised in the neighborhood.

Joey: No? I hadda save you from something looked a lot like a lynch mob a few years ago. What were they on your ass for anyway?

Johnny: I hit this kid.

Joey: You just hit a kid? That's it?

Johnny: He was a cripple.

Pause.

Joey: Why did you hit him?

Johnny: He touched me. I just didn't get the neighborhood. I didn't appreciate it.

Joey: And now you do.

Johnny: That's right. Now I got the knack. Are you going out?

Joey: Haven't made up my mind.

Johnny: Well, do you like to know how to be in a room and not eat up all the light and oxygen? How 'bout sittin down? How 'bout takin a seat?

Joey: No, thank you. *(Goes to imaginary window, looks out.)* What could you find to appreciate about this neighborhood? I never seen so many ugly bastids. And the women. Tough meat. The fat ones look like they ate somebody. The skinny ones look like they had to watch. I mean it! Enlighten me. What the fuck could you find to appreciate about this shithole neighborhood?

Johnny: Our backyard.

Joey: There's nothing back there.

Johnny: There's grass. There's a peach tree hangin over the fence.

Joey: That's the Guzzo's.

Johnny: There's starlings. They wake me up in the morning.

Joey: They wake me up, too.

Johnny: There's tomato plants. There's all that sheepshit Pop put down.

Joey: And you like that?

Johnny: Yeah.

Joey: When the sun hits it?

Johnny: Yeah.

Joey: What are you, Jungle John?

Johnny: Yeah, I'm a real sodbuster. No, there's flowers. There's vines up the wall of MacMurty's garage. Caterpillars, potato bugs, honeybees.

Joey: So that's it? You appreciate the backyard?

Johnny: The Paino's down the street. The smell of their grapevines. I like that, too. I like that a lot.

Joey: So lemme ask you this. Why ain't you in the backyard or down at Paino's sniffin the air? Why you here watchin T.V.?

Johnny: I was at the Parkchester Cafe last night. Everybody I know was there. And they ain't got a fuckin thing to do with me. And the backyard ain't got a fuckin thing to do with me. And neither does Paino's vines.

Joey: What does have to do with you?

Johnny: Nothing.

Joey: I saw that friend of yours. What's his name? Freddie?

Johnny: Yeah, what about him?

Joey: What's his problem?

Johnny: What are you talking about?

Joey: Well, you're seein that girl Patty, right? Right?

Johnny: Yeah?

Joey: Well, he was walking with her, they were talking. It was real chummy.

Johnny: They're friends.

Joey: Maybe that's what she thinks. You know what we should do?

Johnny: What should we do?

Joey: We should beat the shit out of him. Freddie.

Johnny: Freddie's my best friend.

Joey: He's trying to fuck you over with Patty.

Johnny: No, he isn't.

Joey: Yes, he is.

Johnny: No, he isn't.

Joey: What is he? Is he black?

Johnny: No, he's Italian and German.

Joey: I think he's black. He looks black.

Johnny: I guess he does look black.

Joey: He looks very black. The guy's black.

Johnny: No! He's gotta be Italian and German.

Joey: Right! In this neighborhood, he's gotta be Italian and German whether he's Italian and German or not! Like if he was trying to fuck you over with Patty, it would be important it didn't look that way.

Johnny: He's not doing that! That's not what's happening!

Joey: Alright. He isn't. I've seen some shit you haven't, you know.

Johnny: What are you talking about?

Joey: In my life. With these eyes. I've seen some shit.

Johnny: You mean in Vietnam?

Joey: Yeah. In The Nam.

Johnny: You saw shit in Vietnam that makes you better qualified than me to judge whether or not my best friend is after my girl?

Joey: That's right.

Johnny: What did you see? What did you see in Vietnam?

Joey: I don't like to talk about it. I hate this fuckin neighborhood.

Johnny: Yeah, well, it hates you right back.

Joey: It does?

Johnny: You lived here, what, nine years. Did you make a friend? Did you make one friend?

Joey: No. But that was my choice. I didn't have any use for these people.

Johnny: Sounds kinda grand.

Joey: It was my choice! Anyway, I made enough friends in the Corps. You know what they nicknamed me in the Corps?

Johnny: What?

Joey: Dan'el.

Johnny: Dan'el?

Joey: Yup.

Johnny: Why?

Joey: Like Daniel Boone.

Johnny: Daniel Boone? The frontiersman? Daniel Boone?

Joey: And Junior's my friend still. From the old days.

Johnny: But Junior's like an obese criminal devil.

Joey: So?

Johnny: He's more like a tragic flaw than a buddy. Forget me, why ain't you out gettin girls?

Joey: When the Joe decides it's time, the Joe will go. The Boy from New York City.

Johnny: Well, I hope you don't go to the beach.

Joey: Why not? The beach can be excellent. I can do serious damage among the females at the beach.

Johnny: You forget I went with you to the beach. I saw your technique. It don't work to stand in the sand like the Statue a Liberty, starin stone-faced at some girl till she gets so nervous she's gotta leave.

Joey: I got to her.

Johnny: You got to her. You spooked her.

Joey: I got to her exactly as I intended. I unsettled her.

Johnny: She thought you were a weirdo! That's not technique, Joey. That's just nuts.

Joey laughs in that forced way.

Joey: My little brother! So how's your girlfriend doing?

Johnny: What's it to ya?

Joey: Comon, how's she doin? She's cute. Patty. She put a little somethin in her hair, didn't she? She's a little blonder. Did she say it was the sun?

Johnny refers to the t.v.

Johnny: Look at that. They found the gold. End of story.

Joey: Comon, how's she doing?

Johnny: I don't know. We broke up.

Joey: I'm sorry to hear that. Why?

Johnny: Who knows? Why do people break up?

Joey: Why?

Johnny: I caught her with another guy.

Joey: *(Leaping to his feet.)* Wow!

Johnny: Not Freddie! Some clown named Tommy Pinto. And no, let's not go and beat up Tommy Pinto!

Joey: Wow.

Johnny: What's the matter? Does this news trigger a war memory?

Joey: No. So that's why you're in this mood.

Johnny: No, that's not it.

Joey: Then why is it?

Johnny: It's true I'm upset cause I broke up with Patty.

Joey: You want me to fix you up with somebody? I gave these girls your picture and they thought you were cute.

Johnny: What girls?

Joey: You want me to introduce you?

Johnny: No.

Joey: You wanna get a drink?

Johnny: No. When I'm upset and I drink... I hadda unpleasant little episode last night after some gin.

Joey: Whats the matter with you?

Johnny: I guess it's the stuff I've seen. I can't get my head around the stuff I've seen.

Joey: What do you think you've seen?

Johnny: I have seen pretty girls ruined. Handsome guys, just like the greatest guys, destroyed. Sometimes I feel like I'm on a force march. I can hear the wind blowin. We all started out together, and then people just started droppin.

Joey: You haven't seen shit. You should see what I've seen.

Johnny: Think what you want.

Joey: Comon. What are we talkin about? You wanna go some-place and get a drink? It'll do ya good.

Johnny: No, it wouldn't. But thanks.

Joey: That's alright. *(Laughs casually.)* So. Have you taken acid?

Johnny: Once.

Joey: I'm tellin Mom.

Johnny: What!

Joey: *(Goes and sits.)* I'm tellin Mom! It's information I got, it's a responsibility! You're takin drugs and she don't know it!

Johnny: Once!

Joey: I'm tellin!

Johnny: Please don't do that!

Joey: Why shouldn't I? Huh? Why shouldn't I? Is there some reason I don't know?

Johnny: You don't know what I've been through! At least you were in Vietnam! People understand that. They know it was tough. She has these headaches all the time: "Jesus, Mary and Joseph!" Screaming at me. Over nothin! Not that I'm sayin there was never nothin. I admit it. There was a long time when I was doin stuff. Settin fires, breakin windows. And then I was havin all this trouble in school. I was failin everything. They said I had psychological problems, and by the way, fuck them! Showin me inkblots. They said maybe I was retarded, and by the way, fuck them again! And I hadda problem with lyin, I couldn't stop lyin. And I couldn't keep my mouth shut! I stole some records, too, and that turned into a big thing, a regular fuckin witch hunt. I mean, they wanted me DEAD, BROKEN, and RUINED! And if they coulda found a way, these ADULTS—what a fuckin mockery of the word—if they coulda found a way, they woulda EXPUNGED ME. I stole some records from some midget whose life seemed good to me, and these ADULTS, they tried to remount *The Ox Bow Incident*! But I beat their fuckin rap. The school people, the IQ people, the inkblot people, the home people, and by the way, fuck them all! I broke the back of the doomsday squad that was after my ass. If I'm sittin here watchin t.v., with nobody knockin on the door, and Mom quelled, that's a victory. That's fuckin Iwo Jima. I should put my flag up and have a good cry. So yeah, me and Patty broke up, but the good part a that is I'm free. I'm really free. And even though I'm sad, things are a lot better. Even around here. And they're gonna get better yet if I've got anything to say about it.

Joey: You think so?

Johnny: Yeah, I think so. So don't set Mom off with a drug thing. I feel funny sayin it, but the scoop is she's goin through change-a-life. One of the aunts finally told me. You should probably know, too. I thought she was just fuckin crazy.

Joey: So maybe the last thing she needs is you.

Johnny: Or maybe the last thing she needs is YOU. Wavin a fresh red flag in her face. Drugs. I know you've had it hard, Joey. But I've had it hard, too. Okay?

Joey: I'm tellin.

Johnny jumps up.

Johnny: The hell you are! What's the matter with you?

Joey flies out of his chair to confront Johnny.

Joey: You think you can take me?

Johnny: Don't tell her!

Joey: Do you know how crazy I am, you fuckin little shit! I've terrorized people! I could murder you in your sleep tonight, you know that? I could snap your neck and enjoy it!

Johnny: And what does that make you but a fuckin animal!

Joey starts strangling Johnny.

Joey: That's right! I'm a fuckin animal! This is the fuckin jungle!

He's got Johnny on the floor.

Johnny: Go on! Do it, you baboon fuck! You think I give a flier? Do it! DO IT!

Joey, scared, drops him. Johnny is lying on the rug.

Joey: You're crazy.

Johnny: I'm crazy? You're the one's gonna get the certificate!

Joey: I am not!

Johnny: Okay, you strangle me and I'm crazy. I invite you to diagram that fuckin idea.

Joey: You just don't understand me.

Johnny: I understand you a bit. Dan'el.

Johnny gets off the floor and sits back down in his chair.

Joey: I've got big feelings.

Johnny: Congratulations.

Joey: There's things I wanna do. I fell in love with this girl. Nadine. Garvin. She was a Salvation Army lass. I sent her a dozen red roses every Friday.

Johnny: A lass? She was a lass?

Joey: I'm gonna get a Jaguar XKE.

Johnny: We switched, right? We're talking about a car now.

Joey: I wrote an essay about it. "Why I Want A Jaguar XKE". Fuckin high school.

Johnny: You live in a dream world, Joey! I didn't know it now. Just here. But later, man, later I see you clear as you were in this room.

Joey: What good's it do ya?

Johnny: It does me good.

Joey sits down again.

Joey: I hear you got thrown outta college.

Johnny: Sorta. Yeah. The folks were relieved. It cost them money.

Joey: So what are you gonna do?

Johnny: I'm thinkin about joinin the Marine Corps.

Joey: I don't see it.

Johnny: I didn't ask you to see it.

Joey: Johnny, you go in the Corps, they'll throw you out.

Johnny: They will not.

Joey: They threw you outta college.

Johnny: Not the same.

Joey: Threw ya outta the Little League, didn't they?

Johnny: Yeah.

Joey: Kindergarten?

Johnny: Yeah.

Joey: Hot lunch program?

Johnny: Yeah.

Joey: High Schools?

Johnny: Yeah.

Joey: Why'd you get thrown outta so many things?

Johnny: I don't remember.

Joey: But you don't think you'll get thrown outta the Corps?

Johnny: No.

Joey: Why not?

Johnny: I think I'm changing. I think I've changed.

Joey: What about your mental health?

Johnny: My mental health is better.

Joey: What was wrong with you anyway?

Johnny: I'd start to hear this rhythm, and then everything was in this rhythm.

Joey: That doesn't sound so bad.

Johnny: Well, there was something really bad about it. But I can handle it now.

Joey: Well, the Drill Instructor's waitin for you, man.

Ma appears on the landing. She's wearing a sundress. She seems a little spaced out.

Joey: Hey, Mom.

Ma: Hi, Joey.

Johnny: Hi, Ma.

Ma: Have you stolen anything, Johnny?

Johnny: No.

Ma: Have you set anything on fire?

Johnny: No.

Ma: I just washed the floor before Mass and somebody walked all over it.

Johnny: It wasn't me.

Ma: It wasn't?

Johnny: No.

Ma: Are you lying?

Johnny: No.

Ma: Did you sleep with that girl Patty?

Johnny: Yeah.

Ma: Under my roof?

Johnny: No.

Ma: Are you lying?

Johnny: No.

Ma: What are you thinking about?

Johnny: I'm not thinking. I'm thoughtless. When are we gonna get a color t.v.?

Ma: When they perfect it.

Johnny: *(Playfully.)* Hey, Ma?

Ma: What?

Johnny: How 'bout some breast milk?

Ma: *(Chuckles.)* Little late for that, ain't it?

Johnny: What'd you give us, anyway?

Ma: Formula. I gave you formula.

Ma exits the way she came.

Joey: How 'bout lending me some money?

Johnny: No. I only have enough money for myself.

Joey: How 'bout lending me some of it?

Johnny: No.

Joey: How 'bout giving me some of it?

Johnny: Alright.

Johnny gets up, goes to Joey, digs a five out of his pocket, gives it to Joey, and goes back to his own chair.

Joey: Thanks.

Johnny: You're welcome.

Joey gets misted up, pulls out his red bandanna, dabs his eyes and blows his nose.

Joey: That really touched me that you did that.

Johnny: Good.

Joey stows the bandanna.

Joey: How 'bout giving me some more money?

Johnny: No!

Joey: Fuck you! You think I'm not gonna make it? You think I

can't make it on my own? I'm gonna make it! I'm gonna make it!
Johnny: I'm sure you are. And when you do, you're not gonna be beholden to me. And I think that's good.

Enter Ma again.

Ma: What's new?

Joey: Johnny's taken massive amounts of L.S.D.

Ma gives out with a protracted scream.

Ma: Jesus, Mary and Joseph, give me patience!

Joey: And he was the one who walked all over the wet floor. I saw him do it.

Ma: It isn't bad enough, it isn't bad enough, that, that you did it! But you lied! That you boldly barefaced haughty lied to me! You did sleep with that girl under my roof, didn't you?

Johnny: Yes.

Ma: *(Screaming.)* Jesus, Mary and Joseph, give me patience! I have a splitting headache! I'm gonna sob uncontrollably about this for at least three days! Wait till your father gets home! I'm gonna force him to beat you! And if he won't beat you, I'll strip you and whip you myself! Buckle end of the belt! You're not gonna get away with it this time! Well, I gotta go. *(She exits. Joey is about to comment on her behavior when she calls from Off:)* There's a strange stain on the bedspread!

Joey: Well, she keeps you on your toes.

Johnny: *(Gently amused.)* Is that how you see it?

Joey: Johnny?

Johnny: Yeah?

Joey: I love you.

Johnny: I love you, too.

Joey: Do you mean it? Do you genuinely mean it?

Johnny: Yeah.

Joey: You know what the biggest influence in my life has been?

Johnny: What?

Joey: The Beach Boys.

Johnny: You know what the biggest influence in my life has been?

Joey: What?

Johnny: You. *(Thinks.)* The Beach Boys?

Joey: *(Simultaneously.)* Me?

Johnny: That would account for the way you're dressed.

Joey: And me being an influence on you, that would account for the way you're dressed.

Johnny: Exactly, Kimosabe.

Joey: Johnny?

Johnny: Yeah?

Joey: Why don't you hate and despise me?

Johnny: Maybe later. These days, how else can I put it? You're my hero.

Joey: Me? Why?

Johnny: Everybody's gotta have one and around here, the pickins have been mighty slim.

Joey: That sounds kinda cold.

Johnny: Joey, I've licked the water off the underside of every leaf in this fucking desert.

> *Pop appears in the doorway, Left, carrying a double-barreled shotgun, dressed in a sportjacket, tie and sweater vest.*

Pop: Your mother's asleep. Let's let her sleep.

Johnny: Oh.

Joey: Okay.

Pop: I'm going hunting.

Johnny: You're going hunting in the Bronx?

Pop: That's right. I've got the dogs outside.

Johnny: You're taking dogs?

Pop: That's right. Two of 'em. Blackie and Whitey.

Joey: What are you going after?

Pop: I'm gonna get a rabbit. Surprise Mam.

Johnny: Isn't that a big gun for a rabbit?

Pop: I'm gonna blow 'em to kingdom come. Wait. I'm gonna chew on your ear. *(To Joey, holding out the shotgun.)* Hold this.

> *Joey takes the shotgun from Pop. Pop crosses to Johnny and kneels by his chair.*

Johnny: What?

Pop: Lean over. I wanna chew on your ear.

> *Johnny tilts his head to the side. This enables the kneeling Pop to chew it. Johnny takes ticklish pleasure in this.*

Johnny: Stop! Stop!

Pop stops.

Pop: My little gossoon. *(He kisses Johnny's face. Then he wrestles his ring off his finger and holds it out to Johnny.)* Here. Take this. It's my ring.

Johnny: Gee. Thanks.

Pop: It's worth a fortune.

Johnny: Thanks.

Pop: I got it for cheap off a guy he was desperate during the Depression.

Johnny: Thanks, Pop.

Pop: How you doin with the shoes?

Johnny: Good.

Pop: That's the stuff! Shine 'em up! *(Standing.)* Shine 'em till they blind your eye! *(Turns to Joey and orders.)* Sing "Johnny, We Hardly Knew Ya".

Joey is terrified, struggling to remember.

Joey: I know it. I do know it. It just went out of my head.

Pop: Gimme the gun there, dummy. *(He takes the gun from Joey, heads for the door, pauses a moment, chambers a round, and comments.)* Well. Hi Ho.

Pop goes.

Johnny: That guy is like a visitation.

But Joey is frozen, looking after Pop, his fists and jaws clenched. Johnny realizes that Joey isn't going to laugh this off. Joey begins to sing.

Joey: Well ya haven't an arm and ya haven't a leg
O rue! O rue!
Ya haven't an arm and ya haven't a leg
O rue! O rue!
Ya haven't an arm and ya haven't a leg
You're a boneless mindless chickenless egg
And you'll have to be put with a bowl to beg...

(Joey's voice goes dry with emotion. He swallows and observes bleakly.)
He gave you the ring.

Johnny: Yeah.

Joey: To me, that ring is Pop.

Johnny: Hmmm.

Joey: Maybe we should go with him?

Johnny: He's not gonna get any rabbits.

Joey stands up.

Joey: That's not the point. I'm goin with him.

Johnny: Okay. Wait!

Joey: What?

Johnny: Listen. Maybe that ain't such a good idea, Joey.

Joey: He's not gonna be around forever, you know?

Johnny: Promise?

Joey: Hey, that's not funny!

Johnny: Sorry. Okay. But listen. You know. Pop's a bit of a killer.

Joey: Well, I'm a bit of a killer, too.

Johnny: Are you sure?

Joey: Sure. And what about you?

Johnny: You mean really?

Joey: Yeah.

Johnny: I'm a bit of a killer. When I have to be.

Joey: Who isn't?

Johnny: Not everybody is, Joey. Not in the crunch.

Joey: Whadda you know about the crunch?

Johnny: I couldn't tell ya.

Joey: I told you before, little brother. I'm gonna make it.

Johnny: Well, I'll tell you something and I may never say it again. But I don't know about you, Joey. I don't know whether you're gonna make it or not. But I do know this. I'M GONNA MAKE IT! NO MATTER WHAT I HAVETA DO! And that scares me.

A pause.

Joey: YOU'LL NEVER BE POP!

Johnny: I don't wanna be Pop.

Joey: You never could be! Ring or no ring! Why'd he give you that fuckin ring?

Johnny: I don't know.

Joey: I admire that man so much. I wish I knew his secret. Maybe I'll ask him today.

Johnny: His secret of what?

Joey: Happiness. Later on, when you're not around, I intend to steal something from you.

Joey exits. Johnny puts on Pop's ring and looks at it. Then he thinks and says:

Johnny: Happiness.

Ma appears in the entrance in a robe. She's been sleeping.

Ma: Where did they all go?

Johnny: They went hunting, Ma.

Ma: But not you.

Johnny: No.

Ma: I sleep so uneasily. But I sleep. What are you watching?

Johnny: *Lost in Space.*

She comes in.

Ma: Oh, I'll watch that.

She sits down. They watch t.v. She coughs, looks for a reaction from Johnny: None. She repeats the process twice more.

Johnny: You got a cough?

Ma: It's not a cough.

Johnny: Sounds like a cough.

Ma: I thought it was cancer till I went to Dr. Bopp.

Johnny: It's not cancer though, right?

Ma: No. I've been diagnosed. I have a loose esophagus.

Johnny: A loose esophagus.

Ma: It makes me feel like there's an object in my throat but the object is my throat itself.

Johnny: Wow. I don't know how much more of you I can take as a companion.

Ma: I have constant horrible nightmares that men with butcher knives are chasing me. *(She wrestles a ring off her finger and holds it out to Johnny.)* Here.

Johnny: What's this?

Ma: It's a ring. Take it.

He takes it. He inspects it, but doesn't put it on.

Johnny: Well, thanks.

Ma: It's my original wedding ring.

Johnny: Gee. Thank you.

Ma: And I say this to you: "Keep your heart as pure as the gold in this ring."

Johnny: Well, thank you. (*Johnny inspects the ring.*) Fourteen carats.

Ma: Keep your heart as pure as that.

Johnny: That seems doable. (*Pause.*) Maybe I'll write something.

Ma: (*With sudden decision.*) I'm gonna write a book!

Johnny: (*Just fed up.*) Oh, you are not!

Ma: Yeah, I'm gonna write a book. About my life. And times. (*She takes out a big lollipop and starts sucking while watching the t.v. Then she explains.*) This is to soothe the loose esophagus.

> *Johnny nods wearily. She goes back to sucking and staring.*

Johnny: When I was sixteen, seventeen, eighteen fucking years of my life …

Ma: Johnny.

Johnny: In the new house.

Ma: Johnny.

Johnny: I had my family pegged. It was almost over.

Ma: Could you turn up the volume?

> *Johnny goes to the t.v. and turns up the volume. We hear the robot on the program cry out: "Warning! Warning!" Then some sad, yearning, Sixties song of regret over the past, over yesterday, plays. Maybe some song covered by Ray Charles.* As it plays, Johnny starts to leave. He touches his mother's shoulder with sad affection as he goes. The lights fade but for the blue gray light of the t.v., illuminating Ma. Then this light goes out as well. In the dark, the Sixties song segues into dreamy, menacing synthesizer music and sounds of distant destruction. Glass breaking, that kind of thing.*

* See Special Note on copyright page

ACT III

We're in the big black basement of the Old House. No painted drop for this. It's the old, dark-stoned house wall. The old wall has had to be repaired, augmented, with masonry of a newer vintage. But even the newer stuff is a couple of hundred years old.

Through the staves of a rough door in this wall, and through cracks in the wall itself, the red light of a big fire can be seen.

From Off Right, a light shines dimly into the basement; faint 50's music emanates from that direction.

Down left is a door set in the floor, propped open with a bar. Within this entrance into the floor is partially visible some filthy bedding, foul ticking, stained and damp, and perhaps a child's blanket.

John, filthy, asleep, lies in the hole on one side. Joey, even dirtier than John, lies in a ball on the other side. Both are in black jeans and different short-sleeved shirts.

A couple of worklights hang from the invisible ceiling. A couple of wooden spools or crates, suitable for seating, are lying around.

John wakes up suddenly, as from a bad dream, looks around startled and disoriented, and sees Joey.

John: Joey? Joey? What's the matter? Where are we? Why do I feel so scared? Why's everything dirty? What's that smell? Joey, are you asleep? I don't even wanna put my foot on the floor. I feel like there's somethin dead down there. Laugh at me, willya? Ain't you gonna laugh at me?

Joey: Shut up! Shut up! Shut up! Just shut up! Don't even look at me. I don't want you ta see me. I don't wanna be seen.

Johnny: Where's your confidence?

Joey: Gone!

John: Where'd it go?

Joey: You tell me.

John: I don't know. How would I know?

Joey: Stop asking me questions!

John: 'Member when we were kids and we'd talk in the dark?

Joey: We're a long way from that now, Kimosabe.

John: Why?

Joey: Look, I'm just tryin ta ball up here an...

John: Well, we can't just... give up on life.

Joey: Shut up I said! You never got it! Maybe that's your gift. I know, see? Look in my eyes. I know. Lemme tell you what's goin ta happen. I'll stay outta everybody's way. Till I can't anymore. And then I'll be killed. And you won't do a fuckin thing. Even though you love me.

John: Joey.

Joey: 'Cause you'll be like you were a tree. And they'll cut me down. You'll hear my name comin outta your mouth like a knife. And you'll know you were there when they killed your brother.

John: Joey no.

Joey: So don't ask me ta feel for you.

John: Hey, comon Joey, you're my hero brother. You gotta laugh at me when I get scared. *(With sudden passion.)* WHERE ARE WE? We're in the basement of the Old House. Ain't we?

Joey: Yeah. You don't like it here, do ya?

John: No.

Some activity can be heard behind the door in the rear wall.

Joey: Well, why would ya? *(Sensing Pop.)* Be quiet!

John: What?

Joey: It's alright now.

John: Who's that back there?

Joey: I've got nothing, you little shit, and you ask me ta feel for you? What are you, kidding?

John: I'm not asking for nothing.

Joey: And you're not gettin nothin, not from me! Wait! *(Activi-*

ty again.) Shhh!

John: Who is that?

Joey: Look! When I say Shut Up, shut up!

John: It's Dad!

Joey: Please. Shhhh!

John: Dad?

Joey: Don't call him!

John: Why not?

Joey: He's a demon.

John: He's a what?

Joey: He's a demon.

John thinks this over and decides to call anyway.

John: Dad?

Joey: Whaddaya wanna know anymore for?

John: I don't know.

Joey: Don't ask me ta feel for you! I got troubles of my own!

John: I'm callin him.

Joey: Wait a minute. Listen. You did tell me the truth once. When he comes, give him this.

Joey holds out a square wrapped in tin foil.

John: What's this?

Joey: It's a sandwich.

John takes the sandwich.

John: A sandwich? You're kidding.

Joey: He'll want it.

John: Thanks.

Joey: Now leave me outta this all together.

Joey balls up. John steps out of the hole.

John: Dad? DAD?

The rear door opens and a sound like a blast furnace comes up. And a great glow of firelight. Pop enters, in a strap T-shirt and dark trousers, his face red and streaked with soot. He wipes his face with a rag. In his other hand he carries a short stout stick.

Pop: Who summons me?

John: I do.

Pop: So you call me Dad now.

John: What do you want to be called?

Pop: I don't care what you call me. Not down here. So you've arrived. *(He comes closer and points to the sandwich.)* I'll take that.

> *John throws him the sandwich. Pop catches it and smells it through the wrapper.*

John: What are ya doin back there?

Pop: Dealing with the fire.

John: What fire?

Pop: Every house has a fire. This is a big basement. Takes a big fire to keep it warm. I built it against the old wall of the house. That part's Pre-Roman. You like a fire?

John: Yeah.

Pop: Big surprise. I knew as much. *(Peeks within the wrapping.)* Roast beef, lettuce and tomatoes. And a pickle.

John: How did I get back here?

Pop: Oh, you came back. You hadda come back, didn't you? This is your basement.

John: I hear music.

Pop: Yeah! That's a party for the teenagers. There's always a stratum of teenagers. Girls!

John: Do you like girls?

> *Pop laughs. This question almost kills Pop. He chases John, brandishing his stick.*

Pop: God love ya, may ya live ta be a hundred and two and I'll be at your funeral! May ya not die till I kill ya!

John: Hey!

Pop: I should shove ya up a dog's ass and shoot the dog!

John: Whaddaya doin?

Pop: Just the usual jig.

John: Well, stop it!

Pop: Why?

John: You're just saying sayings.

Pop: So? Is that blasphemy?

John: It's nuts. You're scaring me.

Pop: Am I?

John: Yeah.

Pop: Well, if I'm scaring you, what am I doing to your brother? *Pop wheels around and takes in Joey in his hole.*

John: I don't know.

Pop: I'm drivin him into the ground, Johnny boy! I'm killing him! I can smell him, he's shit himself! *(To Joey.)* Ain't I got a heel in your neck, boy! If I had a bat, I'd bat you over the fence home-run! I pulled the bones outta you one by one. *(Starts to walk upstage.)* You're a whipped dog in the corner and you hope that I won't KICK YA!

> *Pop kicks the propped up door savagely. It cracks in half, and half slams down, encasing the lower half of Joey's body. The other half of the door stays propped open. Joey screams in terror.*

Joey: PLEASE, POP!

Pop: *(Simultaneously.)* Ain't that right?

Joey: NO MORE!

John: *(Shouting, partially overlapping.)* LAY OFF HIM!

> *Pop heads for John, getting in his face.*

Pop: Or what?

John: You...

> *Struggles.*

Pop: Cat got your tongue? Why've you come down here do ya think?

John: I don't know.

Pop: You know.

John: Your eyes are like...

Pop: What?

John: Sparks.

Pop: That's right, lad. Have you looked at the world lately? It's something to behold.

John: I haven't looked at anything. I haven't been anywhere.

Pop: You haven't, huh?

John: No.

Pop: You got here. That's something. You're the prince of the slophouse this minute. *(Gently puts his hand on John's shoulder.)* Don't sell yourself too short. Just remember, *(Drives John to his knees.)* I'm the King!

John: Your eyes! Your eyes seem so excited!

> *Pop stalks away. He heads for his sandwich, which he left Upstage.*

Pop: And a beautiful hue a blue, don't ya think? You should see your eyes. I am excited. *(Sits to eat.)* It's chowtime.

John: Are you crazy?

Pop: Not even close.

John: Are you a demon?

Pop: What do you think? What is a demon?

John: Are you here ta show me something?

Pop: I'm no Virgil, but I'm yours.

John: You seem like… completely alone.

Pop: And you're not? In your life?

John: Don't drag me into it!

Pop: Oh, you're in.

John: But you're a father. You have a family.

Pop: You have a family.

John: But you have children.

Pop: I don't know where ta start with you. My children? This is why I shouldn't feel alone? My children, my kids, the fountainhead of my dick, the little ones. But how they do grow! They'd a cut their teeth on my liver if it was put to 'em! They'd grab the sun outta the sky and stash it if they could! Cold comfort in their shade I shall not take. No, thank you. Or should I look to my brothers? My brothers are dead. Do you remember how I shook when they died, one after the other? And I hadda stand there in the suit, them stretched out inna box? While your aunts made jokes and dabbed at their crocodile tears, their heads full of insurance! Where's the soft shoulder for this old man in that? *(Spits.)* I'd rather suck onna stone. Or should I scavenge all the way back to Ireland, searching for something green? My father and mother, always in the middle of a fight. I'd come in. A pail of water'd fly by my face! Whoosh! Or a stool. Yeah! He made furniture and she'd say, You can hide a lot with putty and paint. If she had been my wife! *(Gestures he would have struck her.)* He couldn't get along with anybody. Except me. Even the animals would run away from him. I had a family. And I outwitted them all, Johnny Lad, and you will, too, or you won't. Your mother… *(Joey cries a little and Pop is right on him.)* Was that a whimper? Whimper again and I'll whack you one!

Joey: Please! I'll do anything!

Pop: Anything is not quite enough, boy. Sing "Danny Boy".
SING "DANNY BOY!"

> *Pop smashes back the part of the propped door that remained standing.*

Joey: *(Hysterical with fear.)* I don't know it!

John: Leave him alone!

Pop: *(Suddenly crafty and defensive.)* Why?

John: He can't take it.

Pop: No, he can't.

John: So why don't you pick on somebody who can?

Pop: Oh, I do! I absolutely do! *(Points to Joey.)* But this you notice, you call it cruelty.

John: It is cruelty!

> *Joey has become quite still in what now looks quite like an open coffin. Perhaps his arms are even crossed on his chest.*

Pop: I'm doing the same thing all the time. It's him. He caves in. I hit all of you on the head, John. To see if you were sound. To see if you made a true noise. He fell down, the rest didn't. Think I singled him out? I hit you just the same as him. He fell down.

John: It's not right!

Pop: I'm not sayin it's right! I'm not God. I'm not in charge. I'm down here in the mud with you.

John: You're my father!

Pop: You put a name to me! Yes, and so what? What do you think that signifies?

John: You're my father? I feel frightened!

Pop: Why?

John: Just to be in a room with you.

Pop: Nothin new there.

John: Not because of you, BECAUSE OF ME! BECAUSE OF WHAT'S IN ME!

Pop: What's in you?

John: My hands are cold.

Pop: Don't get distracted by your symptoms now.

John: Why are my hands so cold?

Pop: Come on! No marchin in place! Such visits are rare. Down here. Take advantage. You're smart. You see what you don't wanna. I have bad news for you. You're not God either.

John: I know that.

Pop: Do ya? You do. But you don't. But you do. But you don't. But you DO. I wish I could have a party with you! Upon my operation scars! Men! Men! I wish we could be men together!

John: So what if we were men together, whatever that means? What would we do with that?

Pop: *(Grabs John.)* Where's the fellowship I hunger and can't have and can't request? *(Lets go of John, points to Joey.)* There?

John: What are you, some kinda Celtic rampaging fuckhead or what?

Pop: Sure I am. Paint me blue and set me down on the field of battle! But still! What about fellowship? What about you?

John: What about me?

Pop: How strong are you?

John: I'm strong enough.

Pop: What are you made of?

John: If it came to that, I think I'm stronger than you!

Pop: Do ya? Look who's up on his hind legs! I don't care what you do! I don't care what you do to yourself! I don't care what you do to me! Do your worst!

Throws John his stick.

John: You're not afraid of Death?

Pop: I'm terrified. But maybe death ain't even what you think. Maybe I'll lick it. Remains to be seen. Nothing to brood about. I keep moving. That's my job.

John: What's my job?

Pop: None of my affair.

John: But I have one?

Pop: Yes and no. A job, a legacy. Something.

John: And you think you know what it is.

Pop: There's such a fool in you.

Grabbing his stick back in frustration.

John: Alright, so there's a Fool in me! Fools tell Kings what they don't wanna hear remember!

Pop: What could you say to me? It was me that engendered you! I'm the one with the secrets!

John: I'm not here for you, mister, you're here for me.

Pop: I am not.

John: You serve me.

Pop: I serve no man.

John: Say what you want. You serve me.

Pop: You're not half the man I am!

John: You're not half the man you are! The rest of you's in some hole you call Joey! Enough a this shit. Attend to me, demon.

Pop: You can summon me, boy, but that's all.

John: Look at me! Really look at me!

Pop: I'll do what I want.

John: Gimme your attention.

Pop: You'll not have it.

John: Help me!

Pop: Shove off!

John runs to Pop and grabs his ear. He twists it, bringing Pop to his knees.

John: Gimmee your attention, you spook! You hatchethead!

Pop: Never! You have no claim on it! No!

John drags Pop eight or so feet by his ear.

John: First cough up the answer to my question, Answer Man, what's my job? Will you help me, you ignorant son-of-a-bitch!

Pop: Me ignorant!

John pulls the stick from Pop's hand.

John: Yes, you! Ignorant, dumb as spit! I'm warning you, cough it up! Goddamn you, when I say I need your help, do yourself a favor old man, throw yourself in my way and help me!

Pop: Or what?

John: OR I'LL...

Without realizing it, John has raised the stick to strike his father a mighty blow. Gleefully, his father catches him.

Pop: YES!

Horrified at his own behavior, John drops the stick.

John: No. No.

Pop: What do you imagine that you want from me?

John: If I'm stronger than you, and I know how weak I am, then we're all nothing. What I want is, Tell me what you think I know.

Pop: You'll never understand me, never. I'm deeper away than China. Than a star. If I wanted to, I couldn't tell you who I am. Or who you are, why you are, why Joey broke in two and you did not. I'm a mystery, you dumb son-of-a-bitch. And I can't explain a mystery because I'm not God and you can't explain a mystery because you're not God. And that's why I'm glad I'm a Catholic, because it's a mystery religion!

John: Shitcan the jokes, Pop. I'm askin you now. For my rights. What is it that you think you know?

Pop: Your job is to kill me.

This calms John.

John: So. It's like I thought. Under everything, it's this shit-house idea: It's him. Or me.

Pop: It is.

John makes a seat for himself and sits down.

John: Do I have your attention, Pop?

Pop: Yeah.

John: We could have loved each other.

Pop: No sir.

John: We didn't have to be set against each other!

Pop: Oh yes we did!

John: No we didn't! It was all there. For all of us. The table was full. The places were laid. Everything we needed was there. That's why you came here, right? The land of plenty? *(Indicating Joey.)* It didn't have to be him or me. He didn't have to fall down for me to stand up.

Pop: How do you know?

John: What's the matter with you? What's the matter with your soul? For Chrissakes, we coulda helped each other, Pop. The world is hard enough. Ain't it? Without no haven at all? I look like the Bronx inside. I could vomit up a burning car. You seen them. These dead wrecks everywhere. They've been abandoned. I feel them inside! And I was the lucky one! I was the fortunate son. What have you done to me? What did you do to your boys?

Pop: John.

John: No! Fuck you. You know what I feel when I see a beggar on the street? I wanna kick in his face! I wanna beat him ta death!

Cause that's me! Pathetically waitin with my fuckin cup. But that's over. I've stopped stealin and I've stopped settin fires and I've stopped breakin windows. And now, now I'm gonna stop waitin for you. To reach down to me. To touch my face. To kiss my wounds. There's been a kinda silence fallen between us like a long drop onta sharp rocks. For a long time now. It's been my wait. I've been waitin for something. Words I guess. Some words. Do I have the words even now? *(Pause.)* I will never think of you without being shocked by your lovelessness. I will never think of you without a gasp of wonder. I will never think of you without some pain. And despite everything, in the face of everything, though it personally shames me to say it, I still have love for you.

    Pause.

Pop: What about that I gave you my ring?

John: I didn't want it and I didn't need it.

Pop: But you still got it on I see. What about that I chewed on your ear?

John: I don't know. Why did you do that?

    Pop shakes his head gently by way of answer and then says:

Pop: So.

John: You are a mystery to me.

Pop: Have you had your say?

John: No. How could I? Never. But this one thing I'll say. When you die, and you will, you'll be dead. I won't be you. Not even if I have to cut my own throat.

Pop: You can't dictate nothing. *(Lays a palm on John's breast.)* Maybe you ain't been to the Gypsy, but your fortune's been told. *(Heads for the rustic door.)* I gotta get back.

John: I'm not finished with you! Dad! Dad?

    Pop exits, with fiery effects. The figure of a woman in a party dress appears on the landing, Right. The music, which faded away during John's big speech, returns. It's something from the Fifties, romantic. Little speckled lights flick around the basement. The woman is Ma. She looks younger.

Ma: Let him go.

John: Who are you?

Ma: Don't you know me?

John: Ma?

Ma: Noreen.

John: Noreen?

Ma: That's right. Call me Noreen. That's my name.

John: Noreen.

Ma: Noreen Fitzgerald.

John: Alright. Noreen Fitzgerald. Are you a demon?

Ma: No. No, I wouldn't say so. Did he eat the whole sandwich then?

John: I think so.

Ma: Surprise, surprise. He gobbles up everything. You wouldn't have a lollipop, wouldja?

John: No.

Ma: Hard candy?

John: No.

Ma: Gee whiz. I ain't here for you, stuck up.

John: I can see something in you I could never see before.

Ma: What?

John: I can see the girl in you.

Ma: I'm your mother to the bone.

John: I know, but...

Ma: Let's not have a stupid argument. There's no buts.

John: You're cute in that dress.

Ma: Sure I am.

John: No, you really are. You're sexy.

Ma: No, I'm not.

John: Hey, that's for me to say, Noreen. I'm the guy. I say you're sexy, you're sexy. You may not know, and that's alright. That can be sexy, too.

Ma: Being stupid is sexy?

John: Being innocent.

Ma: I'm not innocent.

John: Sure you are.

Ma: I'm coarse.

A pause.

John: I've never heard anyone call themselves coarse. Before.

Ma: I've never used the word about myself before. It just happens to be the truth.

John: So you're truthful.

Ma: Here and now.

John: That's a nice dress.

Ma: Thank you.

John: See, you're not coarse. You can take a compliment.

Ma: I'm vain.

John: A woman has a right to a little vanity.

Ma: That's right. You'd stand on your head to explain me in a good light.

John: You'll get your lumps.

Ma: When?

John: Trust me. Is that a party I hear?

Ma: Yeah. Teenagers. There's always teenagers. Boys!

John: You like boys?

Ma: *(Explodes.)* Jesus, Mary and Joseph, give me patience! You're giving me a splitting headache! When will you be gone?

John: Never. I'm gonna outlast you, Noreen. I'm gonna bury you. You like boys?

Ma: No.

John: What about Dad?

Ma: That? I can't explain it.

John: What about me?

Ma: I'll tell you one thing. I'm not your guinea pig!

John: Who said you were?

Ma: I spotted you right off. When you'd grunt at me, look me in the eye, shit yourself so satisfied. When you'd waddle around the rug like an old lecher with his belly and his craven face: "What's for me?" You did everything with an eye to how I'd take it. Everything was a test. In the tub you'd look at me, and your pecker'd pop up, and you'd smile! It was like the Devil smirkin in my face! I became afflicted by these awful headaches and horrible dreams of blood and mayhem. But I had your number! I knew you thought only about your functions and your pecker, and I just tried not to look you in the eye cause then you'd give me that big dirty stare. Looking into me. Trying to get at me. Big eyes! I'm not your guinea pig! And then, when you realized that I wouldn't look at you, you wouldn't look at me, and that I found out was dangerous, too! You started doing things. Playing with matches, hiding things, breaking things, stealing things, lying about it all. Mischief! Mischief! I thought I'd go mad!

John: Maybe you did.

Ma: I did not!

John: How do you know?

Ma: I'd've heard.

John: Who from?

Ma: Pop.

John: Maybe.

Ma: Definitely. There's a clock that ticks between us. Oh, I wish I had a lollipop!

John: Why?

Ma: They make my troubles go away. Sweets. Ice cream. Chocolates. Other things, too. Pizza. Do you know, at one time, I could eat a whole pizza pie by myself?

John: Could you tell me something?

Ma: What?

John: What's so great about that?

Ma: I don't know. It was something I had to myself. It was mine. It was my pie. *(Pause.)* So go ahead.

John: What?

Ma: Denounce me. Let's get it over with.

John: No. I'll do that before now, after now, but consider it done. Done to death. What were you doing at that party?

Ma: I don't remember. Just standing there. By the refreshments.

John: I thought it was a party for teenagers. Boys!

Ma: I don't know why I was at it and stop asking me!

John: Did anybody ask you to dance?

Ma: No.

John: This is my last time here. I'm glad. I feel like we were thrown together. Long ago. And now I try to explain.

Ma: Why did you come?

John: To say goodbye.

Ma: Goodbye.

John: No. I didn't come here for you to say goodbye. I came here for me to do it.

Ma: So say it.

John: Shut up. Stop bossing me around. Relax. Be yourself. Fall apart. Do whatever you want. But do it to yourself. Will you dance with me?

Ma: No.

John: Come on.

Ma: No.

John: I think you want to dance.

Ma: That may be true. What's that to do with anything?

John: And I think you feel bad that no one's asked you.

Ma: So what if that's true? So what? I will not dance with you. You're lucky you had me. I am coarse. And I am vain. And I am a bit of a baby. I have crying fits and nightmares and terrible headaches. And I am a pill. And I don't like men. But I'm not your demon, boy. I was a true mother to you. Despite all the temptation. And you were a Temptor, sent to me by the Unseen Hand of God. Despite all the temptation, I did not cripple you. And about that, no matter how I purse my lips and shake my head, about that I am very proud.

John: Come here, let me kiss you!

Ma: No.

John: Just one on the cheek. Let me give you a hug.

Ma: I don't go for the gooey stuff.

Ma walks away from John. He heads her off and makes one last appeal.

John: Then just tell me that you love me.

Ma considers his appeal and then answers honestly but gently.

Ma: It wouldn't sound believable. *(John sinks to his knees, abject.)* You got the only decent thing I had to give, John. Take it and be satisfied. Anyway, I ain't here for you. Joey? Joey?

Joey rouses slightly.

Joey: Yeah?

Ma: Come up here, me boy-o, and give us a dance!

Joey: Really?

John: You're going to dance with him?

Ma: If he'll have me.

John: Then why not me?

Ma: In the bakeshop, they let the ones in the back eat the desserts that are ruined. Let him have his crumb. You have enough. Joey! Dance with your mother.

Joey pulls him up a little.

Joey: Life is hard as a hammer. If I had known what life was like, I never woulda had a good day.

Ma: Do you still like beer, Joe?

She fishes one out of a crate.

Joey: Sure I do.

Ma: Well then here's one for ya. *(She gives it to him. He drinks.)* I don't like it myself. My father always smelled of it. But it's cold like you like it. Commere, son. Let me do a little thing for you.

Danny Boy begins to play. Joey pulls himself up and says gently:

Joey: Why can't it always be like this? How's my ma?

He stands and goes to her, leaving his beer in the hole. He takes her in his arms and dances with her. John looks on. They dance. The rough door opens with the roar and the light of the fire. Pop Emerges. Joey is oblivious. John sees and cries out in helpless warning:

John: JOEY! JOEY! JOEY![

Ma has gently stepped away from Joey. Pop strikes Joey a terrible blow at the base of the neck and Joey falls down dead. This is to the sound of a needle going violently across a record. A second of silence. A different recording of Danny Boy begins to play. Ma and Pop look at each other and begin to dance. John, shaken to his core, sits down on the steps and addresses the audience.

John: I will say this one thing more, my friends, and then I am through with this subject. My parents loved each other. How I do not know. We were alone. We watched them dance. Like dogs at a butcher shop window. *(He picks up a box of kitchen matches and takes out a match.)* Now I am some kind of man. I live in a city where it is difficult to survive. Nothing is new. Some of us walk. Some of us are lying on the ground. *(He strikes the match.)* When I was one, two, twenty, forty years of my life, I stopped to grieve for my fallen brothers.

John looks over at the figure of Joey, and from there to his parents dancing. He blows out the match and the light goes out on him. His parents dance on a moment more in a baby blue spot, at their feet the fallen son. And then all goes dark.

END OF PLAY

A LITTLE NIGHT MUSIC

Music and Lyrics by Stephen Sondheim, Book by Hugh Wheeler

"Heady, civilized, sophisticated and enchanting. Good God! An adult musical."
—Clive Barnes, The New York Times

Cloth $19.95 ISBN: 1-55783-070-3 • Paper $12.95 ISBN: 1-55783-069-X

A FUNNY THING HAPPENED ON THE WAY TO THE FORUM

Music & Lyrics by Stephen Sondheim, Book by Burt Shevelove & Larry Gelbart

"A good, clean, dirty show! Bring back the belly laughs"   —Time
"It's funny, true nonsense! A merry good time!"   —Walter Kerr, Herald Tribune
Cloth $19.95 ISBN: 1-55783-064-9 • Paper $12.95 ISBN: 1-55783-063-0

SUNDAY IN THE PARK WITH GEORGE

Music and Lyrics by Stephen Sondheim, Book by James Lapine

"*Sunday* is itself a modernist creation, perhaps the first truly modernist work of musical theatre that Broadway has produced."
—Frank Rich, The New York Times

Cloth $19.95 ISBN: 1-55783-068-1 • Paper $12.95 ISBN: 1-55783-067-3

SWEENEY TODD

Music and Lyrics by Stephen Sondheim, Book by Hugh Wheeler

"There is more artistic energy, creative personality, and plain excitement than in a dozen average musicals."   —Richard Eder, The New York Times

Cloth $19.95 ISBN: 1-55783-066-5 • Paper $12.95 ISBN: 1-55783-065-7

Now also available all in one volume!

FOUR BY SONDHEIM

Cloth $35 ISBN: 1-55783-407-5

ONE ON ONE

BEST MONOLOGUES FOR THE 90'S
Edited by Jack Temchin

You have finally met your match in Jack Temchin's new collection, **One on One.** Somewhere among the 150 monologues Temchin has recruited, a voice may beckon to you—strange and alluring—waiting for your own voice to give it presence on stage.

"The sadtruth about most monologue books," says Temchin. "is that they don't give actors enough credit. I've compiled my book for serious actors with a passionate appetite for the unknown."

Among the selections:
Wendy Wasserstein THE SISTERS ROSENSWEIG
David Henry Hwang FACE VALUE
Tony Kushner ANGELS IN AMERICA
Alan Bennett TALKING HEADS
Neil Simon JAKE'S WOMEN
David Hirson LA BETE
Herb Gardner CONVERSATIONS WITH MY FATHER
Ariel Dorfman DEATH AND THE MAIDEN
Alan Ayckborn A SMALL FAMILY BUSINESS
Robert Schenkkan THE KENTUCKY CYCLE

$7.95•paper
MEN: ISBN 1-55783-151-3•WOMEN: ISBN: 1-55783152-1

APPLAUSE

THE LIFE OF THE DRAMA
by Eric Bentley

"... Eric Bentley's radical new look at the grammar of theater... is a work of exceptional virtue, and readers who find more in it to disagree with than I do will still, I think, want to call it central, indispensable. ... The book justifies its title by being precisely about the ways in which life manifests itself in the theater. if you see any crucial interest in such topics as the death of Cordelia, Godot's non-arrival... This is a book to be read and read again."

— Frank Kermode
THE NEW YORK REVIEW OF BOOKS

paper • ISBN: 1-55783-110-6

OTHER PEOPLE'S MONEY:
The Ultimate Seduction
by Jerry Sterner

"The best new play I've run across all season.
IT WOULD STAND OUT IN ANY YEAR."
    —**Douglas Watt** ,DAILY NEWS

"Epic grandeur and intimate titillation
combined. **IT IS THE MOST
STIMULATING KIND OF
ENTERTAINMENT"**
    —**John Simon, NEW YORK MAGAZINE**

"*Other People's Money* has a HEART OF
IRON which beats about the cannibalistic
nature of big business."
    —**Mel Gussow,** THE NEW YORK TIMES

 paper• ISBN 1-55783-061-4
cloth• ISBN 1-55783-062-2

THE ACTOR'S MOLIÈRE

A New Series of Translations for the Stage by

Albert Bermel

THE MISER and GEORGE DANDIN

ISBN: 0-936839-75-9

THE DOCTOR IN SPITE OF HIMSELF and THE BOURGEOIS GENTLEMAN

ISBN: 0-936839-77-5

SCAPIN and DON JUAN

ISBN: 0-936839-80-5

COMMEDIA IN PERFORMANCE SERIES

THE THREE CUCKOLDS

by Leon Katz

paper • ISBN: 0-936839-06-6

THE SON OF ARLECCHINO

by Leon Katz

paper • ISBN: 0-936839-07-4

CELESTINA
by Fernando do Rojas

Adapted by Eric Bentley
Translated by James Mabbe

paper • ISBN: 0-936839-01-5

MASTERGATE
&
POWER FAILURE
2 Political Satires for the stage
by Larry Gelbart

REVIEWS OF *MASTERGATE*:

"IF GEORGE ORWELL WERE A GAG WRITER, HE COULD HAVE WRITTEN *MASTERGATE*. Larry Gelbart's scathingly funny takeoff on the Iran-Contra hearings [is] a spiky cactus flower in the desert of American political theatre."
                    —Jack Kroll, NEWSWEEK

"Larry Gelbart has written what may be the MOST PENETRATING, AND IS SURELY THE FUNNIEST, exegesis of the Iran-Contra fiasco to date."
                    —Frank Rick, THE NEW YORK TIMES

REVIEWS OF *POWER FAILURE*:

"There is in his broad etching ALL THE ETHICAL OUTRAGE OF AN ARTHUR MILLER KVETCHING. AND, OH, SO MUCH MORE FUN!"
                    —Carolyn Clay, THE BOSTON PHOENIX

Larry Gelbart, the creator of M*A*S*H, is also the author of *SLY FOX, A FUNNY THING HAPPENED ON THE WAY TO THE FORUM* and *CITY OF ANGELS.*

paper • 1-55783-177-7

CHEKHOV:
THE MAJOR PLAYS

English versions by
Jean–Claude van Itallie

The Cherry Orchard

"A CLASSIC RESTORED TO THE HAND, MIND
AND BLOOD OF THE CREATOR."
—The New York Times

The Seagull

"SUBLIMELY   UNDERSTOOD   CHEKHOV
...ABSOLUTELY   TRUE   TO   THE   ORIGINAL"
—The New York Post

Three Sisters

"CAPTURES CHEKHOV'S EXUBERANCE, MUSIC
AND COMPLEXITY"   *—The Village Voice*

Uncle Vanya

"THE CRISPEST AND MOST POWERFUL
VERSION EXTANT."   *—The New Republic*

Paper•ISBN 1-55783-162-9 • $7.95

THE REDUCED SHAKESPEARE COMPANY'S
COMPLEAT WORKS OF WLLM SHKSPR
(abridged)
by JESS BORGESON, ADAM LONG, and DANIEL SINGER

"ABSL HLRS." —*The Independent* (London)

"Shakespeare writ small, as you might like it! . . . Pithier-than-Python parodies . . . not to be confused with that august English company with the same initials. This iconoclastic American Troupe does more with less."

> — *The New York Times*

"Shakespeare as written by *Reader's Digest*, acted by Monty Python, and performed at the speed of the Minute Waltz. So Forsooth! Get thee to the RSC's delightfully fractured *Compleat Works*."

> — *Los Angeles Herald*

ISBN 1-55783-157-2 • $9.95 • PAPER

The Scarlet Letter

by Nathaniel Hawthorne

Adapted for the stage by
James F. DeMaiolo

Leslie Fiedler pronounced it the first American tragedy. F.O. Mathiessen considered it the "Puritan Faust." Richard B. Sewall compared its inexorable dramatic force to King Lear. These chieftains of American literature were not, as one might suspect referring to a play by O'Neill. They are not in fact, referring to a play at all, but to a masterpiece of nineteenth century fiction. Until now, it appeared that Nathaniel Hawthorne's haunting drama of judgment, alienation and redemption would be forever confined to the page. The Scarlet Letter continues to be the most frequently read novel in American high schools today as well as one of the most widely circulated novels in the American library system. And now comes the stage version to do it justice.

A century and a half after its first incarnation, James DeMaiolo has forged an alliance of craft and spirit so potent in its own right and so faithful to Hawthorne's original that his stage version is certain to compel all non-believers to recant and take heed. The audience joins the chorus as they weigh the American contract of freedom against the fine print of convention and taboo.

Paper•ISBN 1-55783-243-9 • $6.95
Performance rights available from APPLAUSE

WILLIAM GOLDMAN FOUR SCREENPLAYS

William Goldman, master craftsman and two-time Oscar winner continues his irreverent analysis with merciless essays written expressly for this landmark edition of his screen work. Nobody covers the psychic and political terrain behind the Hollywood lot with more cynical wisdom and practical savvy than the much celebrated author of ADVENTURES IN THE SCREEN TRADE.

William Goldman won Academy Awards for BUTCH CASSIDY AND THE SUNDANCE KID and ALL THE PRESIDENT'S MEN

Includes the screenplays:

BUTCH CASSIDY AND THE SUNDANCE KID

THE PRINCESS BRIDE

MARATHON MAN

MISERY

PAPER • ISBN 1-55783-265-X
CLOTH • ISBN 1-55783-198-X